SEX, DISSIDENCE AND DAMNATION

Minority Groups in the Middle Ages

Jeffrey Richards

London and New York

First published 1991
by Routledge
First published in paperback
1994 by Routledge
11 New Fetter Lane, London EC4P 4EE

Simultaneously published in the USA and Canada
by Routledge
29 West 35th Street, New York, NY 10001

Typeset in Bodoni by
Selwood Systems, Midsomer Norton

Printed and bound in Great Britain by
Butler & Tanner Ltd, Frome and London

British Library Cataloguing in Publication Data

A catalogue record for this book is available from the British Library

Library of Congress Cataloging in Publication Data

A catalogue record for this book has been requested

ISBN 0–415–03342–X
0–415–07147–X (pbk)

SEX, DISSIDENCE AND DAMNATION

For
David King
and
Michael Mullett

CONTENTS

ILLUSTRATIONS

PREFACE

At a time when society seems to be growing more intolerant of minority groups and when every day a rabid, unrestrained tabloid press stirs up racism, sexism, jingoism and homophobia, it is perhaps timely to examine the ways in which previous eras viewed and treated the minority groups in their midsts. I seek to make no direct comparisons and will leave it to the reader to draw what conclusions there are to be drawn about the ways in which modern society differs from its medieval counterpart in this area. What can be hazarded is an explanation of the nature, roots, scope and effects of medieval society's treatment of its minority groups.

In attempting this in what is an avowed work of synthesis, I have drawn on the researches of many dedicated scholars. A book like this could not have been written without their work and I am immensely grateful for the labours and the insights of the medievalists who have explored, mapped and signposted this particular historical terrain. I have learned much from them in the course of researching this book and I sincerely hope that readers of this book will be encouraged to turn to their work next. The responsibility for the overarching thesis, however, lies with me.

Many people have helped me over the past two years. I am particularly indebted to my colleagues Dr David King and Dr Michael Mullett who painstakingly read the entire manuscript and made many helpful and constructive comments. The book is dedicated to them with gratitude and respect. Individual chapters were read by Dr Paul Morris, Dr Richard Taylor and Dr John Halloran and I benefited from their pertinent and perceptive remarks. I am grateful for help and advice of various kinds to Dr Paul Heelas, Dr Alexander Grant, Dr Peter Broks, Dr Trevor Dean, Professor Lewis Warren, Mr Gordon Inkster, Dr Luciano Cheles and Mrs Joyce Storer. Thelma Goodman and her colleagues in Lancaster University Inter-Library Loans Department proved as courteous and tireless as ever in tracking down my sometimes obscure requests. I am grateful also to the staffs of the London Library and the British Library, and to Kate Bostock for undertaking the picture research. The following kindly gave permission to reproduce illustrations; the Mary Evans Picture Library, the Mansell Collection, the British Library, the Bodleian Library, the Victoria and Albert Museum, the Wallraf Richartz Museum and the Rheinische Bildarchiv, Cologne, the Museo del Prado, Madrid, the Hamburg Staats- und Universitatsbibliothek and the Biblioteca Nazionale, Florence.

1

THE MEDIEVAL CONTEXT

There have been throughout history recurrent periods of seismic change when the accepted norms and values of society have been decisively challenged and an explosion of new ideas and forms, beliefs and behaviour patterns has been touched off. The sixteenth century with its Renaissance and its Reformation; the era of Romanticism and revolution in the late eighteenth and early nineteenth centuries; and the 1960s with the rise of the counter-culture are examples. In each period, there has been a background of rising economic prosperity, growing materialism and increased leisure allowing the luxury of thought and experimentation. All have involved the idea of rebellion and rejection of the dominant ideology and all have been followed by periods of repression and retrenchment: Renaissance and Reformation were followed by absolutism and Counter-Reformation; revolution and Romanticism by, in England, the rise of evangelicalism and parliamentary democracy; and the counter-culture by the advent of Thatcherism and Reaganism. Each of these eras has centred on a rediscovery of the self and of selfhood, individuality, self-awareness and self-fulfilment. Each has seen the simultaneous assertion of asceticism and libertinism as a means of self-expression.

The twelfth century was another such period. The century saw a rising curve of self-expression in religion and sexuality with men and women explicitly or implicitly seeking greater access to God and greater control of their own bodies. The reaction to this by the authorities was the demand for conformity, religious and sexual. The text was the familiar cry of the totalitarian down the ages – 'Is he one of us?' In the thirteenth century the Church, the municipalities and the emerging national monarchies moved in to curb the freedom that had prevailed in the twelfth. The Church concerned itself particularly with the regulation of sexuality (the campaign against homosexuals, the segregation of prostitutes, the sacralization of marriage) and the regulation of spirituality (the reassertion of the clerical monopoly of access to God).

There are continuing and shaping themes in the Middle Ages: the

1

tension between authority and dissent, between communality and individualism, between materialism and spirituality, between eroticism and asceticism: conflict between these opposing forces ebbs and flows, waxes and wanes, sharing that perpetual oscillation between extremes that Johan Huizinga saw as a prime characteristic of medieval life. It was a society capable of sudden and violent outbursts of hysteria and paranoia, violence and enthusiasm, often against a background of demographic crisis or social dislocation, associated frequently with outbreaks of famine and disease.

But above all two psychological cruces dominate the contours of the period: the passing of the millennium and the coming of the Black Death. It was expected that the world would come to an end a thousand years after Christ. Some imagined it would be in 1000, a thousand years after His birth; yet more expected it in 1033, a thousand years after His death. The monkish chronicler Raoul Glaber captured in his chronicle the rising tide of excitement and apprehension. There were violent storms and serious food shortages in 1033; there were signs and portents in the heavens. 'People', he wrote, 'believed that the ordinary pattern of the seasons and the elements which had reigned since the beginning of time had reverted to chaos once and for all and that the end of mankind had come.' There was a mass movement of pilgrims towards Jerusalem, as people wished to be in the holiest of earthly cities when Christ's second coming would signal the last judgement of all human souls. 'An immense throng began to converge from every corner of the world on the sepulchre of Jesus in Jerusalem.'

But the world did not come to an end. Mankind could breathe again. No one could now be quite certain when the end would come. The official line of the Church had always been that it was not given to mankind to know. But there was no shortage of prophets willing to make predictions. The most influential was Abbot Joachim of Fiore, who divided the history of the world into three ages, the second of which he saw ending amidst violent upheavals in 1260. But there were others who variously predicted the end of the world for 1186, 1229, 1290, 1300, 1310, 1325, 1335, 1346, 1347, 1348, 1360, 1365, 1375, 1387, 1395, 1396, 1400, 1417, 1429 and 1492–4. Even if people did not agree about the date, everyone knew how to recognize its imminence, for Christ himself had told his disciples what the signs would be, according to St Matthew (24 vv. 7–8): 'Nation shall rise against nation; kingdom against kingdom; and there shall be famines and pestilences and earthquakes in divers places. And these are the beginning of sorrow.' Such conditions were not uncommon in the Middle Ages.

At the centre of the medieval apocalyptic world-view was the rise of the concept of Anti-Christ, who from the tenth century onwards became alike a regular theme of theologians and a staple of popular culture,

2

featuring in sermons, poems, histories and plays. Anti-Christ, whose life was a parody of Christ's (born a Jew, Anti-Christ enters Jerusalem, gathers disciples, performs miracles), was an agent of the Devil, who, it was believed, would mislead Christians, persecute the faithful and rule as a tyrant until Christ himself came to rescue mankind in time for the last judgement. The concept appealed to the essentially dualistic nature of medieval popular belief, which saw and understood the idea of life as a permanent battlefield between Good and Evil, God and the Devil, Christ and Anti-Christ, angels and demons. Various figures at various times would be identified with Anti-Christ, not least among them Popes Boniface VIII and John XXII.

The prospect of the millennium which might occur at any time gave rise to two strains of thought. On the one hand there was that radical millenarianism which Norman Cohn has so brilliantly analysed in *The Pursuit of the Millennium*: a belief, often to be found in the lower depths of society, in the arrival of a Golden Age on earth, which would precede the end of the world. Establishments and authorities would be overthrown and an era of equality, purity and plenty would be ushered in. The dream produced a succession of violent outbursts throughout the Middle Ages and it frequently provided inspiration for the militant wing of heretical movements, notably the Hussites. There was a frantic and deluded optimism sustaining those who often had nothing else to look forward to apart from lifelong misery and an early death.

But there was a more generalized apocalypticism. Encouraged by the wandering charismatic preachers who were such a feature of the Middle Ages, people were pessimistic about the future of mankind in general but willing to take thought for their own souls. If the end of the world could happen at any time, it was vital to be prepared for meeting your Maker; hence the impulse towards penance, pilgrimage and in particular personal asceticism. This expectancy generated an atmosphere of puritanism and evangelicalism, conditioning people's reactions to particular circumstances. It concentrated attention on the conquest of sin and on the first principles of the faith, on personal purity and on a rejection of the things of the world. Although the population did not continue in a permanent state of semi-mystical enthusiasm, that mindset remained and it frequently came to the fore at times of crisis.

Despite the permanent presence of the idea of apocalypse in the *mentalité* of the age, after 1033, when it was no longer securely ascertainable, there are abundant signs that Europe shook off its defensive Dark Age mentality and entered upon a period of revival, expansion, and creativity. Darkness was to be dispelled by Light, epitomized by the design, layout and construction of the Gothic cathedrals which arose all over France, symbolizing the spiritual aspirations and sense

3

of liberation of the age and embodying the principle that 'God is Light'. It was of course a combination of social, economic and political forces that achieved the revival but it flowered and flourished in the two centuries following the millennium.

For the first time for centuries, there was peace. The threat from the Arabs, the Vikings and the Magyars which had put the very survival of Christendom at risk had receded. In the wake of peace came demo-graphic growth, agricultural expansion and urban revival. The towns, eclipsed since the heyday of the Roman Empire, destroyed or reduced by the invaders, abandoned by their populations, flared and fizzed into life; none more so than those in northern Italy and the Low Countries, enriched and invigorated by swelling trade and burgeoning industry. A new literate and articulate class, the bourgeoisie, came into being, forming a middle band between the aristocracy and the peasants. The money economy came increasingly to supersede the old barter system. The need for numeracy and literacy, the intellectual stimulus of travel and the interchange of ideas provided a boost to education. The rise of the towns was one of the most influential features of the central Middle Ages.

The consequences of the urban revival were enormous, ramified, and far-reaching. As islands of freedom in a feudal world, the towns stimulated the development of representative assemblies and promoted the idea of self-government. They saw the emergence of a new form of law – commercial law – and more significantly promoted the idea of recourse to the courts instead of to violence and vendetta to settle disputes. They stimulated art, architecture and education. They were fertile sources of new ideas on religion, morality and belief as well as economics. They were potent vehicles for social mobility and oppor-tunity.

The emergence of the national monarchies was the other great feature of the age. In theory, Christian society was unitary and universal, ruled in a harmonious partnership by the Holy Roman Emperor and the Pope. But a succession of violent clashes between Papacy and Empire beginning with the Investiture Contest, a bitter dispute about the appointment of clerics in the eleventh century, made nonsense of that, and the emergence of the new national monarchies with distinctive identities (notably France and England) fractured the theory with tumultuous reality. The Holy Roman Emperor was effectively reduced to being king of Germany and northern Italy. By the eleventh century the ingredients necessary for the emergence of nation-states were present: the stabilization of Europe and the creation of more defined boundaries and borders, the introduction of permanent political insti-tutions particularly to handle finance and justice; and perhaps most important the beginning of a shift of loyalty from the local communities and religious organizations to the monarchy as the symbol of the nation. In France, a definite sense of national identity was engendered, sharpened by war with England, by conflict with the Papacy and by the promotion of Paris as the national capital, centre of learning, justice and administration. Something of the process was undergone by the Papacy, which without relinquishing its claims to supra-national authority, developed in the fourteenth and fifteenth centuries into a bureaucratic and legalistic monarchical power, acquiring a territorial state in central Italy and military and political alliances to implement its foreign policy. All of these embryonic states benefited from the rising population and from increasing wealth, which led to extra revenues flowing into their coffers.

But along with the great economic revival went a spiritual and intellectual revival. The Papacy in the tenth century had been morally bankrupt, the throne of St Peter, the play-thing of rival noble factions who elevated to occupy it a succession of scandalous charlatans. By 1045 there were three rival claimants. The Emperor Henry III stepped in to depose all three. Eventually he appointed his cousin as Pope Leo IX, the first of a succession of able and dedicated pontiffs who set out to reform both the Papacy and the priesthood and to put Rome at the head of the spiritual revival that was stirring. The restoration of the moral and spiritual independence and authority of the Papacy was only one facet of an explosion of religious feeling that took many and varied forms. Existing communities were reformed and reinvigorated, new monastic orders and houses were founded; there was a proliferation of holy hermits and the development of new forms of religious life (canons, friars); there was an upsurge in pilgrimages. The proclamation amidst scenes of wild enthusiasm of the First Crusade, the first of a series which spanned the remainder of the Middle Ages, harnessing the warrior knights of western Europe to the sacred cause of freeing the Holy Land, helped promote a concept of Christian knighthood, with new semi-monastic chivalric orders, sword-blessings, the cult of warrior saints, the sacralization of the process of conferring knighthood and the preaching of 'holy war'. In Spain the Christian kingdoms of the north began the drive to subdue the Moslem states in the centre and south of the country. In eastern Europe, religious missions, followed in due course by military expeditions, sought to convert the heathen Slavs. So far-reaching and deep-rooted was this mood of reform and revival that the historian Brenda Bolton has justly dubbed it 'The Medieval Reformation'.

This 'reformation' was matched by a 'renaissance' which was to open up the mind of man and send it off into all kinds of new and exciting directions. The 'renaissance' was the product of an educational revolution, as numerous urban schools arose to challenge the supremacy of the old monastic schools. From the new schools in the century emerged the universities, where philosophical, theological and intellectual speculation and debate found a permanent home. The 'renaissance' bred a new kind of scholar, dedicated to argument and logic, which found a leading place in the intellectual process for the first time since the fall of the Roman Empire.

Monumental intellectual undertakings were begun, including that of gathering, organizing and harmonizing the legacy of the Christian Roman past in scripture, theology and jurisprudence. Of particular significance, not just for the individual but for political, economic and social life, was the great revival in legal studies. The revival, stimulated by the rediscovery of the law codes of the Roman Emperor Justinian, produced a new breed of professionals – lawyers. They moved out of the universities and into the bureaucracies of the emerging national monarchies and of the Papacy. Around 1140, the canon lawyer Gratian completed his *Decretum*, a systematic code of Church law which was to remain authoritative throughout the Middle Ages.

But as Colin Morris has so persuasively argued, one of the most profound developments of the twelfth-century Renaissance was 'the discovery of the individual'. The early Middle Ages had afforded little scope for individualism. Its essential characteristic was communality, understandable in an age whose primary motivation was defence and resistance to attack from all sides. Organizationally it was a time of the emergence of feudal ties, creating links that bound men together in the interests of mutual defence. It was a time of close-knit monastic communities, banded together to preserve the faith and civilized values against the onslaught of the barbarians. It was a time in which Christianity was pre-eminently interpreted as the community of the faithful, a single unified body within which the individual submerged his distinctiveness to become an obedient identikit servant of God. The dominant literary form of the age was the epic poem, which stressed the need for the loyalty of the individual to larger units; the lord, friends, the family. Thus the keynote of the Dark Ages was obedience and unquestioning faith in authority. But the new emphasis on argument, on reason, and on logic inevitably led to a widespread questioning of established views and this meant a new openness and a new intellectual adventurousness.

One of the central themes of medieval thought now became a search for self and individual fulfilment. 'Know yourself', the alternative title of Peter Abelard's *Ethics*, became the motto of the age. The desire for self-knowledge lay behind the rise of autobiography, a literary form almost unknown in the Ancient World, in the concentration in sermons and treatises on the way in which the individual could relate to God and in the great growth of love literature. The element common to them all is the concern with self-analysis, the discussion of feelings, the experience of emotional and spiritual fulfilment rather than physical and sexual satisfaction.

This search for self-knowledge powerfully reinforced the promotion of penitential confession as a significant feature of religious life. In the early Church, penance for sins required public confession and exclusion from the community until after the penance and formal readmission. The formal, public, and essentially forensic penance took place at one of the great Lenten festivals of the Church. But during the Dark Ages things began to change. Private confession increasingly took over and penance was negotiated with the priest and performed in private. By the twelfth century it had become accepted that outward and formal satisfaction was no substitute for inner repentance. This received additional emphasis from the ruling of the 1215 Lateran Council that annual confession was a minimum requirement for all members of the Church. It was an attempt at one level to introduce the idea of self-examination throughout society. This concern with inner attitudes is illustrated by a new stress on intention in the assessment of conduct. The early penitentials and penal codes of the medieval west prescribed punishment for the action rather than the intention behind it. But during the twelfth century intention became a major consideration in theology and philosophy.

Few aspects of the faith remained immune from the process of individualization. Whereas for the first thousand years of Christianity Christ on the cross had been depicted as triumphant and radiant, redeeming the whole of mankind; from 1050 to 1200 the emphasis in pictures and carvings was on Christ's physical and emotional suffering and his individual love of mankind. At the same time a new position for prayer was adopted – kneeling with the hands together, the position in which the feudal vassal did his individual homage to his lord. This emphasized the individual's quest for salvation and for a private and personal relationship with God. The Church also promoted the concept of individual consent in marriage, a novel idea in an age where marriage was universally arranged by families.

Individualism is the defining characteristic of the key artistic form of the central Middle Ages – the romance, which superseded the epic. The chivalric romance involved the hero in a quest for his real identity and his personal destiny, for self-knowledge and self-fulfilment, based on love rather than the achievement of a family, tribal or national goal like the epic hero.

The political theory of the early Middle Ages was conformist. It had to be to survive. The dominant view was theocracy, with power flowing down from God through his chosen rulers to the people who obey those set in authority over them. But the opening up of society led to the questioning of established order and authority. One form was satire and the twelfth century was the golden age of medieval satire, attacking corruption and abuses. Another was the development of the concept of the citizen, an individual with rights and duties as opposed to the subject, who had no rights and must obey even an unjust superior. This concept evolved following the rediscovery of Aristotle's thought with its emphasis on individual rights and from the implications of the feudal system with its contractual arrangements between lord and vassal. St Thomas Aquinas (c.1225–74) successfully harmonized the new individualism with traditional Christian teachings by emphasising the role of individual conscience.

This newly prominent individualism fuelled the two dominant characteristics which Alexander Murray regards as defining the twelfth and thirteenth centuries: avarice, the habit of desiring more and more money, and ambition, the habit of desiring more and more power. Avarice, the by-product of the return to a money economy, was manifested in the great increase in robbery and simony, mounting hostility to the Jews, and the preoccupation of preachers and satirists alike with the excessive love of money. Ambition was stimulated by the increasing social mobility, most notably in the rise of the literate and numerate professionals (lawyers, administrators, career clerics). It became a theme of sermons from preachers for the first time in the twelfth century.

All this is not to argue that there was a state of rampant and unrestrained individualism. Medieval society continued to be strongly marked by communality – the monastic community, the village community, the parish, confraternities and guilds, knightly orders, urban communes – but most of these organizations were entered into by the free choice of the individual and for the first time there was a wide variety of alternatives to choose from.

For the Church the least welcome by-product of the upsurge of religious feeling and of individualism was heresy. Heresy appeared at every level of society and can be seen as a response to the major developments of the era. The ecclesiastical reform movement had thrown a harsh spotlight on the inadequacies of the existing clerical establishment, riddled with simony (sale of clerical office), nicolaitism (marriage of clergy) and lay investiture (secular control of church appointments). The rise of an urban and money-based life, the social inequalities it produced and the moral and ethical tensions it stimulated all contributed to a crisis of materialism. The reaction of significant sections of the population both in town and country was to reject the new world of avarice and ambition by seeking to practise a life of poverty and personal austerity and to by-pass the existing clerical establishment by entering into a direct personal relationship with God.

Heresy was one of the responses to the intellectual, economic, and social currents of the day but the quest for personal perfection was given added urgency by the ever-present background fear of the apocalypse.

In the universities too, sections of the intelligentsia turned to heresy, using their newly emancipated powers of reason to defend independent interpretations of the scripture, preaching and discussion without official licence and the promotion of unorthodox ideas. Although these developments, influenced by the rediscovery of Greek and the discovery of Islamic texts, rarely percolated down to the population at large, intellectuals often shared the aspirations and principles that received more populist expression in the wider society.

By the thirteenth century the authorities had decided that the time had come to silence the tumult of new ideas and to reintegrate or eliminate dissident religious movements. The emergence of centralized monarchical powers in both Church and state, in whose interests it was to maintain unity and uniformity based on a set of prescribed principles — religious, political and social — ensured that western Europe embarked on the systematic suppression of dissent and disorder in every area of life.

The single most significant event in this movement to limit the freedoms of the twelfth century was the Fourth Lateran Council of 1215. It was one of the most important oecumenical councils of the Middle Ages and it was stamped with the authority and vision of Pope Innocent III, an able, vigorous lawyer-Pope with a grand plan for the re-Christianization of society. It stressed reform of the clergy, the elimination of heresy, and crusade against the infidel. The Council was a major contributor to Innocent's programme and showed him tackling, with a subtle mixture of sophistication and authoritarianism, the problems of an increasingly pluralistic society. The Council's significance was increased by the fact that some of the most important secular rulers of western Europe, the Emperor Frederick II, King Louis VIII of France and King Jaime I of Aragon, incorporated many of the provisions against heretics into their own law codes.

The first group of regulations introduced was aimed at strengthening the Church's control over the lives and beliefs of the laity. The Council ordered the duty of annual confession and communion on every Christian on pain of exclusion from attendance at church and denial of church burial. It introduced the reading of banns for marriages and outlawed clandestine marriage, to further secure clerical control of the marriage ceremony. It prohibited preaching without papal and episcopal licence, in order to maintain ecclesiastical control of the dissemination of religious truth. It permitted public veneration of newly discovered relics only with specific papal permission, in order to control spontaneous outbursts of popular piety. It restricted the granting of

Indulgences to bishops. So marriage, preaching, and popular cults were brought under tight hierarchical control; confession was meant to monitor the lives of the faithful and the control of Indulgences was to prevent them from escaping too easily from the consequences of sin.

At the same time the Council made provision for adequate clerical service. It ordered that bishops appoint enough clergy to ensure proper preaching and confession in every parish. It limited episcopal vacancies to ensure adequate pastoral care. It ordered annual provincial synods and triennial general chapters of the monastic orders to oversee the work of the clergy. It ordered bishops to monitor the level of education and personal conduct of candidates for the priesthood and to provide proper theological instruction. It banned the holding of multiple benefices, because the practice diminished proper pastoral care. Clergy were banned from hunting, falconry, dicing, drinking bouts, excessive feasting and attending theatrical entertainments, all of which had brought them into disrepute. All this was aimed at ensuring that there was proper, trained and effective clerical provision for the people.

Third, the Council took steps to combat heresy. It issued a declaration of faith, anathematized all heretics and issued detailed instructions on how to deal with them. They were to be excommunicated and handed over to the secular power for punishment and their property was to be confiscated. All holders of secular office were to take an oath to exterminate heresy and if they refused, they were to be excommunicated. There were to be yearly episcopal visits to report on heresy. A crusading indulgence was granted to any layman taking up arms to expel heretics. Those who were suspected of being, harbouring, defending or favouring heretics were to be given two warnings or a year of excommunication to reconsider. There was a ban on new religious orders to halt that proliferation which had characterized religious life in the twelfth century and had given rise in some cases to suspicion of heresy.

Fourth, the Council dealt with other minorities. Jews and Moslems were ordered to wear distinctive clothing, to prevent them mingling with Christians unawares. Jews were banned from holding office and practising usury and subjected to curfew in Easter week. In 1179 the Third Lateran Council had imposed penalties on homosexuals (deposition and penitential imprisonment in monasteries for clerical offenders; excommunication for laymen). The Fourth Lateran Council strengthened this by decreeing the 'effective and rigorous' observation of the canonical penalties on all unchaste clergy, especially homosexuals, and decreeing life deposition for anyone who dared to celebrate divine service after suspension for the sin. The 1179 Council had already endorsed the segregation of lepers. Taken together with the action on heretics, this clearly betokens a mentality which sought to segregate,

10

isolate and label deviant or dissident minorities, in order to prevent their contaminating Christians.

The distinctive clothing rule led to the development of the so-called 'badge of infamy', which was applied to all the significant minority groups apart from homosexuals. After 1215, Jews, Moslems and also prostitutes ordered to wear distinctive clothing, took to wearing a badge or sign. The Jews adopted a yellow felt circle known as the *rouelle* and prostitutes a red cord (the *aiguillette*). But there were many local and regional variations of this. Lepers were increasingly ordered to wear special clothes, by, for instance, the Council of Marenac in 1330. Leper hospitals often had uniforms for inmates. But usually it was the lepers' rattle or bell, used to signal their approach, which was their badge. In 1229 the Council of Toulouse ordered heretics who had repented to wear two yellow crosses sewn onto the front of their garments. The order was renewed by subsequent councils and the number increased to three in 1246. The same practice can be found in northern France and Germany. The makers of spells and incantations were ordered to wear two pieces of yellow felt similar to the *rouelle*, and clergy involved in spells, idolatry and witchcraft were to wear four pieces of yellow felt. The regular re-enactment of all these regulations suggests widespread attempts to evade them on the part of minorities and a determination by the authorities to maintain segregation.

Finally, the Fourth Lateran Council institutionalized the process of inquisition, introducing the practice of initiating legal procedures without private accusation and ordering ecclesiastical visitation, inquiry and action. This completed the process begun when Pope Lucius III decreed in 1184 that ecclesiastical inquisitorial tribunals be established all over Christendom and continued in 1199 when Pope Innocent III declared that heretics were traitors to God, branding them with the cardinal sin in the feudal world – faithlessness and betrayal.

It is impossible to overestimate the importance of the legal revolution of the twelfth century and in particular the introduction of the inquisitorial procedure into western Europe. The rediscovery and study of Roman Law restored to the intellectual context the Roman model of a written law code, a formal system of courts, judges and trials with the authorities initiating accusations and a fixed system of penalties.

Previously the system in both church courts and secular courts had been private and communal accusation before a bishop or lord or village elders. If there was no agreement or confession, then trial by ordeal (fire or water), combat or compurgation (formal oath by the accused of his innocence, backed by a group of oath-helpers or supporters) followed. It was a system of communal self-policing based on collective judgement and compensatory payments to the injured. In the twelfth century these old rituals were replaced by a new system, *inquisitio*, a formal procedure, the initiation of action by officials acting on suspicion, denunciation, or their own authority, and including the collection of evidence, the hearing of witnesses and judgement. The new method was proclaimed as early as the Council of Tours (1163) and was strengthened by the enactments of Popes Lucius III, Innocent III and Gregory IX and its use in the inquisition of heretics. As early as 1063 Pope Alexander II had forbidden priests to be subjected to trial by ordeal. But in 1215 the Lateran Council banned it. The secular authorities followed: England in 1218, southern Italy in 1231, and Germany in 1298. Combat continued to be available throughout the Middle Ages but it was an option mainly restricted to the aristocracy and regarded as a mark of their status.

The inquisition system enabled the bishop to discipline his flock swiftly and authoritatively, and the advantages of the system became clear to the secular authorities in Italy, Spain and France, where it was introduced. But it never came to England where the jury system prevailed. However, both in England and on the Continent justice became the king's justice and ceased to be a matter of communal decision. Judges were sent out, records kept and laws codified. Increasingly the king was seen as law-maker and law-enforcer, for adherence to a single system of law with the crown as fount of justice was an ideal way of unifying kingdoms and centralizing authority.

The ordeal had emerged in the sixth century to take the place of vendetta. It was the instrument, in the words of Peter Brown, for maintaining consensus and containing potential disruption, by the employment of ritual and an appeal to supernatural authority. But under the inquisitorial system the nature of crime changed. Crime was no longer seen as an offence against an individual, to be compensated for by financial reparation. It was an offence against society, defined and defended by the king, and a scale of physical penalties (flogging, branding, mutilation, execution) was enforced to encourage the maintenance of order.

The old system did have one particular advantage. It always produced a result one way or another. The new system did not necessarily do so. In the thirteenth century an accused could only be condemned on the testimony of two eye witnesses or by confession. If the evidence was circumstantial or partial, there was no conviction. So to obtain confession, the authorities turned to torture. Pope Gregory the Great had declared invalid confessions obtained under torture, and that decision had been duly inscribed in Gratian's *Decretum*, but it entered the legal process as a way of making the new system work effectively. From the second half of the thirteenth century to the end of the eighteenth torture was part of the ordinary criminal procedure of the Church and most of the states of Europe. Significantly, it is first seen in action in the populous cities of northern Italy and Flanders where there was an urgent need to clear up crimes fast and decisively. It was not introduced into England. Torture was not supposed to inflict death or permanent injury, and clergy, nobles, children and pregnant women were exempt. It was initially not available to the Papal Inquisition, but in 1252 Pope Innocent IV decreed that heretics were thieves and murderers of souls and should be treated in the same way as ordinary thieves and murderers. So torture was made available. Just as confession became central to the Church's means of gaining control of the spiritual life of the laity, it also became central to the state's method of enforcing law and order. The whole process was loaded in favour of the accuser rather than the accused and in favour of authority rather than the community. This was to make the persecution of minorities that much easier.

In his lucid and thoughtful book *The Formation of a Persecuting Society*, R. I. Moore saw the rise of a persecuting society as a direct concomitant of the emergence of the centralizing monarchies. The assertion of legal authority by kings and popes is seen as part of the process of removing judicial authority from the community and from the people to the centralizing powers. Moore sees this as directly paralleling the action against heretics. Heresy expressed communal independence and collective values and had to be suppressed by an authoritarian centralizing Church. Trial by ordeal, the prime method of community policing, was replaced by a system of law courts answerable to the authorities. So Church and state willingly co-operated, establishing a new order in Europe based on nation-states, papal monarchy and noble households. The prime features in the creation of the new order were the replacement of payment in service and kind by payment in money, the superseding of the oral process by written records and displacement of warriors by literate clerks as the chief agents of government. So Moore sees the formation of the persecuting society as a function of the rise of the *literati*, who sought to impose reason, law and uniformity on an undisciplined and ignorant people, identifying and either eliminating or neutralizing by segregation minority groups.

There is a good deal of force in this argument. But it needs to be set in the wider mental and spiritual context of the age. There is a common denominator in all the groups under threat and that is sex. Instead of seeing the persecuting society primarily as a result of the rise of the *literati* I am inclined to see it more as the product of a puritan reformation following the millennium. The continuing movement in the Church to gain control of marriage and eliminate irregular sexual liaisons, the drive to enforce clerical celibacy, the development of a detailed and coherent body of church law on sexual matters, defining

13

and prescribing conduct very precisely, all testify to the desire of the Church to exert control over the sexuality of the faithful. The regulation of prostitutes and homosexuals was an obvious element in this programme. Heretics who often had very different views on sexual matters from those of the Church (enhanced status for women, the unimportance of church marriage, the rejection of procreation) were regularly accused by the Church of addiction to orgies and sodomy. Leprosy was deemed to be a punishment by God for sexual sin and lepers were popularly deemed to be lustful. Jews were said to be agents of the Devil, to have abnormally large sex organs and to be lusting after Christian maidens. Certainly the Church sought theological and spiritual uniformity but it also sought sexual uniformity and was prepared to enlist the secular authorities to impose it. The changeover in the thirteenth century is marked. From the dominant ideas of penance and forgiveness, trial by ordeal and community sanctions in the early Middle Ages, both Church and state went over increasingly to policies of persecution and execution, segregation and isolation. Tolerance is perhaps the chief hallmark of the truly Christian society; tolerance and forgiveness: hating the sin but loving the sinner. Isolation, segregation and persecution are the hallmarks of an authoritarian society, which requires everyone to be the same on pain of death. Two key phenomena of the central Middle Ages, the towns and the national monarchies, shared with an increasingly authoritarian Papacy the desire to deal with dissidents and deviants. The very fact of the rise of the towns focused attention on problems of health and hygiene (lepers), public morality (prostitutes and homosexuals), economic competition (the Jews) and religious uniformity (Jews, heretics, witches), all of which were of significance either to the authorities or the public at large, or both.

The plight of the minorities was, if anything, exacerbated by the second great psychological crux of the Middle Ages, the Black Death. The Black Death (bubonic, pneumonic and septicaemic plague) devastated Europe during the years 1347–9, carrying off, at present estimates, about a third of the population. 'So many died', wrote the Sienese chronicler Agnolo di Tura de Grasso, 'that all believed it was the end of the world.' But this was not an isolated catastrophe; it was part of a pandemic. In 1361–2 a second plague (*pestis secunda*) struck; between 10 and 20 per cent of the population perished. It killed so many young men that it was also known as 'the Boys' Plague' (*pestis puerorum*). In 1369 the third plague (*tertia pestis*) wiped out a further 10–15 per cent of the population. The plague recurred in cycles every five to ten years throughout the Middle Ages. The weakened population fell prey to smallpox, malaria, dysentery and enteric fever, with the result that the European population in 1430 was 50–75 per cent lower

14

than it had been in 1290. It did not recover to its thirteenth-century level until the mid-sixteenth century, after growing slowly from the 1450s onwards.

This demographic catastrophe came on top of major climatic change. The great expansion of population, towns and trade in the eleventh and twelfth centuries had come about in conditions of mild winters, dry summers, and food surpluses. But between 1250 and 1300 the climate changed and a 'Little Ice Age' was ushered in, and echoed in a fourteenth-century prayer which contained the ominous words *frigiscente mundo* ('with the world growing cold'). The colder and wetter weather which was a feature of this period had a disastrous effect on food supplies. Successive harvest failures coupled with soil exhaustion and over-cultivation made famine a fact of life. The population was simply too large for the existing food supplies. In a good year, people could just manage. But there were few good years and in the wake of hunger stalked pestilence. From the 1290s to the 1340s there was a succession of wet summers, harvest failures, animal murrains, and epidemics of typhoid, dysentery and diphtheria.

There was for instance a serious famine in the years 1315–17, which began with prolonged and torrential rain, ruining the harvest of 1315. The severe famine and disease that ensued reduced people to eating cats and dogs, leaves and roots, and in some places to cannibalism. There was an upsurge in crime as people were driven to desperate measures to obtain food. Then a disastrous murrain wiped out many of the cattle. The pattern was repeated in 1316 and 1317. The famine and pestilence in France, England and Germany were worse than any living person could remember. The heavily populated Low Countries suffered particularly badly and at the height of the famine in Ypres something like 18 per cent of the population died.

The plague pandemic multiplied the misery considerably and the later centuries of the Middle Ages were suffused by pessimism, gloom and despair. The reactions of people to the plague are described by Boccaccio in his *Decameron*. Some retired into seclusion, living temperately and hoping thus to escape the plague. Others embarked on a life of frantic debauchery on the 'eat, drink and be merry for tomorrow we die' principle. There were wild bursts of hysterical scapegoatism which culminated in horrific massacres of the Jews, who were accused of spreading the plague.

As the pandemic settled in, the ever-present conviction of the imminent end of the world intensified. Faced with that prospect, there was an upsurge of hedonism, crime rates rose and contemporaries perceived and commented on an increase in immorality. But perhaps more significant was the upsurge of religious activity. In the immediate aftermath of the plague, processions of flagellants took to the streets, savagely scourging themselves and hoping to propitiate the evident wrath of God, and there were outbreaks of tarantism, frantic and compulsive dancing, a grotesque 'dance of death'. There was a burst of pilgrimage activity and the proclamation of new saints, like St Roch, an inhabitant of Montpellier who devoted himself to nursing plague victims. There was also a notable increase in charitable donations and foundations. In London, the amount of the average charity bequest in wills increased by 40 per cent between 1350 and 1360. But in the longer term there was a powerful impulse towards personal asceticism and of course an almost inevitable return to heresy, which in the most famous case (Hussism) took on a national dimension.

The Black Death intensified the medieval preoccupation with 'the four last things', death, judgement, heaven and hell. It had a marked effect on art and literature, which became saturated in images of pain and death. Mystery plays with religious themes became common and usually told of human decay and the torments of hell. Funerals became great events, marked by lavish ceremonial. Revealingly, where the pictorial calendars of the thirteenth and fourteenth centuries had emphasized spring and summer, in the late fourteenth and fifteenth centuries they highlighted autumn and winter. With death and the end seemingly closer than ever, salvation became more and more important. The established Church failed to meet the challenge. It had already suffered a loss of prestige. The Papacy lost credibility as an independent force when it moved to Avignon in 1309 and was widely seen to be under the thumb of the French king. In the eyes of many it ceased to be the moral and spiritual leader of Christendom and became just another bureaucratic state, preoccupied with finance and law. This perception was intensified by the Great Schism (1378–1415) in which a succession of rival popes in Rome and Avignon, divided not by doctrine but by power politics, fought it out until a council of the Church at Constance (1414–17) resolved it by deposing the rival claimants and installing a new Pope. The organization of the Church was seriously impaired by the ravages of the Black Death. Many of its best intellects died and large numbers of parish priests fled. Under the circumstances, the people looked to themselves for spiritual deliverance.

The social order was seriously affected by the plague. But the effects of pestilence were compounded by those of war. The Hundred Years War (which actually lasted, though intermittently, for 116 years) subjected England and France to a succession of campaigns between 1337 and 1453 which were ruinously costly in men and money. France, where the war was fought out, was ravaged by roving war bands and riven by murderous factional rivalry within the aristocracy. The flower of French chivalry was wiped out in the successive defeats at Crécy (1346), Poitiers (1356) and Agincourt (1415). In England the Hundred Years

War was no sooner ended than the Wars of the Roses filled the country with civil strife. So in addition to death by disease, there was man-made death on a large scale.

However, widespread death gave new men the opportunity to rise up and make fortunes. The *nouveaux riches* like the de la Poles in England and the Florentine Medicis seized the chance to rise to dizzy heights of power and social pre-eminence. At the same time acute labour shortage meant that labour costs shot up. Post-Black Death societies passed a succession of sumptuary laws, regulating people's dress, so that they did not seek to get above their station, and sought to hold down wages for fear of bankrupting the aristocracy. But these strategies did not work, and indeed exacerbated the situation which in some areas gave rise to revolutionary millenarian ideas. In others change and crisis led to major revolts, notably of the peasants in the Jacquerie Revolt in France in 1358, and in England in 1381, and of the urban poor in the rising of the *Ciompi*, the Florentine textile workers, in 1378. Where there had been few rebellions up to the late thirteenth century, there were to be many in the years following the Black Death, as class conflict sharpened. Not only this but there was a general breakdown in law and order. The incidence of homicide in England, for instance, in the period 1349–69 was twice what it had been in the period 1320–40, despite the loss of a third of the population.

The great reduction in the population meant the end of the sub-sistence crisis. Low prices, high wages and sufficient food supplies enabled the lower orders, if they had survived the plague, to flourish. This had various knock-on effects. The manorial system was under-mined in western Europe and a substantial free peasantry emerged. For depopulation meant that peasants worked all the land they could and paid rent. Labour services were commuted into money and other duties were replaced by money payments and long-term leases. The lords in consequence became *rentiers* and absentee landlords, seeking their fortunes at the royal courts. In Eastern Europe, the reverse happened. The lords kept the peasants down by force and imposed an even harsher serfdom to ensure prosperous grain production. Depopu-lation also accelerated the laicization of society, with secular schools making the running in education, lawyers and bureaucrats tightening their control over the governments and theories of royal authority being articulated.

Like every other aspect of existence, intellectual life suffered from the ravages of the plague. Twenty universities disappeared between 1350 and 1400. Many highly skilled and highly trained people perished and could not be replaced. The crisis in scholarship hastened the growth of vernacular languages to replace Latin as the language of government and official business. In the realm of ideas, there was a growth of conservatism and scepticism. The clear and dominant ideas of reason and logic that had held sway since the early thirteenth century were eclipsed. William of Ockham's thought-system displaced Aristotelianism. He rejected the process of abstract reasoning and argued that knowledge could only be intuitive and individual. He saw only two possible alternatives for confronting the mysteries of the universe: unquestioning faith in those truths which could not be demonstrated, such as the existence of God, or logical deduction, applied to what could be observed in the created world. The promotion of faith over reason encouraged the individual search for God and further diminished the role of the priesthood, while the sharp differentiation of sacred from profane encouraged both the secularization of science and the promotion of realism in art. It was a very different thought-world from that of St Thomas Aquinas and St Albertus Magnus.

Lynn White Jr has described the period from 1300 to 1650 as 'the most psychically disturbed in European history', a time of heightened anxiety due to rapid cultural change and a succession of disasters. This is certainly true of the latter half of the Middle Ages. The twelfth and thirteenth centuries, the era which had seen the building of the Gothic cathedrals, the expansion of the towns, the rise of the universities, the growth of courtly love literature and vernacular poetry, the revival in Roman law, the recapture of the Holy Land, the Medieval Reformation and the Medieval Renaissance, was replaced by an era of doubt, fear and uncertainty, war, destruction and depopulation, disease, decay and death.

In the context of the optimism and expansion of the central Middle Ages and the recession and pessimism of the later Middle Ages, what was the position of minorities? They suffered under both dispensations. The desire of the Church, the state and the municipalities to promote unity, order and uniformity coupled with the rise of Christian fundamentalism and religious enthusiasm in the central Middle Ages created an atmosphere ripe for the persecution of the minorities. The overwhelming air of approaching apocalypse and the need for scapegoats in the later Middle Ages maintained it.

Minority groups have notoriously been susceptible to stereotyping. Stereotypes are a way of making sense of a disordered universe, imposing order, defining self, personalizing fears. As Sander L. Gilman has written:

Everyone creates stereotypes. We cannot function in the world without them. They buffer us against our most urgent fears by extending them, making it possible for us to act as though their source were beyond our control. Stereotypes are a crude set of mental representations of the world. They perpetuate a needed sense of difference between 'the self' and 'the other'.

This was particularly true of the Middle Ages which was much given to the making of lists, creation of hierarchies and rank ordering of things. There were positive stereotypes of the knight and the holy man, role models to live up to. But there were also negative stereotypes. The negative stereotype, according to Gilman, appears in the adult as a response to anxiety, 'an anxiety having its roots in the potential disintegration of the mental representations the individual has created and internalized'.

Thus threats to the established social structure or to the existing ideological structure of society provoked the creation of negative stereotypes embodying the threat. The stereotype arose specifically from the social context, its form and content dictated by the society that produced it. It constituted what was different, and difference was what threatened order and control.

> This mental representation of difference is but the projection
> of the tension between control and its loss present within each
> individual in every group. That tension produced an anxiety that
> is given shape by the other.

Gilman sees the stereotypes of 'The Other' as incorporating the basic categories by which the self is defined – the sense of personal mutability, the central role of sexuality and the relationship to the larger groups: broadly illness, sexuality and race. Awareness of the fragility of human organization lay not just in its mortality but its susceptibility to disease, corruption, pollution and alteration. Human sexuality when out of control defies agreed norms. In racial terms, 'The Other' is defined as physical antithesis of the self, the threat to the group. The three frequently overlap, with racial difference seen in terms of sexual threat and sexual difference perceived in terms of illness.

This was peculiarly true of the Middle Ages where a racial minority (the Jews), an illness (leprosy), and a sexual minority (homosexuals) were seen as threats to the self defined as Christian, healthy and heterosexual. But given the overwhelming importance of religion, there was a predominant other – the Devil – who lay behind awareness of the activity of minorities, inspiring them to seek to encompass the destruction of God's order.

Just as in modern times, there was an overlap between minority groups in the Middle Ages in popular perception. Pope Gregory the Great and St Isidore of Seville in the early Middle Ages used the term 'leprosy' to describe heresy, a disease infecting the healthy body of believers. The metaphor of disease was applied regularly to heresy, as

R. I. Moore has demonstrated. He discovered that the word *pestis* (plague) was used of almost every significant outbreak of heresy in the twelfth century. Eckbert of Schönau, for instance, complained that the Cathars

> have multiplied in every land and the church is now greatly endangered by the foul poison which flows against it from every side. Their message spreads like a cancer, runs far and wide like a leprosy, infecting the limbs of Christ as it goes.

This was a well-established usage dating back to the Ancient World: Augustine, Origen, Bede and Rabanus Maurus all used it. In the sixth century Bishop Caesarius of Arles spoke of the Jews being infected with 'the leprosy of sin'. In the eleventh century, William the Monk declared to the heresiarch Henry of Lausanne:

> You too are a leper, scarred by heresy, excluded from communion by the judgement of the priest according to the law, bare-headed, with ragged clothing, your body is covered by an infected and filthy garment; it befits you to shout increasingly that you are a leper, a heretic and unclean and must live outside the church.

In the twelfth century, according to Beryl Smalley, theological writers 'used the word "leprosy" almost interchangeably with "sin"'. But the most interesting aspect of the relationship is heresy–leprosy–sex. Leprosy was believed to be sexually transmitted, hence the ban on lepers entering brothels and statutes of leper-houses seeking to curb their promiscuous natures. Heresiarchs like Tanchelm and Henry of Lausanne were accused of promiscuous sexual behaviour.

The Council of Ancyra, St Peter Damian, and Pope Gregory IX all used the term 'leprosy' to apply to sodomy. Bishop Jacques de Vitry of Acre compared prostitution to 'an incurable leprosy'. A thirteenth-century description of leprosy included a reference to the victim being 'horned' thus linking lepers to Jews and magicians, who were believed to be similarly endowed, and at one remove to the horned Devil, their master.

Other linkages were made. The Jewish terms 'synagogue' and 'sabbat' were applied to the meetings of witches. Witches and heretics were regularly accused of staging homosexual orgies. The laws of thirteenth-century England linked Jews, sodomites, sorcerers and heretics together as deserving of death. Lepers, Moslems and Jews were accused in 1321 of trying to poison the wells of France. Witches in Hungary were sentenced for their first offence to wear a Jew's hat in public. Prostitutes in one southern French town were confined in the local leper-house during Easter week. The chronicler Salimbene called the heretical Apostolic Brethren of Gerard Segarelli 'the synagogue of Satan'. In

1 Last Judgement by Stefan Lochner, Cologne c. 1430. (Reproduced by kind permission of the Wallraf Richartz Museum and the Rheinische Bildarchiv, Cologne.)

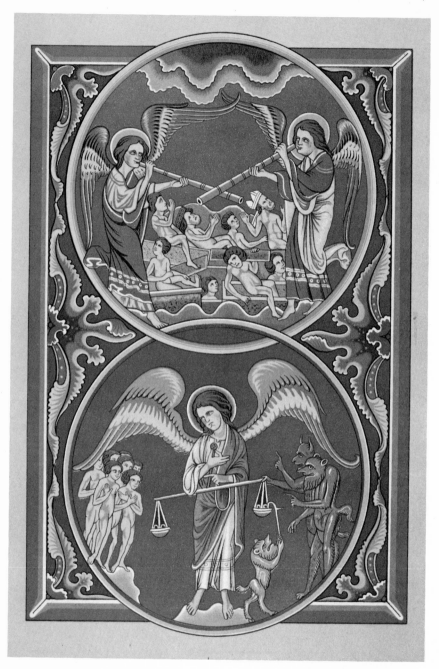

2 Representation of the Last Judgement and the weighing of souls, from a thirteenth century psalter. (Reproduced by kind permission of the Mary Evans Picture Library.)

3 Confession: the confessional became an increasingly important feature of religious life in the Middle Ages. Anonymous woodcut, 1482. (Reproduced by kind permission of the Mary Evans Picture Library.)

4 The angel holding the keys of Hell enchains the devil, in the form of a dragon, from a twelfth-century commentary on the Apocalypse. (Reproduced by kind permission of the Mary Evans Picture Library.)

5 Virginity: St Aldhem, a Saxon priest offers his poem *De Virginitate* to the nuns of Barking. English, eleventh century. (Reproduced by kind permission of the Bodleian Library MS. Bodley 577, fol. 1v.)

6 The storming of the Castle of Love, from a fifteenth-century romance *Champion des dames*. (Reproduced by kind permission of the Mary Evans Picture Library.)

7 Lovers in a garden, 1525. The figures on this Italian majolica dish were taken from a popular engraving by Robetta known as *The Stream of Life*. (Reproduced by kind permission of the Victoria and Albert Museum.)

8 The kiss. Drug bottle inscribed *Aqua capillorum Veneris*. Faenza, 1535. (Reproduced by kind permission of the Victoria and Albert Museum.)

9 Erotic pleasures. An anonymous woodcut, Basle *c.*1430. (Reproduced by kind permission of the Mary Evans Picture Library.)

10 Preparing the feast for a wedding. This twelfth century illustration to a St Albans manuscript of Terence's *Woman of Andros* derived from a much earlier classical version. (Reproduced by kind permission of the Bodleian Library, M S. Auct. F.2.13, fol. 4 v.)

11 Marriage ceremony performed by a bishop, English, fourteenth century. (Reproduced by kind permission of the British Library.)

12 Heretics depicted as demons attacking the Christian Trinity. From an English thirteenth-century manuscript. (Reproduced by kind permission of the British Library.)

13 Albigensian heretics and their lovers. The accompanying commentary accused them of devil worship and sodomy. From a late thirteenth-century manuscript, northern France: left hand column, second roundel with accompanying commentary. (Reproduced by kind permission of the Bodleian Library M S. Bodley 270b, fol. 123 v.)

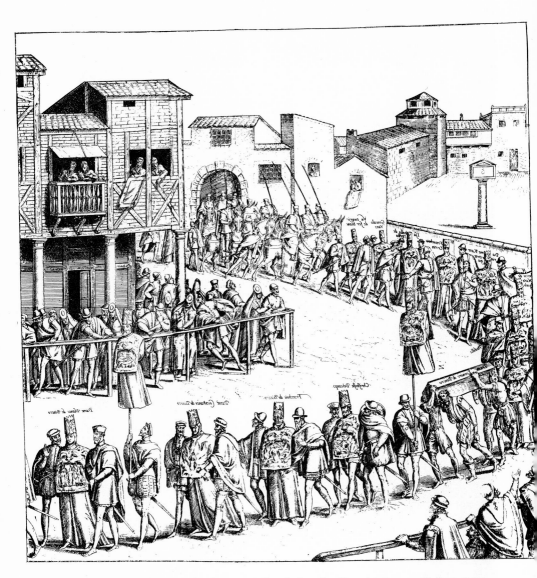

14 Heretics about to be burnt to death by the Inquisition at Valladolid in
1559. (Reproduced by kind permission of the Mary Evans Picture Library.)

15 St Dominic presiding over an auto-da-fé to exterminate heresy, by Pedro Berruguete *c.* 1450–1503. (Reproduced by kind permission of the Museo del Prado, Madrid.)

16 Demons assist at the conceiving of Anti-Christ. From a German pamphlet *Der Entchrist*, 1475. (Reproduced by kind permission of the Mary Evans Picture Library.)

17 Instruments of torture used for the witch trials at Bamberg in 1508. Torture ws accepted practice for the Church and secular courts in most of Europe from the thirteenth to the end of the eighteenth century. (Reproduced by kind permission of the Mansell Collection.)

Tortosa in 1346, Jews, Saracens, and prostitutes were forbidden to use the public baths except on specified days of the week.

In her book *Purity and Danger*, Mary Douglas writes:

> The whole universe is harnessed in man's attempts to force one another into good citizenship. Thus we find certain moral values are upheld and certain social rules defined by beliefs in dangerous contagion, as when the glance or touch of an adulterer is held to bring illness to his neighbours or his children.

The threat of danger from the unclean is used to coerce others into line. Medieval society fitted this picture exactly. There was a moral and physical threat of contagion from dangerous minorities, hence the segregation and labelling with the 'badge of infamy' of Jews, lepers, and prostitutes. The attribution of leprosy to sexual sin, the blaming of sodomy for disasters like the Great Flood and the Black Death, the use of cleansing fire to destroy heretics, sodomites and witches all reinforce the warnings to avoid deviation from the norm. But increasingly in the later Middle Ages the moral contagion came to be seen as an actual one, with Jews and/or prostitutes in Perpignan (1299), Lerida (1350), Cervera (1399) and Solsona (1434), forbidden to touch foodstuffs unless they bought them.

The six groups who are the subject of this study broadly fit into religious (Jews, witches, heretics) and sexual (homosexuals, prostitutes and lepers) categories. But one common factor links them all – sex. It was the stereotype of the lustful deviant closely linked with the Devil that was used to demonize them all. The Devil is the ultimate 'Other', the inspirer of evil, the antithesis of the Christian God and it was he who, by exploiting the susceptibility of the weak-willed to sex and by poisoning their minds, was portrayed as seeking to use them to overturn God's natural order.

2

SEX IN THE MIDDLE AGES

For centuries historians have studied war and money, law and religion, art and power, the working out of some basic human instincts – but only recently have they turned to study in depth humankind's primal instinct, the urge to reproduce itself and thereby perpetuate the race through sex. This intellectual taboo testifies powerfully to the legacy of Christian teaching and thinking upon western civilization. In the nineteenth century passages dealing with sexual matters in ancient texts were left in the 'decent obscurity of a classical language'. That obscurity is now being dispelled as the searching lamps of historical investigation are trained on the darkness, lamps which have thus far shone brightest in the universities of France and America. Massive and authoritative studies pour regularly from the presses. These works survey the sources in depth, place them in context and seek to recreate for us something of the sexual experience and sensibilities of the Middle Ages: James A. Brundage's *Law, Sex and Christian Society*, Jacques Rossiaud's *Medieval Prostitution*, John Boswell's *Christianity, Homosexuality and Social Tolerance*, Pierre Payer's *Sex and the Penitentials* are just a few of the key works in this area, joined most recently by Peter Brown's dazzling *The Body and Society*, which concentrates on the Ancient World but highlights themes and preoccupations that continue into the Middle Ages.

What evidence is there for medieval attitudes to sex and sexuality? It comes under three main headings: theoretical (medical texts, theological treatises, law codes), practical (court records, the Church's penitential handbooks), and cultural (poetry, prose, jokes, rhymes). It was the Church, the dominant force in the moral and spiritual lives of medieval people, which took the lead in prescribing what sexual acts people might indulge in and regulating where, when, and with whom sex could take place. The degree to which churchmen achieved their aims is unlikely to be known with any precision. But then precise estimates of the degree of people's conformity to social and sexual norms in any age are hard to come by. However, from the Church's actions and reactions, preoccupations and pronouncements, we can deduce something of the attitudes and practices which churchmen were seeking to combat.

The Church prescribed in full knowledge of the power of the sex drive. One eminent cleric wrote in one of his prayers:

> There is one evil, an evil above all other evils, that I am aware is always with me, that grievously and piteously lacerates and afflicts my soul. It was with me from the cradle, it grew with me in childhood, in adolescence, in my youth and it always stuck to me, and it does not desert me even now that my limbs are failing because of my old age. This evil is sexual desire, carnal delight, the storm of lust that has smashed and battered my unhappy soul, drained it of all strength and left it weak and empty.

This was none other than St Anselm, Archbishop of Canterbury (1033–1109).

The attitude to sex he expressed is typical of the Christian Church as a whole. For Christianity was from its early days a sex-negative religion. That is to say, Christian thinkers regarded sex as at best a kind of necessary evil, regrettably indispensable for human reproduction but interfering with a person's true vocation – the search for spiritual perfection, which is by definition non-sexual, transcending the flesh. That is why Christian teaching exalted celibacy and virginity as the highest forms of life. This marked a decisive break with the pagan Ancient World which was preoccupied with the maintenance of the population and perpetuating the family; it therefore placed little value on perpetual virginity. Christ had said nothing about Original Sin but in the second century Clement of Alexandria linked it directly to the discovery of sex by Adam and Eve. St Augustine refined this, identifying Original Sin with sexual desire rather than simply sex. But popular preachers, confessors, and priests continued to make the simple equation that Original Sin equals sex. This entered the popular consciousness.

Sexuality was, according to Christian teaching, given to people solely for the purposes of reproduction and for no other reason. Christ had envisaged marriage as the normal state for people and pronounced it indissoluble, except in cases of adultery. St Paul stressed that celibacy was the highest ideal, the most desirable form of life, but that marriage was an acceptable second best. 'It is better to marry than to burn,' he said. Marriage thus became the basic Christian means of regulating sexual desire, combating fornication and perpetuating the race.

Sex was not to be used for mere pleasure. By this definition, all sex outside marriage, both heterosexual and homosexual, was a sin and inside marriage sex was to be used only for procreation. Medieval theologians stressed that it was a mortal sin to embrace one's wife solely for pleasure. 'A man who is too passionately in love with his wife is an

23

adulterer,' said St Jerome in the fourth century, an opinion regularly reiterated throughout the Middle Ages. It was not until the end of the sixteenth century that the idea of sex purely for pleasure was advanced as a serious theoretical proposition.

The Church's bid to control sexuality had a positive aspect and a negative aspect. The positive aspect was to channel sexual activity into marriage and to extend Church control over marriage, transforming it from a largely secular institution into a sacrament. This process has been sensitively traced by Georges Duby.

It was in ninth-century France that the Church began the long process of sacralization. This took the form of asserting priestly control of the marriage ceremony, which had until then been a largely secular affair, a matter of negotiation and contract between families with the priest only tangentially involved, usually blessing the marriage bed. Sacralization also involved the enforcing of new rules designed to increase the stabilizing effect of marriage on society: the enforcement of monogamy, indissolubility of marriage, the prohibition of marriage to the seventh degree of blood relationship, the discouragement of remarriage and the promotion of the idea of consent by the marrying couple. The emphasis on the consent of the couple was a new development. In the Germanic and Roman marriage traditions, consent was a much broader concept in which emphasis was frequently placed on the agreement of the father of the bride.

It may be that we should see the promotion of consent by the couple as part of the rise of individualism which characterized the twelfth century. That is more plausible than Jack Goody's suggestion that the Church's marriage regulations were designed to ensure that vast amounts of land were left to the Church because the restrictions ensured that many families died out for lack of heirs. The Church did acquire vast tracts of land by inheritance from childless couples or single women but to erect that consequence into a cause is a classic example of *post hoc ergo propter hoc*. It seems more likely that the promotion of consent was part of the process of sacralization. Someone had to ensure that the consent was freely given and accepted and that someone was the priest. The new centrality of the priest's role in the marriage ceremony was symbolized by the fact that instead of handing the bride directly to the husband, the parents now handed her to the priest who joined her with her husband.

It took several centuries for the Church's interpretation of marriage to be accepted and there were bitter and sometimes protracted struggles with the aristocracy, who for reasons of securing the succession and acquiring ever more land favoured the easy dissolubility of marriage and regular remarriage. But by the twelfth century the Church had effectively gained legal, moral and organizational control of marriage.

The ceremony of marriage had been transferred from the home to the Church (though still outside the doors), the banns had been introduced to allow the registering of canonical objections to the nuptials, registers had been started to record the event officially, and minimum age limits for the marriage (12 for girls, 14 for boys) and specific days of the week for the ceremony had been introduced.

In 1150 the theologian Peter Lombard definitively expressed the view that marriage was a sacrament, a dual union of man and woman, a spiritual and physical union. This meant the need to be clear about the role of sex. Theologians advanced the idea of sex as an obligation, an idea that goes back to St Paul who, using the legal language of debtor and creditor, said that the husband must give the wife what he owed her and vice versa. The wife could not claim her body as her own; it was her husband's and vice versa. The Dominican, St Albertus Magnus, argued that if a husband recognized a desire for sex in his partner he must act to fulfil it even if he had not been asked for it. This might again seem to imply equality but it also suggests that the husband had to take the lead, with the woman being assumed to be the passive partner. It was also clear that people's bodies were not their own to be used with anyone else as they wished, but belonged to their partners.

In all this the woman's role remained subordinate. When Gratian wrote 'The woman has no power, but in everything she is subject to the control of her husband', he was merely expressing one of the universally held beliefs of the Middle Ages, the inherent and inescapable inferiority of women. The theories of women's role had been developed by the Church Fathers. Woman was the daughter and heiress of Eve, the source of Original Sin and an instrument of the Devil. She was at once inferior (since created from Adam's rib) and evil (since she succumbed to the serpent, causing Adam to be driven from Paradise and had discovered and introduced Adam to carnal delight). This view of women's inferiority was uniformly propagated in theological, medical and scientific treatises and no one questioned it. Because of her inherent evil, woman needed to be disciplined. Canon law specifically allowed wife-beating and this took place at every level of society. Legally, a woman could not hold public office or serve as military commander, lawyer or judge. Secular law justified this on the grounds that women were by nature light-minded, wily, avaricious and of limited intelligence. Ecclesiastical law justified it on the grounds of Original Sin. The literature of the estates, which defined the roles of various groups in society, declared explicitly: 'Women must be kept out of all public office. They must devote themselves to their feminine and domestic occupations.' The promotion of the cult of the Virgin Mary from the eleventh and twelfth centuries onwards provided women with two ennobling role models: virginity, through which the sin of Eve could be most absolutely resisted, and motherhood, the perfect function for women not suited to the life of a religious celibate.

Marriage was, then, the expected fate of most women. But love, which is today assumed in the western world to be a precondition of marriage, was rarely involved in this. In general, love did not often precede or indeed follow marriage. Marriages were arranged by families at every social level for they almost all involved property, or later money, changing hands. Marriage was a matter of business or politics, with love as an optional extra. Only at the lower depths of society was nothing involved apart from sex and companionship, and then the people involved rarely bothered with marriage, settling for floating and transitory concubinage.

The twelfth century was notable for its extensive discussion of love in many different guises. There was the love of God, which in some cases became passionate and almost erotic; love between men of an emotional but non-sexual kind and based on mutual affection and respect; courtly love in which an unmarried man did gallant deeds in the name of a married woman and the keynote of which was yearning and suffering. None of these versions involved sexual fulfilment.

There was a theory of erotic love based on sexual pleasure but it was made clear that this was strictly outside marriage. It was influenced by pagan authors, particularly Ovid, whose *Art of Love* had a great vogue in the twelfth and thirteenth centuries as a handbook of seduction, with many translations, adaptations, and updatings to apply to contemporary scenes and manners. As Norman Shapiro makes clear in his collection of medieval erotic writings, *The Comedy of Eros*, these versions are slick and cynical and imply that everyone, married and single alike, is sexually active. These poems give advice on how, where, and when to seduce women, treating sex as a game. The anonymous 'Key to Love', for instance, leaves one in no doubt about the ultimate objective of the male. It advises on his appearance: neat, cut hair, clean teeth, sweet breath, no paint or powder, a languishing expression to signify that he is dying for love. It advises the cultivation of letter writing, charm, wit, flattery, a display of weeping – an onion is recommended to obtain the desired effect – and also enlisting the aid of the lady's maid to advance his case. But once he gets a kiss, he must press on until he gets what is known in football parlance as a result.

It is possible that the necessity for consent improved the chances of there being love in marriage but not by that much, for family pressure remained a major factor in the arrangement of marriage. But in the thirteenth century the Church did develop a concept of marriage as a matter of loving companionship. St Thomas Aquinas argued that there should be love between husband and wife based on companionship, the recognition of virtue in each other, the creation of a family and house-

26

hold, and the sex act which could give pleasure but only in pursuit of procreation. The idea was developed by St Bernardino of Siena (1380–1444) who urged husbands to show great compassion and consideration towards their wives, to love them as much as they had been loved by their entire families. 'Between husband and wife there should be the most singular friendship in the world,' he said. The wife had been made from Adam's rib to be her husband's loving companion. They were equal in spirit, but in the flesh, the husband was greater than the wife and she should obey him.

When in the twelfth century, Gratian codified and systematized canon law in a collection which remained authoritative throughout the Middle Ages, he endorsed the by now established Church position. Marriage existed to produce children and to curb sexual temptation. There were two stages necessary for its validation: consent (spiritual) and consummation (physical). If either were not present, the marriage was invalid. He stressed the idea of marital debt, opposed remarriage, considered the sex urge a defect, and condemned excessive sex in marriage.

Yet the role of sex within marriage continued to be a matter of debate amongst theologians. Three separate viewpoints emerged. There was a rigorist position, expressed by the twelfth-century canon lawyer, Bishop Huguccio, who took the view that every act of sexual intercourse, even inside marriage, involved sin, though he saw marital sex as a venial rather than a mortal sin. Jean Gerson (1363–1429), allowing marital sex for procreation, to pay the debt and to avoid fornication, said that if nothing but pleasure was sought, so long as it remained within the limits of matrimony and did not occur in otherwise prohibited circumstances, it was either no sin or only a venial sin. But these were both minority positions. The mainstream view remained the one expressed in the thirteenth century by St Thomas Aquinas and St Albertus Magnus, that sex had an integral part to play in marriage for the prescribed purposes so long as it was not 'excessive'.

This was, then, the positive side of the Church's sex teaching. The negative side was the Church's prohibitions on what it disapproved of. Now here we have not only the Church's view but some evidence about what actually went on. This comes in the penitentials, of which Aron Gurevich has written that they 'permit the cultural historian in a way to eavesdrop on the private conversations of medieval people'. Confession and penance were central institutions of the Church. They ensured ecclesiastical control and discipline of the laity but also provided an outlet for the individual suffering from a guilty conscience. In the early Church, confession, penance and reconciliation had been public events. But between the late sixth and thirteenth centuries this changed. Confession increasingly became private and penance an arbitrary matter, awarded at the discretion of the individual priest. To help priests decide on the seriousness of sins and how to deal with them, detailed penance books or penitentials were drawn up. Although they varied in detail, the general attitude remained consistent. They provided, in Pierre Payer's words, 'a broadly based and relatively homogeneous code of sexual behaviour'. What is of added interest is that they were the products of experience. They listed the matters which would be expected to come in confession and that the authors themselves had encountered. St Albertus Magnus justified going into detail 'by the monstrous things heard these days in confession', though Robert of Flamborough and St Raymond of Penaforte, both authors of handbooks for confessors, warned against going into too great detail lest it gave ideas to people who had not previously thought of them.

In the ninth century the penitentials were condemned by Church councils as having neither official standing nor scriptural warrant. But they continued in use until the twelfth century, when Gratian drew up his *Decretum* and there was a much more scientific and sophisticated approach to Church law-making. In 1215 the Lateran Council made annual confession compulsory for all Christians and this and the extensive work of commentary coming out of the universities prompted a new breed of handbooks for confessors, the *Summae Confessorum*, which put within the reach of the ordinary priest in a comprehensive and accessible form an encyclopedic compendium of Church law and teachings on all moral matters. The *Summae* listed and discussed sins, and the methods of dealing with them, then prescribed the questions to be asked and thus provided a coherent and enforceable moral code for society. But they were heavily influenced by the preceding penitentials, particularly in sexual matters.

Payer points out that sexual matters formed the largest single category of offences in the penitentials. The penances involved varied in severity but they were all based on the idea of fasting on bread and water and avoiding sex for a number of consecutive days in multiples of ten. When a penance of a number of years was given, this meant penance on the three annual fasts of Christmas, Easter and Pentecost and on the Wednesday, Friday and Saturday of every week. There was a sliding scale of punishment depending on whether you were old or young, married or single, layman or cleric, and whether the sin was isolated or habitual. The old were punished more than the young, the married more than the single and the cleric more than the layman because of the responsibility, maturity and obligation to set an example attached to the former groups. For instance, when it came to adultery, sex by a married man with another's wife or virgin daughter, with a nun or a female slave, usually incurred a penance of about five years. But a priest got ten years and a bishop twelve years and deposition into the bargain. On the other hand, fornication between two unmarried persons, male and female, evoked only one to two years' penance and this was halved if it was with a servant girl, suggesting that servant girls were more or less fair game. But then fornication was comparatively rarely covered and always more leniently than adultery.

The Church regulated sexual activity within marriage, forbidding it on all feast days and fast days (of which there were 273 in the seventh century though this had shrunk to 140 by the sixteenth century), on Sundays and in periods when the wife was deemed to be unclean (during menstrual periods, during pregnancy, during breast-feeding and for forty days after childbirth). This would generally allow married couples to have sex less than once a week. Failure to keep these rules invoked a forty-day penance.

The Church prescribed the proper form of intercourse. The only permitted form was what is now known as 'the missionary position', face to face with the man on top and the woman underneath. All other variations were penalized. Anal intercourse incurred seven years' penance. There was three years' penance for dorsal intercourse, with the woman on top; that was deemed to be contrary to nature which prescribed that the man should hold the dominant position. There was three years too for oral intercourse and rear-entry intercourse, heterosexual intercourse from behind, deemed to reduce man to the level of the beast because horses and dogs copulate in that way. Anal and oral intercourse were also probably deemed to be contraceptive, though this is not specifically mentioned. The penitentials encouraged couples to have sex only at night and then only partially unclothed. It is clear that it was seen as something essentially shameful.

But to look at just one highly influential eleventh-century penitential, the *Decretum* of Burchard of Worms (*d*.1025), who drew heavily on previous penitentials, we can see how he grades sexual sins in terms of their seriousness. Burchard tries to keep as close as possible to ordinary morality and to ensure its conformity with Christian teaching. His questions about sexual matters often contain the phrase 'Have you done, as some are accustomed to do', suggesting evidence from confessions.

Ten days on bread and water was the penalty applied by Burchard to male masturbation by the hand. For the use of a perforated piece of wood, you got twenty days (and probably splinters). The penalty for fornicating with a maid servant or unmarried woman was also ten days. These are in his view the least serious of sins and it is clear that he is reflecting the view of a society which regarded the sexual sins of unmarried young men with great indulgence. Other penitentials penalized masturbation with between forty days and a year, depending on the age and status of the offender and the frequency of the habit.

Similarly there was a penance of ten days on bread and water for making love to one's wife in a forbidden position and when she was menstruating or pregnant. Four days on bread and water was the penance for having sex on a Sunday, but forty days if it took place on one of the holy days, though this was halved if the husband was drunk, again a recognition of an all too likely occurrence.

The highest penalty was inflicted on incest, sodomy, and bestiality: fifteen years for habitual offenders. But there were lesser penalties for other homosexual offences, such as mutual masturbation and inter-femoral sex. In other penitentials, anal intercourse carried a seven year penalty; lesser homosexual offences two to three years. Boys were much less seriously penalized than adults.

Burchard also explicitly recognized female sexuality by prescribing questions to women about whether they had used aphrodisiacs (two years' penance), engaged in lesbian acts (five years), copulated with beasts (seven years), masturbated themselves with dildos (one year, notably more severe than for masturbation by men), secured abortions (ten years), consumed their husbands' semen in order to inflame their lust (seven years) or put their menstrual blood in their husbands' food or drink to inflame them (five years).

Burchard observed that any act leading to sexual arousal or sexual pleasure was sinful and listed them, indicating again his awareness of what people got up to. The provocative acts he singled out were telling or laughing at dirty jokes, singing or listening to suggestive songs, performing in or attending lewd entertainments, bathing in mixed company and touching, fondling or kissing breasts and genitals.

Burchard, like the other penitentialists, rank-orders sins. In descending order of seriousness, they were incest, sodomy and bestiality, adultery, fornication and masturbation. Gratian in his *Decretum* confirmed this scale, and so did most other theologians. There remained debates and discussions among commentators and glossators but the underlying principles remained standard. The scale of sins was accepted and continued to be judged according to whether the offence was secret or notorious, continuous or intermittent, involving one partner or many. What this suggests is that far from being monolithic on the subject of sexual sin, the Church adopted a sophisticated and flexible approach, responsive to everyday realities.

There were two significant developments with regard to sexual sins in the Middle Ages and they concern rape and masturbation. Rape was not condemned by the penitentials but *raptus* was. In Roman law, *raptus* was abduction and did not necessarily involve sex. The offence was a property offence – stealing a female from her family or guardian. It was a private rather than a public crime. The early penitentials took the same view of *raptus*, and rape as we understand it did not appear.

But Gratian, when codifying Church law, had access to the law codes of Justinian, who had defined *raptus* as a sexual crime against unmarried women, widows and nuns and prescribed the death penalty. Gratian and his successors redefined the crime to bring it closer to what we now see as rape. They considered it a major crime not against property but against the person and defined it as having four constituent elements: abduction, violence, sexual intercourse, and the absence of consent. This strongly suggests that we should see the development of the offence of rape as a corollary of the Church's development of the idea of consent in marriage. Contradictorily though, the Church held that it was not possible for a husband to rape his wife since she had given her consent to sex by marrying. They also held it was not possible to rape a prostitute, since she was in the sex business and had no justification in refusing.

The second change came about in the case of masturbation. It was then as now virtually universal. In the early Middle Ages, it was seen as a fairly trivial sin to be dealt with by the parish priest. However, in the later Middle Ages, it was seen as far more serious. Archbishop Guy de Roye of Sens actually suggested in 1388 that it should be reserved to bishops to deal with. It is likely that the bishops would have been kept pretty busy. But this did not happen. Nevertheless Jean Gerson, Chancellor of the University of Paris and a leading fifteenth-century theologian, wrote an entire treatise on hearing the confessions of masturbators. It was the first such manual. Gerson described it as an abominable and horrid sin and expressed his concern that habitual indulgence led to more serious sins such as sodomy. In prescribing the exact procedure to be followed by the confessor, Gerson went into great detail. 'Friend, didn't you touch or rub your member the way boys usually do,' he asked. He went on

If he denies that he ever held it or rubbed it in [the erect] state, it is not possible to proceed further except in expressing amazement and saying that it is not credible; exhorting him to remember his salvation; that he is before God; and it is most serious to lie in confession and the like.

Many adults committed the sin, said Gerson, and youths of 13 to 15 were strongly inclined to this vice, presumably before they moved on to fornication. He urged parents and teachers to lecture against it, warning of the danger of perpetual damnation. His suggested remedies included cold baths, flagellation, sobriety, prayer and good company. He sounds like an obsessive Victorian headmaster. But he was not alone. St Thomas Aquinas ranked it as one of the most serious sins, the sins against nature (bestiality, sodomy, masturbation, deviation from the prescribed position for intercourse), so called because they frustrated

31

the natural purpose of sex – procreation. It seems likely that the increased anxiety about masturbation was tied to the wasting of seed and this reflected the high level of concern about population decline, particularly in the wake of the Black Death, when a third of the population of western Europe died, and which ecclesiastical commentators and popular preachers attributed to the judgement of God on mankind for its sexual irregularities.

There was a parallel increase in concern in the later Middle Ages about contraceptive practices, particularly *coitus interruptus*. Contraception and abortion were as well known in the Middle Ages as they had been in the Ancient World. Various forms of contraception, whether actually effective or not, were known about and presumably practised: potions distilled from assorted plants, gymnastic exercises performed after intercourse, ointments smeared on the male genitals, liquid introduced into the womb before or after intercourse, pessaries. In addition to this there were magic amulets to prevent conception and the practice of *coitus interruptus*, the Biblical sin of Onan, spilling the seed 'on the ground' rather than allowing it to fertilize the ovum. Abortion similarly was known in the Middle Ages and was practised by gymnastic exercises, carrying heavy loads, hot baths, liquids introduced into the womb, potions, and other such abortifacients.

Theologians regarded birth control as a major sin and here, as in so many other areas, the teachings of St Augustine shaped medieval thinking. He had defined marriage as being for 'offspring, fidelity and symbolic stability' and the interference with the procreative aspect of marital sex could not therefore be other than sinful. Augustine's attitude was transferred direct into canon law, the law of the Church, codified *c*.1140 by Gratian and holding sway as authoritative until 1917, and also direct into theology, through inclusion in the *Sentences* of Peter Lombard (also mid-twelfth century), the basic handbook of Catholic theology until the sixteenth century. The rationale that the opponents of birth control put forward was that it was homicide to kill an unborn child, that it was contrary to nature since nature prescribed insemination as an integral and inescapable part of intercourse, and that it destroyed the marital relationship, which had been ordained specifically for procreation.

Contraception and abortion were regularly denounced by the penitentials. Burchard of Worms imposed a ten-year penance on them. The *Summae* of the central and later Middle Ages similarly denounced the practices. But John Noonan, the historian of contraception, has discerned a significant change of emphasis. In the penitentials, which held sway in the early Middle Ages, potions and magical practices were what preoccupied the clerical writers in the area of contraception; in the central and later Middle Ages it was *coitus interruptus*.

Warnings about deviating from the norm in marital sexuality and in sexuality in general became more urgent in the twelfth century because Catholic teachings were under threat from two different directions. Courtly love, which exalted the love of a young unmarried man for a married woman, was believed by the Church to promote adultery and the use of contraception to prevent the birth of unwanted bastards. Catharism, the principal heretical challenge to Catholicism in this period, held that sex, marriage and procreation were inventions of the Devil and they exalted celibacy as the highest state. But if lust burned, they thought it should be assuaged by non-procreative sexual acts.

When the threat from the Cathars receded, another problem arose to worry the Church, the massive depopulation in the wake of the Black Death and the plague pandemic. Preachers and theologians denounced the practice of birth control now as exacerbating population decline. The added urgency is reflected in the escalation in seriousness with which *coitus interruptus* was regarded. Like masturbation, it came to be seen as extremely serious and destructive. Where St Thomas Aquinas and St Albertus Magnus in the thirteenth century had reserved the term sodomy to refer to sex between two males, John Gerson and St Antoninus of Florence in the fifteenth century described as sodomy any act which involved the spilling or misuse of the seed, including homosexual masturbation and *coitus interruptus*. Noonan concludes: 'There is enough pastoral advice on the sin against nature to suggest that in the period 1232–1480 many persons in marriage sought intercourse but avoided procreation.' Peter Biller has drawn attention to a saying common in the thirteenth century and first encountered as early as 1049: 'If not chastely, at least with precautions', the medieval equivalent of 'if you can't be good, be careful.'

The Church institutionalized the reporting of sex offences. In England from the mid-thirteenth century parish clergymen were charged with reporting notorious fornicators to the archdeacon who would call them in, and either fine and censure them or persuade them to marry. Where they have been studied, the bulk of Church court registers seems to have been concerned with adultery and fornication.

But the state and the municipalities began to concern themselves with sexual matters too. The European monarchies took a hand as part of their emergence as law-makers and law-givers, under the influence of the Roman Imperial law codes, as did the municipalities, often under the stimulus of the mendicant friars, whose influence was important in the shaping of bourgeois morality. Kings and other rulers were also interested in preventing people taking the law into their own hands, given the tendency of cuckolded husbands or offended families to castrate or murder to avenge their honour. The influence of bourgeois morality can be seen in the difference in the treatment of adulterous

33

couples between town and country. In urban Brabant, adulterous couples were fined, flogged and put in the stocks and in some towns in southern France, were forced to run through the streets naked, being lashed as they went. This indicates the severity of communal disapproval of breaches of the marriage vow. In rural areas, by contrast, the punishment was simply a fine, suggesting a greater degree of rural tolerance of sexual misbehaviour.

The Church's views of sexual practices are fully recorded and can be explored and assessed. But how far did these ideas take root? This is more difficult to ascertain but there are indications. First, the Church's view of marriage as the cornerstone of a stable Christian society was generally accepted. This was partly a matter of self-interest, for aristocracy, bourgeoisie and the higher peasantry all had property interests to consider, along with the need for alliances and mergers of families and interests, a concern enhanced by the adoption of primogeniture and the creation of stable and defined blocks of property rather than shifting, divided territory that equal division of inheritances had caused. But while indissolubility was accepted, the Church's discouragement of remarriage was widely ignored by both the aristocracy and the bourgeoisie, given the high level of mortality and the need for children as heirs. Sexual adventurism outside marriage endangered property settlements and the purity of bloodlines as well as compromising family honour, so there was a practical objection to adultery. Consent seems to have been accepted by the public as the basis for viable marriage and indeed increasingly demanded, as is evidenced by the fact that English court records of the late thirteenth and fourteenth centuries show that marriage cases almost always centred on the issue of consent.

As for marriage itself, medieval popular culture regarded it in much the same way as comic seaside postcards and music hall comedians of the twentieth century. Few medieval love stories end in marriage and secular writings rarely see marriage as a source of happiness. Marriage was a trap, the end of freedom and the beginning of care. 'No man marries without regretting it' was one popular saying of the age. The *fabliaux*, the bawdy and satirical rhymed stories of the towns and cities, presented a familiar cast of cuckolded and often elderly husbands, lustful young wives, lecherous priests and amorous young gallants. They showed a world in which everyone was in hot pursuit of extramarital sex. But the main thrust of the humour is of embarrassment and humiliation and the impression given is that sex is a huge dirty joke, with people constantly being caught literally with their trousers down or their private parts trapped in painful apertures. But allowing for the exaggeration, there are elements of truth in the picture they paint. Urban married couples were frequently disparate in age, with older men marrying a succession of younger women, as the wives died in childbirth or the husbands deferred marriage until they had made their fortunes. Lecherous and non-celibate priests were a recurrent problem for the church authorities. The clergy, according to Jacques Rossiaud, made up an estimated 20 per cent of the clientele of the private brothels and bath-houses of Dijon. Fornication was regarded as a universal youthful pursuit.

But tenderness within marriage was possible. We get one of those rare and precious snapshots of intimacy in the writings of Christine de Pisan (c.1364–c.1430), the first professional woman writer, who, after she was widowed, described her married life. She paints a convincing picture of a relationship based on affection, respect and mutual consideration. In one passage she describes the gentleness of her husband on the wedding night, when she was 15 and he was 24. He did not demand sex on the first night, wanting to let her get used to his presence. Only on the next day did he kiss her lingeringly and promise that God had created him only to be good to her. During their marriage love and affection grew between them. One of the fifteenth-century Burgundian collection of stories, *Les Cent Nouvelles Nouvelles* goes into detail on the 'first night fears' of a 15-year-old virgin who, instructed on her wedding day by her mother in the mysteries of the marriage bed, finds herself unable to go through with sexual intercourse either on the marriage night or thereafter. When her parents seek to have the marriage annulled on the grounds of non-consummation, the husband protests his willingness to consummate and the judge sets up a bed in his house, carefully instructing the bride to fulfil her marital obligation. The marriage is successfully consummated with the husband worn out much sooner by the 'joustings' than the wife. This encapsulates what must have been a not uncommon problem for young newly-weds.

The idea of behaving too passionately with one's wife was considered shocking because the ideal wife was expected to be chaste and demure. Another of the *Cent Nouvelles* lends support to this view. The value of such stories is that they depend for their humour on the acceptance of a set of social norms. The story tells of a young man, newly married, whose desire for sex is so great that he takes his wife continually, wherever and whenever he wants and not just at night, as was proper. Although she does not always want it, she dutifully obeys. One day he takes her into the woods in broad daylight and before having sex strips her in order to inspect and comment on her finer points, a procedure she roundly denounces. They are spotted by a farmer out looking for his lost calf. The humour of the story derives implicitly from the grossness of the behaviour: too much sex, sex during the day instead of at night and stripping the wife, all of which transcend the canons of modest and decorous marital behaviour.

35

The attitude of women towards love seems to have been shared by both the upper and lower classes. The fourteenth-century peasant women of the southern French village of Montaillou, whose attitudes were minutely analysed by Emmanuel Le Roy Ladurie, never speak of love in connection with their feelings towards their husbands. They seem to have regarded love as something which existed outside marriage. Andrew the Chaplain in his treatise *The Art of Courtly Love*, which dates from the 1180s, writes of the rules of love as applied to the middle and upper classes:

> We declare and hold as firmly established that love cannot exert its powers between two people who are married to each other. For lovers give each other everything freely, under no compulsion of necessity, but married people are in duty bound to give in to each other's desires and deny themselves to each other in nothing.

This is clear evidence of the acceptance of the idea of the marital debt. Indeed it looks very much as if the laity, like the theologians, drew a distinction between marriage (for procreation) and extra-marital affairs (for pleasure): the difference being that the Church disapproved of the latter and lay people did not.

Le Roy Ladurie's study of Montaillou also reveals the entrenchment in the countryside of an alternative morality to the one preached by the Church. It was the morality of pre-Christian tribal and peasant society, in which sexual life was free and easy, fornication and concubinage common. Marriage was often informal and easily dissolved. The sex act was widely believed to be innocent if performed for money with a prostitute or by two people if they got pleasure from it. The idea was that if sex was agreeable to the partners, it was not disagreeable to God.

Nevertheless, just as in ecclesiastical thinking, the double standard applied in secular society. Johannes Teutonicus, author of the standard commentary on Gratian, said that adultery was more detestable when committed by a woman than by a man. St Thomas Aquinas said that women should be more severely punished for adultery than men; Huguccio declared that virginity should be demanded from women but not from men. They all believed that women were more inclined to lust and sexual excess than men. The general public similarly believed that it was acceptable for men to be unchaste but not for women, as a story in *Les Cent Nouvelles Nouvelles* demonstrates. A Picard apprentice in Brussels impregnates the daughter of his merchant master and promptly leaves to return to his native village. The girl, who confesses to her mother what has happened, is turned out, follows the apprentice and arrives in his village on the day he is due to be married to another. When his new wife questions the apprentice about the girl she saw him talking to, he explains what happened and says that the girl told her mother about him. The wife does not berate her husband but pours scorn on the girl, saying that the carriage driver has slept with her dozens of times but she would never dream of telling her mother this. On hearing this, the apprentice leaves his wife immediately in a fury and returns to the other girl. The story hinges on the acceptance of the husband's fornication as a natural occurrence, the rejection of similar behaviour on the part of women and a recognition of the inherent stupidity of the women in talking in both cases.

Masturbation seems to have been universal but it was sometimes given an interesting justification. Gerson wrote: 'many adults were polluted with the sin and had never confessed it ... many apologized for their ignorance, saying that they had never known such touching, whereby they did not have the desire to know women, was a sin.' If true and not merely said to mislead the confessor, it means that the penitents understood that fornication was considered wrong but that masturbation, which avoided contact with women, was somehow an acceptable substitute. It may have been this kind of thinking which lay behind the modest penances ascribed to the sin by Burchard of Worms.

Contraception seems to have been widely practised and not recognized as a sin by the laity, much like masturbation. St Bernardino of Siena lectured his congregations:

> You will see that you will have many sins in this state of matrimony which you have never confessed nor did you know it to be a sin or sins.... Listen, each time you come together in a way where you cannot generate, each time is a mortal sin.

Where contraception was practised, the evidence suggests that it was used for four main reasons. The first was poverty and the desire to limit family size. This was acknowledged by medieval theologians. The Venerable Bede and Burchard of Worms declared abortion less serious a sin when undertaken to limit family size for reasons of poverty than when used to conceal the evidence of fornication. The practice of *coitus interruptus* to limit family size was mentioned by the fourteenth-century Dominican Peter de Palude and the fifteenth-century Dominicans Johan Nider and St Antoninus of Florence.

Contraception was also practised for medical reasons (to avoid death or injury to a woman for whom pregnancy was medically undesirable), for reasons of fashion (a woman wanting to avoid pregnancy because it interfered with her social life or threatened her beauty) and to avoid the consequences of fornication. This was stated by Thomas of Chobham in his *Summa* (c.1210), which was extremely influential in the Middle Ages, surviving in over one hundred manuscript copies.

37

Jean-Louis Flandrin has suggested that since contraception within marriage invited charges of heresy and since men married late, contraception was generally practised in illicit extra-marital relationships preceding marriage. But this begs the question: how far did people worry about charges of heresy for what took place in the marriage bed? It also flies in the face of the weight of evidence from fourteenth- and fifteenth-century Tuscany, for instance, of voluntary limitation of family size. St Bernardino of Siena denounced it as a cause of Italian population decline. It is clear that contraception was a continuing and widely practised activity.

The clerical authorities were united in their view that fornication, sex committed by the young and unmarried men, was universal and it seems likely that their view reflects reality. Johannes Teutonicus observed in the early thirteenth century that nearly everyone committed fornication and that people were more prone to this offence than to any other. Bishop Bartholomew of Exeter, author of a twelfth-century penitential, wrote that most people considered fornication to be no sin. Bishop Jacques de Vitry of Acre claimed that students especially believed this. But it also emerges as a general view among the peasants of Montaillou. Thomas of Chobham in his *Summa*, complaining that many penitents considered fornication to be a minor sin or no sin at all, insisted that the priests must make it clear that it definitely was a sin. So widespread was the view of the sinlessness of fornicators that the Church was moved to declare this view heretical in 1287. It made little difference. The popular late-fifteenth-century preachers Olivier Maillard and Michel Menot were still lamenting that most people considered fornication to be no sin at all. St Vincent Ferrer (1350–1419) opined that all boys had lost their virginity by the age of 15.

John of Tynemouth thought that the young were wholly incapable of sexual continence because of their susceptibility to female allure; though Alain of Lille argued that it was a lesser offence to have sex with a beautiful woman because the temptation was greater than with an ugly one. Johannes Teutonicus claimed that students went to church not to worship but to ogle the women. Huguccio said that two young persons discovered in circumstances in which sexual activity was possible should be assumed to have engaged in it, whereas older persons should not. 'Few adults are to be found who are innocent of fornication,' he said. Whatever the Church may have said about it, there was clearly widespread social tolerance of male pre-marital and extra-marital sexual activity in the medieval world.

Jacques Rossiaud has identified the existence of a specific male youth culture in Dijon, a culture of local bachelors: journeyman, apprentices, male servants, the sons of the bourgeoisie and immigrant workers.

Gangs of these young men wandered Dijon at night seeking to dispel boredom by fighting, drinking, gaming, dicing, taunting the watch, and staging gang rapes. Between 1436 and 1486, 125 rapes – 80 per cent of them gang rapes – are recorded for Dijon, probably only a proportion of those actually committed, because of non-reporting. The gangs broke into houses, dragged young women out and raped them. The records show that 85 per cent of the offenders were unmarried and half of them were aged 18 to 24. Rossiaud estimates that half the young men of Dijon were involved at one time or another in one of these rapes. The activity was spread throughout the year, took place once or twice a month and was a regular feature of the life of the young, a *rite de passage*.

The women involved were often the wives and daughters of day labourers or textile workers or servant girls. Rossiaud suggests that there is here a deliberate desire by bachelors to deny the social order by destroying the marriageability of the girls. But this seems unnecessarily elaborate. The evidence suggests that they rarely took wives, prominent or respectable women, or children, but concentrated their attentions on women who were already 'tainted' and therefore 'fair game' – priests' concubines, girls with bad reputations, widows or separated women (who traditionally had a reputation for flightiness) and servants (commonly believed to be the mistresses of their masters). These rapists are not social rebels but unbridled young men whose definition of masculinity hinges on drink and sex. The punishment for such rapes – if the victim was not prominent – was a fine or a short period in prison.

This pattern of young male behaviour was not confined to Burgundy. In his fascinating book, *The Boundaries of Eros*, Guido Ruggiero has demonstrated that violence against women was also part of the sexuality of young males in late medieval Venice. Rape in Venice tended to be regarded as serious if it involved children, the elderly or the upper classes, but rape between social equals was not regarded as too serious and in some cases almost as part of the courtship ritual. A recurrent pattern of rape followed by the promise of marriage, followed by fornication, can be seen as the behaviour pattern of some young Venetian males. Only 14 per cent of rape cases in late medieval Venice earned the culprit more than two years in jail or major corporal punishment. Most cases resulted in fines or brief imprisonment. The heaviest punishment was usually reserved for the rape of someone in the upper classes. An illicit but widely practised sexual culture, centred on prostitution, rape, and concubinage emerged in Venice to cater for late-marrying males.

The attitude of sexual bravado was not limited to any one class, but seems to have been the norm. It became part of the lifestyle of the young knights of north-western France, studied by Georges Duby. Duby identified the existence in that region of an aristocratic group he called 'the youth', young men who had been made knights but were not yet married. They were typical of a whole class in medieval chivalric society. It was marriage which gave them the right to be called men and until then, whatever age they reached, they remained 'youths'. But with primogeniture the rule and the family estates going intact to the eldest son, the younger sons often had to fend for themselves and so took to the road in knight errantry. Often the young knights went round in groups, filling their days with tournaments, hunting, war, gambling, brawling and sex. Their ultimate objective was military reputation and the hand of a rich heiress to secure their futures. But for them, too, like the unmarried journeyman or merchant's son, sexual satisfaction would be provided by rape, concubines or prostitutes. Andrew the Chaplain confirms this in *The Art of Courtly Love*. If a man is unfaithful to his beloved – not in order to find a new love but because of an irresistible passion – that is permissible. If a man meets a woman at a time when 'Venus is urging him on', if he should meet 'a little strumpet or somebody's servant girl' and take her then and there on the grass, he will not lose his beloved.

> We can say without fear of contradiction that just for this a lover is not considered unworthy of the love of his beloved unless he indulges in so many excesses with a number of women that we may conclude that he is over-passionate.

Although Duby calls this group 'the youth', a better description in English would be the colloquialism 'the lads'. Laddishness is a concept well known today. The lads go round in groups, earning a reputation for drinking, fighting and wenching, and they exist at every social level. Encouragement by society to use a brothel and the services of a prostitute, implied by the municipalization of the houses of ill-fame in the later Middle Ages, could well be seen as a defence against the committing of too many and too indiscriminate rapes. For innocent women and respectable girls did fall victim to the rapists and as a result lost status and marriageability and even less 'innocent' victims could often be shunned socially and driven to prostitution.

Both secular and ecclesiastical courts claimed jurisdiction and rape cases might appear before both. The Church courts did not impose the death penalty but could impose a wide variety of penalties (excommunication, public penance, imprisonment, whipping, fines), depending on the degree of force used and the extent of prior commitment between the couples. Commitment to marriage before or after the rape might mitigate the sentence. The secular courts maintained the Roman penalty of death when the emerging national monarchies began to introduce their law codes. But it was rarely applied and the usual penalty was a fine. Judging by the evidence for England in the thirteenth and fourteenth centuries, which has been studied in detail, rape cases rarely came to court. The shame factor will have operated as much then as now. Sometimes the family took it into their own hands to avenge its honour. But it was widely accepted as part of youthful male sexuality.

The Church associated illicit sex with the Devil and his legion of demons who haunted the world causing mischief and putting temptation before ordinary Christians. One of the most popular books in medieval Germany was the *Dialogue on Miracles* by the Cistercian Prior Caesarius of Heisterbach (*c.*1180–*c.*1250). More than fifty manuscript copies of it survive. To illustrate the miracles of the confession, Caesarius recounted several stories of demon-induced sexual encounters. A married woman of Nantes confessed that for six years she had been 'tormented with incredible lust' by a demon who appeared in the form of a comely knight and with whom she had had sex. She confessed to St Bernard of Clairvaux who helped her to overcome the power of the demon. The daughter of the priest, Arnold of Bonn, was much pursued by the local young men, so he locked her up. But a demon came to her in the form of a man who seduced her and had sex with her many times until she confessed, whereupon her father sent her across the river to escape the demon. A woman of Breisach confessed on her death-bed that she had been having sex with a demon (in human form) for seven years. It is clear that Caesarius believed implicitly in these demons, who had all been repelled by confession. It is equally clear to us that all these were simply actual events with human seducers and that when the women repented and broke off the relationships, they denounced their seducers as demons in human form. Whether they actually believed it or were playing to priestly prejudices is something we will never know. But certainly not everyone believed in demons, as a salutary story told by Caesarius reminds us. John, the *scholasticus* of Prüm, 'a very learned man but of a light and wanton character', slept with a woman well known to him, who soon after said: 'Do you know who you've been sleeping with – the Devil.' Caesarius continues solemnly: 'To this John, who was a strange man, replied with a strange word, which modesty forbids me to repeat, scoffing at the Devil and no whit disturbed.' One eminent professor of medieval history has suggested that the word in question was probably, given the context, the equivalent of 'bollocks'.

3

HERETICS

The Catholic Church in the Middle Ages was a totalitarian organization. It had a defined and comprehensive body of doctrine, an organized hierarchy, established rituals and a clear view of its authority and responsibility. Any divergence from these fundamentals constituted a challenge to the divinely ordained world order and could not therefore be tolerated. It was heresy, defined in the thirteenth century by Bishop Robert Grosseteste as 'an opinion chosen by human perception, contrary to holy scripture, publicly avowed and obstinately defended'. Heresy was therefore specifically to be recognized as the product of fallible human choice and public defiance of the will of God, expressed in the Bible and interpreted by the legitimately appointed authorities.

Popular heresy seems not to have been a problem that the Church had to face in the Dark Ages, when survival was the first priority, when society was static and on the defensive against attack by outside forces, and there was little time for religious experimentation or intellectual debate. But circumstances changed with the return of peace and with the urban expansion, economic revival, and spiritual awakening that accompanied it. There was a great upsurge of intellectual activity which scholars have dubbed 'the twelfth-century Renaissance'. But this was accompanied by a religious ferment which properly deserves the description bestowed by Brenda Bolton 'the Medieval Reformation'. Both Renaissance and Reformation shared a concentration on the individual and in religion this took the form of the individual search for redemption and the desire of the ordinary lay Christian for a more direct and personal relationship with God.

The great spiritual revival of the Middle Ages, beginning in the late eleventh century and continuing into the twelfth and thirteenth centuries, took many forms: the crusading movement, the great increase in pilgrimages, the rising number of new monastic orders and houses, the popularity of itinerant preachers and holy hermits, and above all perhaps the spiritualization of the laity, whose desires in this area seemed not to be fully met by existing religious forms and ecclesiastical institutions.

At the same time, the Church began to reform itself. The Papacy, rescued from decadence by the later eleventh century by a succession of vigorous reforming popes, took the lead in setting its house in order. It launched a campaign against simony (the sale of clerical office), secular control of sees and benefices, marriage of clergy, and clerical unchastity. But this had two serious consequences. It focused attention on the unsatisfactory lives of many of the clergy and on the inadequacy of the system and it transformed the Papacy into an organized monarchical institution, bureaucratic and legalistic, with the clergy becoming a closed, exclusive caste.

There is a school of thought which regards all western heresy as essentially Manichaean. But the most likely interpretation, and one advanced with great force and clarity by R. I. Moore in his brilliant book *The Origins of European Dissent* (1977), is that the attitudes and opinions of western heretics were a gospel-based evangelicalism provoked by a reaction to the perceived worldliness and corruption of the Church.

Both the failings of the clergy, highlighted by the Reform movement, and the increasing wealth, bureaucracy and politicization of the Papacy, with its heavy involvement in warfare, lawsuits and taxation, served to emphasize the desirability of an alternative view, which was increasingly propounded. This was the desire to return to Christian first principles, to the ideals of the life lived by Christ and his followers (the *vita apostolica*), a life which stressed above all asceticism, poverty and preaching. There was a desire to follow literally the commandment of Christ, recorded in Matthew 19 v. 21: 'If thou wilt be perfect, go and sell that thou hast, and give to the poor, and thou shalt have treasure in heaven; and come and follow me.' This generally took the form of a life lived by soliciting alms or by basic manual labour. It involved the renunciation of wealth and property, the desire to emulate Christ in suffering and spirituality, and the impulse to encourage others to follow suit by preaching and expounding the truth of the gospels. It was animated by a mood at once evangelical, fundamentalist, and puritanical, one that was not met by simple church attendance or even by entry into a monastery or nunnery. It was a truly religious life lived 'in the world, but not of it'.

This apostolic mindset encouraged free access to the Bible, hitherto a monopoly of the educated priesthood, by means of translations from Latin into the vernacular and through widespread and indiscriminate preaching by self-taught, unauthorized preachers. It sought to dispense with anything not in the gospels, frequently rejecting the whole range of ideas and practices sanctioned merely by tradition or by academic rationalization: prayers for the dead, infant baptism, confession, and transubstantiation for instance. It thus substituted scripture for authority. It advocated personal chastity. This was inadvertently given a powerful boost by the official papal campaign to promote priestly celibacy and received notable expression in the cult of the Virgin Mary, greatest of medieval saints, which began to develop in the eleventh century. Churches began to be fitted with 'lady chapels' for the specific veneration of Mary. All the churches of the Cistercian order were dedicated to Mary and an order of pious laymen 'The Slaves of the Blessed Virgin Mary' was founded. Mary as a symbol of virginity was an inspiring and emotionally powerful role model. But the desire of many lay men and women to adopt a life without sex seemed at one level to reduce the special nature of monasticism, whose celibacy had been one of the principal characteristics distinguishing it from the rest of society. Above all, the apostolic outlook promoted the idea that personal perfection was the chief aim of religion and that anyone could make contact with God by living a pure life rather than communicating through the priesthood. The ultimate logic of its ideas was to dispense with hierarchy and formal rituals altogether. Since it deprived the Catholic Church of its *raison d'être*, there could be no more serious threat to the existing establishment. Yet the apostolic renewal answered a deep hunger in the laity for a life of spirituality, a hunger that burned throughout the Middle Ages and was met by a succession of heretical movements.

In all these movements, the quest for a more complete and fulfilling religious life through personal austerity, adherence to the gospels and preaching was the central theme. It was the refusal of the Church fully to recognize these aspirations and these practices that turned their adherents into heretics. From the eleventh century to the fifteenth the pattern was the same. A group would appear, often inspired by a charismatic leader, who would advocate apostolic views and then – for various reasons – having failed to get recognition, the group would be driven into opposition. It would adopt more and more extreme anti-hierarchical and anti-sacerdotal views and the Church would turn the full weight of its authority and might against the group until it had been harried and battered into submission or extinction or driven out to seek survival as a persecuted heretical sect. Only in one case, that of Catharism, was there an imported, non-Christian belief system and most of the followers even of that movement believed it to be a purer form of Christianity.

Medieval heresy grew out of the conditions and psyche of medieval society. It was religious dissent and it was for the most part popular religious dissent. It was not usually an outgrowth of the intellectual disagreements about the faith or philosophical disputations that arose among university elites. These occurred periodically, had minimum support, and were generally swiftly exterminated. A notable exception to this pattern was Lollardy, a genuinely popular movement, inspired by the ideas and arguments of an Oxford University academic, John Wyclif. In general, it was the deep-rooted and recurrent desire of ordinary people to attain a state of religious perfection by their own acts, to be totally involved in a religious and spiritual life, while often remaining in the world, that gave rise to dissent and heresy. Heresy was not a matter of anti-Christian disbelief or of secularization. It was a fundamentalist Christian impulse of the purest kind, to return to the truth of the gospels, the lifestyle of the apostles, and the imitation of Christ. It was given added impetus and urgency by the continuing belief in the imminence of the end of the world, the second coming of Christ, and the onset of the millennium. It was this conviction and the desire to attain a state of pure spirituality in preparation for these events that in part explain the tenacity with which heretics held to their views.

CENTRAL MIDDLE AGES

There are only four recorded cases of heresy occurring between 970 and 1018. There was a flurry of heresies between 1018 and 1050; then the sources are silent until 1100. The outbreaks were isolated and seem to have been rapidly repressed. But they have certain features in common: concern for purity, rejection of sex and materialism, denial of the structures and practices of the existing Church. It is clear that these heretics were puritan reformers of the type that were to become familiar later in the Middle Ages. But these upsurges of puritanism more or less coincide with the first outbreaks of violence against the Jews. Both can legitimately be seen as products of a heightened religious sensibility inspired by an awareness of the imminence of the millennium. When 1033, the thousandth anniversary of the Crucifixion, passed and Christendom breathed again, many resolved to be worthy of their second chance and determined to prepare properly for the end whenever it should come.

When heresy returned in the early twelfth century, it was almost certainly a response both to this underlying millenarianism and to the ecclesiastical reform movement, which unleashed expectations, feelings and emotions in the laity which the existing Church could not satisfy. Popular wandering preachers, encouraged by Pope Gregory VII to counteract the apathy of local clergy and to combat the sins he was seeking to eradicate from the body of the Church, continually played upon these emotions. The hordes of followers such preachers attracted, inspired by their message and their example, saw the adoption of an apostolic lifestyle as the key to salvation. Many of the preachers, men like Norbert of Xanten and Robert of Arbrissel, were entirely orthodox and their aim was the positive promotion of the Church's views and policies. They channelled their supporters towards the rigorous new monastic orders and houses that they founded. But other preachers were much more critical and outspokenly anti-clerical. The first heresiarchs of the age were themselves renegade clerics: the monk Henry of Lausanne and the priest Peter of Bruys. Henry first appeared in the region of Le Mans in 1116 and Peter was active in the 1120s and 1130s. Both were radical reformers and both remained at liberty for twenty to thirty years, wandering the south of France and stirring up feelings against the Church until they were finally apprehended and imprisoned. Peter was burned to death and Henry died in prison. It is clear that they filled a gap in an inadequate and unresponsive system. The south of France in the 1140s was graphically described as a country of 'churches without people, people without priests, priests without reverence due to them and Christians without Christ'. This is an exaggeration and some good priests and well-supported churches existed but the general picture was one of corruption and neglect.

The basis of both Peter's and Henry's views was their rejection of what they saw as a wealthy and corrupt Church. They denied the idea of priestly mediation between God and man, the need for special Church buildings and most of the sacraments and practices of the Church. Henry believed that the faithful could hear each other's confessions; that marriage was binding by the consent of the couple; and that anyone deemed worthy could baptize. They both based their ideas squarely on the New Testament, envisaging communities of the faithful, regulating themselves and communing directly with God. It was a total denial of the institutional role of the Church. There is little evidence that the heresies of Peter and Henry long survived their passing. But they were the precursors. The Albigensian heresy was to flourish in just the areas that Peter and Henry evangelized. So the new heretics would be sowing their seed in fertile ground.

One of the most durable and inspiring elements in the Medieval Reformation was the tradition of lay piety. Perhaps the most notable example of this is Waldensianism. The Waldensians were the followers of a Lyons usurer, Valdès, who was inspired by hearing the story of St Alexis, a wealthy man who renounced his riches and became a beggar. Valdès did the same, embarking on a life of poverty and preaching to encourage others to follow suit. He had the gospels translated from Latin into the vernacular and used them as the basis of his message. His followers, known as 'The Poor Men of Lyons', renounced personal property, lived on charity and sought to convert the people to a simple life of faith. In 1184 they were condemned as heretics but despite savage persecution, they took root in southern France and northern Italy and spread from there to Spain, Germany and Austria.

The Waldensians had no ordained clergy. They were divided into two groups. The elite, known variously as 'the apostles', 'the masters', 'the elders', 'the brothers and sisters', were the preachers, who underwent a rigorous training programme lasting several years, pledged themselves to renounce the world, to model their lives on the apostles, to remain chaste, to live on alms and to lead the life of itinerant preachers. The rest, 'the friends', provided them with support and congregations. They elected their own ministers from amongst themselves.

They based their beliefs on the New Testament, recognizing only three sacraments (infant baptism, marriage and the eucharist). They refused to take oaths, rejected capital punishment and opposed military service. Their principal value was poverty and they believed that the Church of Rome was failing in its duty in neglecting to impose absolute poverty on the clergy. They rejected all the impedimenta of Catholic worship (buildings, rituals, music, singing, cemeteries) and ideas based on tradition, academic elaboration, or Church authority, such as purgatory, prayers for the dead and saints' days. They believed in minimum ritual (communion once a year, observing Sunday).

But doctrinally they were entirely orthodox and initially took a leading role in combating dualist heresy. Their heterodoxy stemmed from other sources. They rejected the Catholic Church and hierarchy as established. Their creed was communal rather than institutional. They believed in the 'priesthood of all believers'. Their translations of the Bible breached the priesthood's monopoly of God's word. They indulged in preaching without permission and threatened the official dissemination of the message of Christ. Thus they struck at the very roots of the Church's authority and control of the faith.

The Waldensian preachers were generally not learned men but peasants and artisans, who devoted their lives to intensive study of the scriptures, learning large sections by heart. They were much respected, were the only international dissident movement to attract the peasantry in large numbers, and allowed women as well as men to become preachers. 'Above all', says Malcolm Lambert in his authoritative study of medieval heresy, 'Waldensianism was the religion of the little man, whether in town or country.' The Waldensians were the first sect to survive the death of their founder and the only twelfth-century heresy to survive in unbroken continuity, to link up, somewhat awkwardly, with the Protestant Reformation in the sixteenth century. In Italy and the United States, they have survived down to the present day.

The Waldensians had their internal doctrinal disagreements and there was a split between the French and Italian Waldensians in 1205.

A council held at Bergamo in 1218 to resolve their differences failed and the two groups remained separate while adhering to broadly the same principles. The Waldensians were ferociously persecuted and frequently members of the community were burned. A contemporary chronicler recorded in the early fourteenth century that they 'all showed an incredible stubbornness, even to death; they went joyfully to execution'. By the fourteenth century persecution had broken the back of the French Waldensians and they withdrew to the Cottian Alps, where they held out until the sixteenth century. In Germany and Austria savage assault in the late thirteenth and late fourteenth centuries came close to exterminating them but they survived, thanks to the tenacity and mobility of their preachers who moved in secret and in disguise, keeping up the spirits of the believers.

Their unadorned, sincere and accessible preaching, their apostolic lifestyle, their humble origins and the contrast between them and the often poorly instructed and neglectful parish clergy all helped the Waldensians to instil their message. The Passau Anonymous, a cleric involved in the Inquisition in Austria in the 1260s, described the Waldensians:

> Heretics are to be recognized by their morals and their words. In moral behaviour they are composed and modest. They take no pride in their clothing, which is neither too rich nor too abject. They do not undertake any business because they seek to avoid lying and oaths and fraud, but they often make their living by the work of their hands, as craftsmen: their learned men are weavers and textile workers. They do not increase their riches, but are satisfied with necessities. They go neither to taverns, nor to shows, nor to any such vanities. They avoid anger. They are always working, teaching or learning.

It is an attractive picture of a sober and pious people.

Around the middle of the twelfth century the tradition of Catholic asceticism which had given rise to the puritan reform movements was infiltrated by another and alien tradition. This was to pose the greatest threat that the Catholic Church had to face in the central Middle Ages. The importation was Manichaeanism. It was the religion of the third-century Persian sage Mani, who taught that the universe was the work not of one creator but of two. One was responsible for what was spiritual and good, the other for what was material and evil. It was a dualist world-view which saw each man as a battlefield within which the forces of the two gods were at war. The life of the Manichaean was aimed at suppressing that within him which was evil. Matter and the body were the kingdom of evil, the spirit the kingdom of good. All life-forms were believed to be a mixture of both, and the aim of each individual was to disentangle the dark elements (matter) from the light (spirit), enabling the pure light to be returned to the kingdom of light whence it had originally come. The achievement of this was accomplished by the observance of basic rules, centred on the avoidance of matter (meat, sex, wealth). The true Manichaean, then, was celibate, pacifist and vegetarian, living a life of austerity so demanding that it was enjoined only on the elite, the 'elect', who were supported by the rest of the believers, 'the hearers', who were permitted to eat meat and to marry, but were expected to fast periodically and practise sexual abstinence from time to time.

In the tenth century a Manichaean type heresy, Bogomilism, appeared in Bulgaria. Its founder, the preacher Bogomil, based his teachings on the New Testament and thus rejected all practices not described in it (confession, the Catholic celebration of communion, infant baptism, the developed liturgy). Bogomils particularly hated the cross, which they saw as the symbol of Christ's torment. But beyond this they believed in a dualistic universe where the material world was the domain of Lucifer, God's eldest son who had fallen from grace and the spiritual world, the domain of God and his second son, Jesus Christ.

Bogomilism, arriving in the west down the Rhine–Danube trade routes, fastened on an existing tradition of anti-clerical dissent and gave it a different structure. The first evidence of its arrival in the west comes in 1143 when Eberwin, prior of Steinfeld, appealed to St Bernard of Clairvaux for help in combating the new heresy. Eckbert of Schönau's *13 Sermons against the Cathars* (1163) introduces us to the name of the heretics, Cathars (from the Greek *katharos*: pure) and gives a full account of their organization. The heresy took root in the Low Countries and the Rhineland and became even more important in the south of France. There Cathar missionaries organized a Cathar Church in the 1170s. The heretics in the south became known as Albigensians, from one of their strongholds, Albi.

The Cathar Church was never a monolithic alternative to the Catholic Church. Splits appeared in its ranks due to personal and geographical rivalries. There were six Cathar churches in Italy, for instance. Nevertheless Catharism did provide its own hierarchies to rival those of Catholicism. There were Cathar bishops, Cathar dioceses, Cathar councils, even a Cathar pope. Despite internal divisions and doctrinal differences (some Cathars believed in reincarnation; others did not), they all held the same basic principles. They believed that the body and the soul were creations of different forces; the body by Evil, the soul by Good. They rejected all things material (notably meat, sex and wealth) as intrinsically evil. They denied purgatory, masses for the dead, transubstantiation and infant baptism. Their central ceremony was the *consolamentum*, the laying on of hands, the ceremony by which a believer was freed from the flesh and reunited with the spirit and made pure (catharized) and sinless. For the majority of Cathars, this took place on their deathbeds. It was administered by one group of the elite, the *perfects*, who lived the ideal Cathar life and were rather like monks. The great appeal of Catharism was its vivid image of a perpetual struggle between the forces of light and the forces of darkness, the stress on gospel truth, the veneration of poverty, chastity and simplicity, and the involvement of individuals in the everyday search for spiritual purity.

Catharism remained the chief internal threat to medieval Catholicism. For although its dualistic theology was fundamentally at odds with Christian belief, the values and attitudes of the Cathars coincided with the puritanical religious climate of the day, capitalizing on the atmosphere of anti-clericalism, the growing religious enthusiasm, the disorientation in social and economic conditions and the traditional respect for ascetics. The sect had limited intellectual appeal but immense popular appeal, since anyone, man or woman, upper class or lower class, could become a *perfect* if he or she lived the right kind of life. Despite the dualism, Cathars thought of themselves as Christians, indeed as adherents of a purer form of Christianity than that practised by the Church, whose wealth, power and politicization had taken it from the truth of the gospels. They believed that Christ had appeared on earth to deliver the souls trapped in the material world. Cathar preachers used the Bible to support their arguments, exhorted their followers to live a moral life and remain faithful to Christ and administered the *consolamentum* rather like the Catholic sacrament of extreme unction. So while the theology may have been suspect, the spirit and the practices and the justification seemed genuinely Christian to the movement's followers.

Faced with the continual threat of dissent and heresy, how did the Church react? It evolved three principal strategies: persuasion, repression and demonization. Persuasion involved a programme of preaching and conversion by missionary activity. Repression ranged from the imposition of penances to death and exile. Demonization involved the promotion of propaganda that stigmatized the heretics as sexual deviants and orgiasts.

Initially the reaction to heresy was haphazard and sporadic, but Pope Alexander III (1159–81) initiated a comprehensive policy based on the teachings of Augustine, arguing that coercion of wrongdoers was permissible if exercised by a properly constituted authority and if undertaken not out of a desire for vengeance but out of a spirit of justice and love of the offender. In 1163 the Council of Tours under the same pope drew attention to the clergy's duty to enquire into heretical sects and to imprison their members and confiscate their goods. By the time of the Third Lateran Council of 1179 Pope Alexander was calling on Catholic princes to use force, and giving the faithful who took up arms against heretics the privileges of crusaders.

After Alexander's death, there was a hardening of attitude. Pope Lucius III and the Emperor Frederick Barbarossa agreed on a joint policy of secular and ecclesiastical repression and at the Council of Verona (1184) the bull *Ad abolendam* was issued. It was the first attempt in the century to deal with heresy on a supra-national basis. The bull condemned an assortment of heretics by name, including Cathars, Waldensians and Humiliati, all who dared to preach without Papal or episcopal permission, all whose beliefs were at variance with approved doctrine and all those who aided heretics. It was a blanket ban and it also effectively institutionalized the process of inquisition in its prescriptions. Bishops were to investigate parishes rumoured to contain heretics and any individuals who were behaving suspiciously. Refusal to take an oath was to be regarded as an automatic indication of heresy. The convicted were to be excommunicated and handed over for punishment to the secular authorities. This legislation lumped together both the doctrinal heretics and apostolic evangelicals.

But this was too far-reaching and in consequence did not work. Pope Innocent III (1198–1216) changed the policy. He had a clear-sighted and comprehensive policy for the reform of Christian society, which involved calling a crusade, eliminating heresy, and summoning a general council to codify the disciplinary regulations of the Church, all in implementation of the theory of a unitary and universal Christendom. To this end, he introduced a more flexible and enlightened policy towards reformists. Innocent understood the difference between disbelief and disobedience and he separated the heretics into two groups, making obedience the key test. Loyalty to the Pope and acceptance of the hierarchy could excuse the adoption of certain practices. To groups of young men and women who had taken up a life of voluntary poverty and preached without permission but otherwise remained doctrinally orthodox, he proved sympathetic. They could, he saw, perform a positive role, meeting the spiritual needs of the people, substituting for an inadequate priesthood, undertaking missions against the entrenched heretics, playing them at their own game by surpassing them in personal asceticism; so long as they recognized and accepted in future the authority of the Pope. By applying this policy he achieved a measure of success.

He approved and organized the Humiliati of Lombardy. These were lay men and women, some of them rich and educated, who bound themselves to a life of austerity, poverty, prayer and fellowship. They adopted simple undyed cloth garments as a symbol of humility, reinforced by their choice of the Lamb of God as the symbol of their

51

movement. Some lived at home and moved among the people; others lived in voluntary religious communities. They fed and clothed the poor, cared for the sick and did manual labour. They had been condemned by Lucius III in 1184, not for doctrinal heresy but for preaching without the licence that would certify that they were theologically competent. In 1201 Innocent III released them from this condemnation and formed them into three orders, which effectively anticipated the structure of the Franciscan and Dominican friars. The first order received the tonsure and enjoyed the status of canons; the second order comprised lay men and women living separately in religious communities; the third order (Tertiaries) were ordinary lay people living at home with their families but regulating their lives according to strict evangelical principles. Uniquely, they were even allowed to preach, provided they kept off theological questions and stuck to exhortation. They repaid this confidence by fighting the heretics in northern Italy. This is the first example of a group of laymen being officially organized by the Church.

Several groups of Waldensians were also reconciled with the Church under a similar arrangement. One group in France under Durand of Huesca, organized as the Poor Catholics, were evangelical anti-heretic preachers and another group in Italy under Bernard Prim became the Poor Lombards, laymen engaged in penitential preaching. By mid-century both groups had been merged with other religious orders.

But the Papacy's principal weapon in the battle against heretics of all kinds was the friars. The Franciscans and Dominicans provided within the Catholic Church the exemplars of apostolic poverty, chastity and simplicity that so appealed to the heightened sensibilities of the spiritually inclined laity. The Dominicans, founded by the Spanish canon St Dominic (c.1170–1221), were devoted to practical evangelical work, and St Dominic laid stress on academic training, simple apostolic lifestyle and the preaching mission. The principal inspiration of the Franciscans was poverty. St Francis of Assisi (1181–1226), rejecting the worldliness and materialism of the commercial world in which he grew up, sought to imitate Christ in his nakedness and his poverty. His ideals were vagrancy, chastity, poverty and simplicity. The Franciscans thus brought to fulfilment the quest for spirituality based on voluntary poverty which had been a dominant theme in religious thought in the eleventh and twelfth centuries. However, Francis laid heavy stress on orthodoxy of belief and loyalty to the existing hierarchy and particularly the Pope. This enabled Innocent III to recognize and authorize the Franciscans, in 1210. The Dominican Order, which also received encouragement from Innocent, was formally approved by Pope Honorius III in 1217. The two orders, initially different, came increasingly to resemble each other, as the Dominicans took up and elaborated the

Franciscan ideal of poverty and the Franciscans took on, particularly after their somewhat anti-academic founder's death, the academic training and organizational ideas that characterized the Dominicans.

It is hard to over-estimate the contribution of the friars to the maintenance and extension of the Catholic Church and faith. Their activities were geared to rebutting heresy and removing the conditions in which it flourished. Their strength lay in the inspiration provided by their remarkable founders, their continuing close and direct links with Rome, and their provision within the Church of a legitimate outlet for the desire for poverty, asceticism and service to the community. They appealed particularly to the dynamic elements in society: to the young, to the merchant class, to the universities, but their espousal of poverty endeared them to the populace at large.

They made a major contribution to the intellectual life of the Church, staffing university faculties, harmonizing Catholicism with the new philosophical ideas and providing some of the most influential theologians of the central Middle Ages, men like the Dominican St Thomas Aquinas (c.1225–77) and St Albertus Magnus (1206–80), and the Franciscan St Bonaventure (1221–74). But their work was far more than just theoretical. They decisively helped to resolve the feeling of rejection and isolation that the merchant class suffered because of the long-standing prohibition on usury and the often reiterated view that 'avarice is the root of all evil'. This sense of alienation, encapsulated in the dictum recorded by Gratian 'the merchant is rarely or never able to please God', came eventually to be seen as counter-productive, even as one of the conditions that made the towns happy hunting grounds for heretics. The mendicants, who had begun in revulsion from and rejection of materialist modern society, gradually evolved an ethical justification for money-making as a way of reintegrating the merchant class and ensuring that money-making was directed towards appropriately moral and spiritual ends. If a merchant made profit honestly to support himself and his family, if he made profit to give to charity, if he charged interest to compensate for delay in repayment, his activities were justified. In 1199 Innocent provided a role model in the lifelong merchant St Homobonus of Cremona (d.1197), who had spent his life in trade but had devoted his time also to good and charitable works. Not only did the friars provide justification for trade, they also provided an institutional outlet for merchant piety with the establishment of the lay confraternities, associations of laymen who attended mass and confession together, observed the same fasts as the friars, carried out co-operative works of charity and became an essential element in the creation of a bourgeois mentality and in the implementation of the mendicants' plan to moralize and purify urban society.

The friars were also great preachers, their study programmes preparing them for the active ministry. Their ministry was targeted specifically on the towns, which, according to Humbert of Romans, Minister-General of the Dominicans, needed them most because the level of sin was qualitatively and quantitatively higher, and because the message preached there would inevitably percolate out to the countryside. The friars tackled not just heresy but what Alexander Murray calls that 'dogmatic materialism' that suffused the cities of Italy – a concern for the day not the morrow, desire for money, sex and advancement, and failure to attend church, listen to sermons or pray. So friars became an integral and ubiquitous element in town life.

Textbooks on the art of preaching, concordances of the Bible for use in preparing sermons, collections of model sermons and illustrative *exempla* (moral anecdotes), proliferated. The preaching of the friars was accessible, straightforward, and vivid, avoiding theological subtlety but appealing to the vernacular, to humour, to emotion and to everyday life. Each generation produced mendicant preaching stars who travelled Europe, attracting crowds of thousands and disseminating the Catholic message: for instance St Anthony of Padua (1195–1231), St Vincent Ferrer (c.1350–1419), and St Bernardino of Siena (1380–1444) became legends in their own lifetimes. The effect of the sermons could be electric. When St Vincent Ferrer preached of sin, death, hell and the imminent appearance of the day of judgement, members of his congregation fainted with fear and he often had to stop his oration because of the uncontrollable sobbing of the crowds. The renowned Franciscan Berthold of Regensburg attracted, according to the chronicler Salimbene, audiences of 60–100,000, spoke from a wooden tower, and inspired a dedicated following. One woman followed him from town to town for six years just to hear his sermons. With confession mandatory from 1215, the doctrine of intention newly accepted by theologians and preachers coming to terms with the psychology of the crowds, the mendicants concentrated on confession, penance, and repentance, and provided the kind of spiritual and emotional climate in which heresy could be routed.

If preaching and teaching did not work, there was always the Inquisition. The mendicants were to play a leading part in that institution too, because of their pastoral and theological training, their intellectual weight and their understanding of the popular mind.

From the time of Innocent III on, the Papacy employed the full range of repressive measures to eradicate heresy, concentrating initially and particularly on the Cathars. In 1199 Innocent equated heresy with treason for the first time and threatened the perpetual disinheritance of the heirs of heretics. The Cathars, however, continued to flourish. In Languedoc, Innocent put his faith in the Cistercians, explaining in a bull of 1204 that he did so because preaching, in order to be effective, needed to be undertaken by men full of zeal for God, learned in theology, powerful in word and in works, by men who were exemplary and above reproach. The Abbot of Citeaux himself, Arnaud-Amaury, was appointed papal legate and two monks, Peter of Castelnau and Ralph of Fontfroide, were chosen to conduct an intensive preaching mission. They were empowered to discipline local bishops and clergy, and the quality of the higher clergy notably improved under their impact. But the Cathars remained obdurate.

In 1208 the Papal envoy Peter of Castelnau was assassinated and Pope Innocent lost patience. He proclaimed a crusade against the heretics, the so-called Albigensian Crusade. He called on the northern French aristocracy to descend on the south and root out the Cathars. Arnaud-Amaury was put in command and he was described as fervently desiring the death of Christ's enemies. The Abbot led the army which took Béziers in 1209. There was some debate about how to distinguish heretics from Catholics. The Abbot is said to have replied: 'Kill them all; for the Lord knoweth them that are His.' The town was pillaged and burned and the population massacred. But the Albigensian Crusade dragged on inconclusively for years, mainly as a succession of sieges. Eventually the French king intervened and assumed direct rule over most of the territory. But the crusade broke the Cathars. By the 1240s Cathar *perfects* had stopped wearing their distinctive black robes and taken to wearing instead a girdle next to the skin and moving about in secret. By 1275 no Cathar bishop survived in France and in 1326 the last known French Cathar was burned at Carcassonne. In Italy Catharism survived longer with the last surviving Cathar bishop captured in 1321.

In 1215 Innocent held his great Council at the Lateran, designed in part to codify the Church's regulations for dealing with heresy and to enlist the aid of the secular powers to deal with it. Only two countries had enacted laws against heresy before this time – England and Aragon. But in 1220 Emperor Frederick II incorporated canon law enactments on heresy into the laws of the Holy Roman Empire and in 1224 decreed burning for convicted heretics. In 1226 Louis VIII of France enacted that supporters of heretics should be debarred from public office and have their lands confiscated. In 1233 Jaime I of Aragon incorporated many of the Lateran Council's provisions into the laws of his kingdom and Alfonso X of Castile (1252–84) decreed that all unrepentant heretics be burned. Thus the leading secular rulers of western Europe fell into line behind the Papacy.

Although the kings of France and Aragon allowed Inquisitors to operate freely in their states and authorized royal officials to render full co-operation, rulers often supported the Church's anti-heresy drive most vigorously when there was something in it for them. Philip

Augustus of France (1180–1223) took over control of the Albigensian Crusade with territorial aggrandizement in mind. Frederick Barbarossa (1152–90) suppressed the heretical movement of Arnold of Brescia because he wanted imperial coronation at the hands of the Pope. Arnold, a radical reformist canon who argued that no monk or bishop who owned property could be saved, demonstrated the political threat that heresy could develop into. When his increasingly virulent campaign against the wealth and worldliness of the Papacy failed to bring about reform, he threw in his lot with the communal revolt of the city of Rome against the Pope. The revolt was suppressed by Barbarossa who handed Arnold over for execution in 1155. Frederick II was unwilling to allow the papal Inquisition to operate within his territories. But after his death in 1250, Charles of Anjou took over Sicily with papal backing; the Inquisition was established in 1269 and Charles gave military aid to the papal anti-heresy drive in northern and central Italy.

But the Church was developing its own machinery to deal with heresy, and that came to fruition under Pope Gregory IX. Gregory turned to the Dominicans and Franciscans to staff a formal Inquisition. It was founded around 1233 primarily to combat Catharism and its powers were extensive. The Inquisitors had jurisdiction over everybody in the area to which they were assigned except the bishops and their officials. They were accountable only to the Pope and they depended on the co-operation of local secular officials. But there was no centralized co-ordinating authority before 1542 when Pope Paul III set up the Holy Office, and the Inquisition never operated in areas where heresy was thought to be non-existent, such as England and Castile. Their aim was to establish guilt or innocence by lengthy questioning and then try to persuade the offenders to recant. If they failed, they handed over the offenders to the secular authorities for punishment. The Inquisition acted on denunciation and in secret. It employed full-time agents, part-time informers and repented heretics.

In 1252 the Inquisition was given power to apply torture, though Pope Innocent IV authorized its application only provided that it did not cause mutilation, bleeding, or death. Inquisitors were not permitted to pass sentence because they had no legal training. They had to take the advice of the bishops and professional lawyers. They imposed a range of penances on those who repented, including fasting, public scourging and pilgrimage. The Inquisitors devised a new form of penance – that of wearing large yellow crosses on clothing – singling out punished heretics. The most serious offenders were sentenced to perpetual imprisonment. The Inquisition was the first court to award this penalty on a large scale and special prisons had to be built for its use. The unrepentant were handed over to the secular arm for punishment. They were usually burned and their property confiscated.

Despite the fearsome reputation that has retrospectively attached itself to the Papal Inquisition, Bernard Hamilton in his carefully argued *The Medieval Inquisition* (1981) insists that 90 per cent of the sentences were canonical penances, that only a small minority of the accused were imprisoned or killed, and that the secular authorities burned heretics too on their own responsibility. He argues that the Inquisition set out to, and succeeded in, substituting the rule of law for mob rule. It is true that heretics had been destroyed over the protests of local bishops by lynch mobs of Catholic zealots in Milan (*c.*1028), Cambrai (*c.*1077), Soissons (*c.*1114), and Cologne (1143). But the atmosphere of fear and repression established by the campaigns of the early Inquisitors Conrad of Marburg and Robert le Bougre lingered long. The Dominican friar, Robert le Bougre, first Inquisitor in France, was a fiery ex-heretic who earned the nickname 'The Hammer of the Heretics'. He was supposed to be able to tell unbelievers by their speech and their gestures alone. He was despatched to Northern France to root out heresy in 1232–3. Despite opposition from local bishops, he established his headquarters in Cambrai and travelled round, burning heretics as he went. The climax of his career came in 1239 when at Mont-Aimé in Champagne he burned 180 Cathars after they had received the *consolamentum* from their 'archbishop'. But he seems to have over-reached himself. Soon afterwards he was confined by the friars in Paris and ended his days doing menial duties in Clairvaux as a punishment for his conduct. Conrad of Marburg at around the same time initiated a reign of terror in Germany, rooting out and burning alleged heretics and witches until he was murdered.

Taken in conjunction with these inquisitorial campaigns, the regular use of torture and events like the Albigensian Crusade confirmed in the popular mind the image of the Inquisition as a ruthless instrument of papal repression. The measure of the fear the Inquisitors inspired is the regularity with which they were murdered. Besides Conrad of Marburg, murdered in 1233, other early victims of vengeance were the papal Inquisitors in Avignonet, murdered in 1242, and the founder of the north Italian Inquisition, Peter of Verona, murdered in 1252 and promptly canonized as St Peter Martyr.

Within ninety years Catharism had died out, the victim of the Crusade, of missionary activity by the friars, of the Inquisition, and of the loss of its powerful secular protectors in the south of France. By the early fourteenth century it survived only in Bosnia. The Inquisition, however, continued, pursuing the Waldensians, Beguines and Beghards, the heretics of the Free Spirit, the 'Pseudo-Apostles', the *Fraticelli* and other groups.

Persecution was accompanied by demonization, in the form of

propaganda that stigmatized heretics as sexual deviants and orgiasts. The charge of sexual licence stemmed from the characteristic Catholic view of heretics as hypocrites, who preached one thing but did another, and from either deliberate or genuine misinterpretation of the belief of many groups that it was possible to attain a state of freedom from sin. This was interpreted as meaning the ability to indulge in any sin without penalty, whereas it usually meant the practice of rigorous asceticism to attain a state of oneness with God.

Such charges were made almost as soon as heresy appeared in the medieval west. The beliefs of a group of respected Orléans canons, burned for heresy in 1022, were entirely consistent with the movement to greater spirituality. They rejected the ceremonies and sacraments of the Church and laid stress on personal asceticism and mysticism. But contemporary chroniclers made the standard accusations against them. The monk Paul of St Père de Chartres accused them of holding meetings where indiscriminate sex orgies took place and the children born to these unions were killed and burned. However, that account seems to be lifted from the early Christian writer Justin Martyr's description of the calumnies alleged against Christians by pagan propagandists. The monastic chronicler Adhemar of Chabannes claimed that the Devil appeared at the ceremonies of the Orléans group, first as an Ethiopian and later as an angel of light, and brought them money, and that they rejected Christ and 'secretly practised unspeakable abominations'. So we get the classic linkage of Devil-worship and sex orgies. The accounts of these orgies, which are entirely fantastic, become standard, sometimes even word for word. The logic behind them can be seen readily enough. Since heresy is intended to disrupt Christianity, it must be the work of the Devil; therefore heretics must be Devil-worshippers. Since heretics are by nature hypocrites and since they invariably preach personal chastity, they must in fact be indulging in orgies.

Tanchelm was another radical reforming preacher in the Low Countries. Rejecting veneration of images, ecclesiastical hierarchy and tithes, he insisted that the personal merits of the priest determined the efficacy of the sacraments. He attracted an adoring following, so devoted that allegedly they drank his bathwater. The canons of Utrecht denounced him in a letter to the archbishop of Cologne, calling him 'the angel of Satan' and 'the precursor of Anti-Christ' and claiming that he 'spread his errors by way of matrons and harlots, whose intimacies, confidential conversation and private couch he was most willing to enjoy'. The clerical continuator of the chronicle of Sigebert of Gembloux recorded that Tanchelm was 'so incontinent and beastly that he violated girls in the presence of their mothers and wives in the sight of their husbands, asserting that this was a spiritual act'. But the canons' account of Tanchelm is based on Gregory of Tours' description of a false prophet in sixth-century Gaul, and there was what looks suspiciously like deliberate misrepresentation of the preaching mission to prostitutes and married women that was a regular part of the work of these charismatic preachers. Tanchelm's career was cut short when he was murdered by a furious priest in about 1115.

Abbot Guibert of Nogent, relating the story of anti-clerical reformers near Soissons around 1114, was the first to introduce charges of sodomy against dissidents. The brothers Clement and Evrard, uneducated but clearly ascetic, preached a message based on the rejection of marriage and procreation, infant baptism and the role of the priest. Guibert introduced the standard account of secret meetings, sex orgies and burning of unwanted babies but also included allegations of homosexual acts, presumably on the grounds of the rejection of marriage and of legitimate intercourse.

Around 1120, at Ivois near Trier, a group of heretics who denied transubstantiation and infant baptism were questioned. One of them, a priest, Dominic William, denied the views charged against him and was acquitted, but returned to encouraging the heresy until 'seduced by the spirit of fornication, he was taken in adultery not long afterwards and suffered a death befitting his iniquity'.

The first great medieval western heresiarch, Henry of Lausanne, 'a great snare of the Devil and armour-bearer of Anti-Christ', according to Bishop Hildebert of Le Mans, was a barefoot charismatic preacher whose appeal according to his clerical opponents was partly sexual.

Matrons and adolescent boys (for he enjoyed the pandering of both sexes) attending him at different times, avowed openly their aberrations and increased them, caressed his feet, his buttocks, his groin, with tender hands. Completely carried away by this fellow's wantonness and by the enormity of adultery, they publicly proclaimed that they had never touched a man of such strength, such humanity, such power.

Apart from his indiscriminate bisexual promiscuity, Henry was accused of an affair with a knight's wife and was said to be 'wholly given over to sensuality'.

As individual heretics gave way to heretical groups, all of them devoted to personal asceticism, so the charges of sexual irregularity became attached to whole movements. In the twelfth century Alain of Lille wrote in *De Fide Catholica* (Concerning the Catholic Faith) that the Waldensians were

incontinent ... for in their assemblies they indulge in gluttony and other excesses, as those who have ceased to consort with them testify; lovers of pleasure, putting carnal delight before the spiritual. These are also they who creep into the houses of widows and lead them astray.

Nicholas Eymeric, the fourteenth-century Aragonese Inquisitor, declared that one of the Waldensians' articles of faith was:

It is better to satisfy one's lust by any kind of evil act than to be harassed by the goadings of the flesh. In the dark it is lawful for any man to mate with any woman without distinction; whenever and as often as they are moved by carnal desires. This they both say and do.

Bernard Gui, Dominican friar and Inquisitor, in his *Conduct of the Inquisition of Heretical Depravity* (1323–4), said of the Waldensians:

The Waldenses praise continence to their believers, yet they admit that burning passion must be satisfied, however base the means.... They declare that it is better to satisfy passion by any means, however shameful, than to be tempted within the heart. This however they keep very secret lest they fall into disrepute with their believers.

He went on to repeat the standard story of indiscriminate sexual orgies in darkness and the appearance of a cat (the Devil) at their celebrations.

The Cathars were similarly accused. In 1150 Geoffrey of Auxerre wrote that the Cathars taught free sex. The Council of Rheims in 1157 condemned sex orgies as part of the heresy. Caesarius of Heisterbach wrote of the Cathars defiantly holding nocturnal meetings and orgies in Verona in 1184 even as Pope Lucius III and Frederick Barbarossa met to concert plans to extinguish them. Peter of Vaux-de-Cernay, a Cistercian monk, wrote in his *Historia Albigensis* (c.1213) that the Cathars were 'limbs of Anti-Christ, the first born of Satan', that the *perfects'* claim to remain chaste was false and that the heretics argued that no one could sin from the waist down. In his *Disputation between a Catholic and a Patarine Heretic* (c.1240), the layman George of Florence accused the heretics of 'preferring the sodomitic vice or the copulation of men'.

Walter Map, archdeacon of Oxford, writing in his *De Nugis Curialium* (Courtiers' Trifles), between 1181 and 1192, did a classic demonization job on the *Publicani*, a dualist sect similar to the Cathars who sent missionaries from Germany to England. He related the story as told by those who had returned to the faith:

About the first watch of the night ... each family sits waiting in silence in each of their synagogues; and there descends by a rope which hangs in their midst a black cat of wondrous size. On sight of it they put out the lights and do not sing or distinctly repeat

60

hymns, but hum them with closed teeth, and draw near to the place where they saw their master, feeling after him and when they have found him they kiss him. The hotter the feelings the lower their aim; some go for his feet, but most for his tail and privy parts. Then as though this noisome contact unleashed their appetites, each lays hold of his neighbour and takes his fill of him or her for all he is worth. Their elders maintain indeed, and teach each new entry that perfect love consists in give and take, as brother or sister may request or require, each putting out one another's fire.

This is the first known mention of the obscene kiss. It is also a literal case of demonization, for the cat that was said to be worshipped was the Devil, and to add insult to injury the heretical assemblies were called synagogues, thus branding them with the malign influence of the Jews, who were also emerging at that time as alleged agents of the Devil. The story of the obscene kiss was given Papal endorsement in the bull *Vox in Rama* (1233) by Pope Gregory IX. Abbot Ralph of Coggeshall, recounting an upsurge of *Publicani* in Rheims in 1176–80, claimed that 'they preach virginity as a cover for their lasciviousness'. The fourteenth-century Franciscan chronicler John of Winterthur claimed as fact that 'heretics are the special sons of Satan because they carry out and imitate his words and works'. Caesarius of Heisterbach recounts Bishop Bertrand of Metz in about 1200 denouncing Waldensian preachers: 'I see the Devil's messengers among you.' The relationship between the Devil, heretics and lechery thus became a standard charge.

In the first half of the thirteenth century, Philip, Chancellor of the University of Paris, put forward the interpretation that the cause of all heresy was 'lechery, cupidity or pride'. He claimed that the Beguines, lay women who partly adopted the life of nuns and were supposedly chaste, were in fact constantly pregnant through consorting with male heretics, who regularly claimed that sins of the flesh were not sinful. It was reiterated in sermons like those of the influential Augustinian Jordan of Quedlinburg that heretics believed above all in pleasure and particularly sexual pleasure.

In the fourteenth century the adherents of the Free Spirit movement, based on the Beguine-Beghard groups, were accused of libertinism because of their belief in potential sinlessness. All the surviving confessions of the Free Spirits include acknowledgement of freedom to have sex promiscuously, incestuously and sodomitically. The confession of John of Brunn, for instance, argued that freedom of spirit allowed an adept to be released from all moral laws. In the matter of sex, they might satisfy their lusts with women, indulge in homosexual relations and drown with impunity any child illicitly conceived. But the similarity of the confessions can of course be explained by the standard questions put to the accused, often under torture, and contrived to produce these answers.

Allegations similar to those levelled against the heretics of the Free Spirit were made against the scholarly Amalricians, a group of clerics in early thirteenth-century Paris. These followers of Amaury of Bène, who believed in the ability to attain absolute freedom from sin, were accused by Abbot John of St Victor of promiscuity: 'They committed rapes and adulteries and other acts which gave pleasure to the body and to the women with whom they sinned and to the simple people whom they promised that sins would not be punished.'

Similarly the Apostolic Brethren or 'Pseudo-Apostles' were stigmatized in the fourteenth century. The Inquisitor Bernard Gui wrote:

> They believe that any man or woman may lie naked together in one and the same bed and lawfully touch each other in every part and may without sin, caress each other. It is no sin for them to engage in carnal intercourse with each other to put an end to temptation, if the man is carnally stimulated. Also that to lie with a woman and to enjoy carnal intercourse with her is a greater deed than to bring the dead back to life.

The Franciscan friar and chronicler Salimbene claimed that Gerard Segarelli, leader of the 'Pseudo-Apostles', had a host of boy followers whom he sodomized. Salimbene called the Apostolics 'deceivers, robbers and fornicators ... the synagogue of Satan – a congregation of fools and lewd folk and forerunners of the disciples of Anti-Christ'. The slur was the by now customary mixture of sex, Satanism, and the Jews. The fifteenth-century Franciscan dissidents, the *Fraticelli*, were also accused of orgiastic behaviour.

The extent to which these libels stuck can be seen etymologically. In the late twelfth century the Albigensians became known in France as 'Les Bougres' from their reputed place of origin (Bulgaria). But the word crossed the Channel in due course to give rise to the English word 'bugger' meaning a sodomite, though the usage gained ground only after Catharism had been extinguished. Yet it testifies to the persistence of a popular view of the link between their deviant beliefs and practices. In south Germany, likewise, the dialect term *Ketzerei* could mean either heresy or sodomy.

It should be said that some more moderate scholarly opinion acquitted heretics of leading sinful lives. The Franciscan Giacomo Capelli wrote of the Cathars in 1240 in his *Summa contra Haereticos*:

> They are most chaste of body. For men and women observing the

vow and way of life of this sect are in no way soiled by the corruption of debauchery. Whence, if any one of them, man or woman, happens to be fouled by fornication, if convicted by two or three witnesses, he forthwith is either ejected from their group or, if he repents, is reconsoled by the imposition of the hands, and a heavy penitential burden is placed upon him as amends for sin. Actually the rumour of the fornication which is said to prevail among them is most false.

Their monthly meetings were not, he averred, as some 'lyingly said for purposes of fornication but for preaching and confession'.

The Dominican Moneta of Cremona in a massive treatise against heresy *Adversus Catharos et Valdenses libri quinque* acknowledged the Cathars' utter rejection of 'every form of sexual activity', even the merest touching of women, though he also went on to defend the Catholic view of sexuality (defence of procreation, intercourse within marriage, and God's creation of sexual differences).

THE LATER MIDDLE AGES

In the later Middle Ages, a major feature of Christian religion in the west was a rising interest, not least on the part of the laity, in emotive piety, meditation, and mysticism. This individual search for God tended to play down the mediation of the priesthood and complemented the life of withdrawal from the world. Mysticism was particularly strong in the Low Countries and in the Rhineland, where its greatest exponent was Meister Eckhart, a German Dominican, not a heretic – though under suspicion of heresy – who laid stress on the accessibility of God to the individual soul. Mysticism was associated with almost every heretical movement in every land.

The most serious potential threat which the Church believed itself to be facing between the fall of the Cathars and the rise of the Hussites was the movement of the Beguines and Beghards, the latest exponents of the idea of lay piety, practising the *vita apostolica* of poverty, mendicancy, and preaching, and seeking an individual relationship with God. The 1215 ban on new orders led to their proliferation. For they did not find the existing forms of religious life satisfactory. They belonged to no order, took no binding vows, and followed no common rule. But they wore religious habits and lived a religious regime, practising apostolic principles and committing themselves to chastity for the duration of their service. The females, the Beguines (a name possibly deriving from Albigensians and if so indicating the suspicion of heresy attaching to them), were townswomen, often well-to-do, who sometimes lived in houses known as *beguinages* from which they embarked on good works such as care of the sick. Their male equivalents, the Beghards (from which the name beggar probably derives) were wandering mendicants, effectively lay equivalents of the early Franciscan friars. These groups were suspected of heresy and often condemned and persecuted, but they were for the most part merely harmless contemplatives and mystics. In 1216 Pope Honorius III, persuaded of this fact, gave Jacques de Vitry, confessor of one of the leading Beguines, permission to organize the religious women into a common life in France, Germany, and the Low Countries, and communities of such women begin to appear and spread in those areas. By the mid-thirteenth century early hostility had subsided. In 1233 Pope Gregory IX permitted them to live a cloistered life and although not recognized as an order, they were accepted as following a virtuous regime. But hostility revived after the Second Council of Lyons (1274) repeated the ban on new orders.

Some of the Beguines and Beghards were accused and convicted of being adherents of 'the heresy of the Free Spirit'. The Free Spirits were misunderstood and have been misappropriated both then and since. In a lucid and scholarly study, Robert E. Lerner has disentangled the truth about them. They were not revolutionaries or millenarian communists or anarchists, but pious and ascetic mystics. Lerner persuasively argues that they were never even a sect or homogeneous organization. 'The Free Spirit' was a state of mind, closely related to the orthodox mystical movement. Its adherents were individuals, many of them women, and their main motivation was the search for spiritual perfection. They hoped to achieve it by imitating the apostolic life and reaching a total and permanent union with God during their lifetimes. They did believe that reaching this state of perfection made them incapable of sin and freed them from conventional moral restraint and from obedience to the Church ('where the spirit is, there is freedom'). This position of theoretical amoralism made it easy for the Free Spirit's foes to deduce a pattern of actual and active immorality. But in fact they believed that perfection could be reached only by the practice of extreme asceticism and an apostolic life.

The fear of this heresy crystallized around Marguerite Porete, a wandering Beguine, who produced a book called *The Mirror of Simple Souls*. Accused of heresy, she refused to recant, and she and her book were burned in 1310. But copies of it survived to inspire her followers. At the Council of Vienne (1311–12), Pope Clement V issued a bull denouncing the heresy of the Free Spirit and condemning the Beguines because they violated the ban on new orders. Bishops and Inquisitors were ordered to pursue those Beguines who held heretical beliefs. Under the pressure and threat of persecution, many Beguines became Franciscan tertiaries.

The Papacy sought to deal with the Free Spirit heresy by attacking the Beguines and Beghards. For a hundred years they were subjected to cyclical attacks by the authorities. The refrain was always the same. Their mendicancy (symbolized by their cry 'Bread for God's Sake'), their promotion of the doctrine of the Free Spirit which was an incitement to libertinism, and their disobedience (rejection of the authority of the Church in their personal pursuit of holiness) made them heretics.

Some Popes (John XXII, Gregory XI) sought to distinguish between heretical and non-heretical Beguines and Beghards. Others (Innocent VI, Urban V, Boniface IX) sought to eliminate Beguines and Beghards totally. Persecution of 'Free Spirit' Beguines and Beghards in Strasbourg in the fourteenth century was so savage that by 1400 none were left. Ferocious persecution in Bohemia provoked a revolt against the Inquisition in 1339. The Papal Inquisitors in Silesia and Bohemia were murdered in 1341 and 1350 respectively. In the 1390s and 1400s central Europe witnessed sustained and bloody campaigns of repression during which the hapless victims were regularly forced to confess to sexual malpractices. The friars were particularly hostile to them, perhaps seeing them as rivals to the Franciscan tradition. By the fifteenth century they had largely disappeared.

Even the Franciscans, pillars of the Catholic campaign against heresy, were not immune from the 'virus of heresy'. The development of the Franciscan organization at the service of the Papacy, based on convents and property-ownership, caused a split. Two tendencies developed after the death of St Francis; the Spirituals who sought to adhere strictly to his ideal of holy poverty and the Conventuals who were prepared to accept a modified Franciscan rule based on the organizational needs that they faced and some, albeit vicarious, acceptance of property. The tendencies broke into open conflict in the period 1280–1320.

The Spirituals appropriated and even distorted the apocalyptic doctrines of Joachim of Fiore (1145–1202), the Calabrian abbot whose views were very influential in the later Middle Ages. In a complex but highly symmetrical scheme, he envisaged the world passing through three ages: the first was the Age of the Father, the Old Testament, the flesh, and the law; the second was the Age of the Son, the New Testament, the flesh, and the spirit. Then there was the Third Age, the Age of the Holy Spirit, when the people of the world would be converted into a race of monks living in a state of mystical ecstasy. This would be followed by the Second Coming and the Last Judgement. Joachim suggested 1260 as the date when the Second Age would end and be succeeded by the Third Age. But the Third Age would be ushered in by a period of turmoil in which Anti-Christ would arise. The Spirituals saw themselves as the champions of the Third Age and when in 1317 Pope John XXII issued a bull rejecting their position, they identified

65

him as Anti-Christ. He ordered their revolt suppressed. The Spirituals gained strong support in the south of France, particularly in the towns, where their followers were known as Beguins (a term derived from Albigensians), because they were the exemplars of the apostolic poverty that was revered and filled the gap left by the crushing of the Cathars. But the Spirituals never gained the mass support the Cathars had enjoyed. The Spirituals were in their turn crushed and the Beguins subjected to intense pressure from the Inquisition. After 1320 the remnants fled to southern Italy, where they were last attested in 1466.

Ironically, the Franciscan authorities who were engaged in suppressing the Spiritual dissidents also found themselves at odds with the Pope. In 1323 the authoritarian John XXII issued a bull rejecting the doctrine of the absolute poverty of Christ and the apostles and declaring it a heresy. Since this was the basis of the Franciscans' belief, the general of the order, Michael of Cesena, and leading Franciscan theologians like William of Ockham rejected the Pope's views and fled to the court of the anti-Papal Emperor Louis IV of Bavaria, where they lent intellectual support to the anti-Papal cause. But they remained an intellectual elite, never gathering the popular support of the Spirituals. The dissident friars were known as the *Fraticelli*, the Spirituals as *Fraticelli de paupere vita*, and Michaelists (followers of Michael of Cesena) as the *Fraticelli de opinione*.

The ideas of the Spirituals and the Joachimites found another outlet in 1260 in the Apostolic Brethren or 'Pseudo-Apostles', founded in Parma by Gerard Segarelli. A simple, uneducated man, refused admission to the Franciscans, he set up his own grouping, practising the Franciscan ideas of absolute poverty and rigorous observance. But the 1215 Lateran Council had placed a ban on the creation of new orders and, as we have seen, this was reiterated by the Council of Lyons in 1274. In 1285 Pope Honorius IV banned the Apostolic Brethren and Segarelli was captured and burned in 1300. Segarelli was succeeded by Fra Dolcino, bastard son of a priest from Novara, who issued a manifesto in 1300, claiming the direct inspiration of the Holy Spirit, and said that the Apostolics would play a key role in the new age. He predicted the extermination of the ecclesiastical hierarchy within three years and the introduction of that new age. Dolcino took to the hills in violent rebellion to bring it about. He was taken and burned in 1307.

There was no heresy in England until the fourteenth century when abuses in the Church (simony, pluralism, non-residence), the decline of the friars, and the rise of literate laymen provided conditions favourable to the emergence of religious dissidence. It came in the form of the Lollards. Similar to the Waldensians in their adherence to the apostolic tradition, their inspiration was the Oxford academic John Wyclif. Wyclif's heresy was not derived from existing heretical movements. It developed from his study of the Bible, but by using scripture as his only authority, stressing apostolic principles, and rejecting tradition and Church laws, he came up with a set of ideas similar to those of previous dissident groups.

In political matters, Wyclif was an authoritarian statist, supporting the existing establishment and thereby gaining the protection of some of its senior members. But in religion, he was a radical, rejecting the entire clerical hierarchy and advancing the priesthood of all believers. He did not write in the vernacular or organize preaching missions. But he inspired the production of a vernacular Bible and attracted followers who launched a programme of evangelization. He died in 1384, still a communicating member of the church, but in 1411 he was condemned as a heretic. In 1428 his body was exhumed, burned, and the ashes thrown into a stream.

As they became more openly and obviously heretical, Wyclif's ideas lost intellectual and academic support but gained widespread following among both the gentry and the rural and urban population. His appeal was his puritanism, his fundamentalism, his anti-clericalism, and his desire for a vernacular Bible. His views were simplified and popularized by preachers. Lollardy was not centrally organized but consisted of individual conventicles and wandering evangelists. Nationwide persecution turned it into a clandestine sect.

The Inquisition did not operate in England and although in 1401 parliament passed an act, *de haeretico comburendo*, authorizing the handing over of recalcitrant heretics to the secular power for burning, under Henry IV only two were burned. Torture was not used, captives were given time to reflect, and some recanted. There was even some sympathy for them in high places, though this was dispelled after Sir John Oldcastle, a prominent Lollard rescued from the Tower by his followers, raised rebellion in 1414. The rising was crushed and Oldcastle was eventually executed but Lollardy was now effectively linked with sedition. However, there was no sustained and systematic persecution, and the accusations of sexual immorality, frequent against heretics on the Continent, were rarely made in England against the Lollards.

Lollardy appealed most strongly to the craftsmen, skilled artisans, and their families in the textile industries and was most strongly based in the south, the west and the Midlands, particularly London, Bristol, and Coventry. The Lollards were kept firm in their faith by a succession of dedicated travelling preachers and thus survived into the sixteenth century to merge with Protestantism.

Partly inspired by the ideas of Wyclif, Hussism was the climax of medieval heresy. It repudiated the close control of the Papacy in doctrinal matters, was notable in merging Church protest and national revolt, and successful in establishing a measure of religious tolerance.

The background was hostility between native Czechs and ethnic Germans in Bohemia and the questioning of the validity of the current ecclesiastical hierarchy in the wake of the Great Schism, which for four decades saw rival popes in Rome and Avignon. It was given an extra fillip by the development of humanism in Bohemia.

Wyclif's ideas surfaced in the Charles University in Prague and inspired the Rector of the University, Jan Hus, who was really a moralist and moderate reformer rather than a revolutionary. Hus launched a call for a return to apostolic simplicity and reliance on the Bible as a source of authority. He went to plead his case before the assembled dignitaries of the Church at the Council of Constance in 1415 and was burned at the stake. The execution stirred national feelings of outrage and 452 nobles of Bohemia and Moravia signed a letter of protest.

Two groups developed; one were the moderate Utraquists – noblemen, burgesses and university men – whose demands centred on communion in both kinds being available to the laity, which it currently was not. The other group, the Taborites, were largely peasant radicals opposed to the wealth and power of the Bohemian Church. They broke with the Church completely, abolished Catholic rites, and elected their own bishop. The two groups came to an agreement in 1419 on the basis of the Four Articles of Prague, requiring communion in both kinds for all, freedom of preaching, the renunciation of all property by the Church, and punishment of all who committed mortal sin. The German Emperor Sigismund, Bohemia's would-be ruler, launched successive attacks on Bohemia to suppress the Hussite revolt but under the brilliant generalship of John Žižka, the invading German armies, which had been given the status of crusaders by Pope Martin V, were defeated. It was the first heretical movement to defeat a Catholic crusade. But war-weariness and increasing internal divisions with conservative factions, alarmed at the Taborite excesses, led to a split. The Utraquists negotiated a settlement with the Council of Basle in 1436, allowing them to have communion in both kinds, and they returned to the Catholic fold. The Taborite army was decisively defeated by conservative Utraquists in battle in 1434 and Hussite radicalism was suppressed. The next major departure from Catholic authority would be the Protestant Reformation.

At the extreme end of heresy was the continuing trend of millenarianism which Norman Cohn has so brilliantly expounded in his *Pursuit of the Millennium* (1975). There was a great variety of millenarians, some pacifists, some violent anarchists, and millenarianism appealed to all classes. But its adherents all believed that Christ was about to return to establish his kingdom on earth in anticipation of the last judgement.

A tradition of revolutionary millenarianism is to be found in the Low Countries, the Rhineland, northern France, and later, southern and central Germany, areas that were becoming overpopulated and were involved in a process of rapid social and economic change. There were the poor, beggars, exploited and insecure unskilled workers, and the deracinated and marginal figures in urban society, disorientated by loss of custom, tradition, and support systems, and with no means of voicing their grievances. Such groups were particularly susceptible to the appearance of charismatic preachers promising the kingdom of the saints and such messianic preachers appealed particularly in times of upheaval, revolts, crusades, plague, and famine. These leaders drew on a tradition of apocalyptic prophecy which required the removal of unbelievers before the Second Coming could occur; hence the desire to destroy Jews and Moslems.

The preaching of the crusades was accompanied by millenarian fervour, and unregulated hordes moved off to the Holy Land slaughtering Jews en route. The idea of crusade continued to exert its appeal to the people and many unofficial crusades were launched which capitalized on hysterical popular enthusiasms: the Children's Crusade in 1212, the Shepherds' Crusade in 1251, the People's Crusade in 1309, and another Shepherds' Crusade in 1320. Many of these movements, inspired by messianic teaching and occurring at times of famine and distress, turned into episodes of rape, slaughter, and plunder directed against the rich and powerful.

There was an upsurge of millenarianism around 1260 when, according to Abbot Joachim of Fiore, the Second Age would end and the Third Age would begin. It took its most dramatic form in the appearance of the Flagellants, who spread rapidly through Italy and into central Europe and the Balkans. The non-appearance of the Third Age led to the disappearance of the Flagellants until 1349 when a new threat of the end of the world in the form of the Black Death stimulated their return. Flagellantism was a spontaneous movement, provoked by the atmosphere of general hysteria. The Flagellants had a strict ritual, an oath, a uniform, and a sense of divine mission. They marched with banners and candles from town to town, flogging themselves for hours on end in front of the churches. All classes joined in but the poor persevered longest and in the end alone remained.

Flagellation has been known since the early days of Christianity. What was new was its organized character and mass involvement. The aim of the Flagellants was to imitate the sufferings of Christ and to induce God to forgive them their sins and spare them greater chastisement. But they were seen as a threat to the authority of the Church. Pope Clement VI banned them in 1349, complaining that they transcended the ban on new orders and sought to circumvent the Church's control of salvation.

The Flagellants then underwent the characteristic evolution from popular piety to heterodoxy. The people revered them for taking on their shoulders the sins of the world. But the social composition of the movement changed, as nobles and burghers dropped out, leaving peasants, artisans, vagabonds, and outcasts. Flagellantism became an anti-clerical, messianic movement, rejecting all church rituals other than the Flagellants' own and claiming to be in direct communication with the Holy Spirit. The Flagellants attacked the Jews and the rich. But the ban by the Pope, the arrest of their leaders and the suppression of the processions by the bishops and secular authorities effectively suppressed the movement, which by 1357 had subsided. Nevertheless there were upsurges of Flagellantism in the 1360s and 1390s in Germany and in the 1390s in France, Italy, and Spain, in response to social conditions such as plague, the Great Schism and the threat to Christendom from the Turks.

The Hussite revolution had its radical messianic wing, the Taborites. They rejected the Church, feudalism, and the dogmas of purgatory, prayers, and masses for the dead, relics, images, and oaths. They affirmed the right of everyone to interpret the gospels as they chose. From the beginning, they developed millenarian and apocalyptic fantasies, and alarmed conservatives moved in to suppress them.

CONCLUSION

There were reasons why heresy found a better reception in some places than in others. One of the linking characteristics of heresy was its deep rooting in areas where political authority was diffused and there was no strong centralizing force. Heresy never took secure hold in those areas in which authority was concentrated (England, Sicily, Capetian France) for there the secular authorities co-operated with the Church to eliminate movements which were seen to threaten the unity and stability of Christendom. But in the Low Countries, southern France and northern Italy, heresy took hold and flourished, and came to constitute a grave threat to the authority of the Catholic Church. These were areas of intensive urban growth, industrialization, ease of movement, concentrations of wealth, and reserves of support.

But more generally heresy was the product of a drastically changed social and economic situation, as Janet Nelson has so cogently argued. Early medieval society had been stable, hierarchic, and conservative. It was constructed around recognized and accepted roles and functions with kinship groups, village communities, kingship, and lordship, holding society together and providing the necessary support systems.

Early medieval religion fitted into this system, endorsing tradition and stability, sanctioning established authority, dealing with sin and the supernatural by ritual practices. But from 1000 onwards a series of seismic changes occurred in the social and economic structures, caused initially by population growth. This led to widespread migration and the disruption of established patterns. The rise of primogeniture created a great reservoir of rootless young men. The new urban society promoted competition and individualism.

As R. I. Moore points out, the appeal of heresy was not class-based. It could appeal to all classes.

> It was not simply a revolt of the urban poor against nascent capitalism, of the rural poor against the elaboration of seignorial control and exploitation, of women against the growing domination of men, or laymen against the growing domination of churchmen, or of a rising bourgeoisie against ecclesiastical control of their activities and communities.

These were all elements in the rise of heresy. But most of all, perhaps, it was the victims of change who turned to heresy. In the cities, small traders and artisans and old patrician families furnished the most enthusiastic supporters of heresy. The knights and nobles of the south of France, impoverished by partible inheritance and deprived of the chance to exploit church property by Papal reforms, were similarly attracted to heresy. The dissolution of the old ties of community and family, which was a byproduct of the rise of towns, could be compensated for by the community of heretic groups.

Many women joined heretical sects and followed popular preachers. The surplus of women over men, the scarcity of legitimate female vocations, and the inability to enter the priesthood all provided sociological reasons for this. Women found that they could gain status and authority in heretical sects. Both Cathars and Waldensians gave women equal rights in their movements as preachers and participants. In the Cathar Church women could be *perfects* and administer the *consolamentum*. But it would be wrong to suppose that women turned to heresy just because they felt excluded by the clerical establishment or victimized by the social structure. Many found positive spiritual attractions in the lifestyles and values being propounded.

The Church had not been geared to the rapid urban expansion and its parish system failed to meet the needs of people flooding into the towns in search of a new life. Equally the Church could not cope with the upsurge of the money economy and this provoked a crisis of materialism, a phenomenon sensitively and illuminatingly explored by Lester K. Little in *Religious Poverty and the Profit Economy in Medieval*

Europe (1978). The Church's first reaction was a rejection of the new world. The received ecclesiastical tradition was hostility to the towns, money, and the urban professions. Until the end of the tenth century pride had been the most serious of the seven deadly sins, but it was displaced in the eleventh by avarice. 'Avarice is the root of all evil,' said St Peter Damian and was echoed in this by St Bernard of Clairvaux and John of Salisbury. Peter Lombard said that a merchant could not perform his work without sinning. The popular *Dives and Lazarus* story showed the rich man ignoring the poor man and in consequence going to hell. The theme of Christ driving the money-changers out of the temple cropped up regularly in sermons. Usury was regularly denounced by Church councils, preachers, and theologians. A regular and recurrent image in the popular culture of the time was of people or animals vomiting or defecating coins, thus associating money with filth.

The reaction to this was the spontaneous adoption of poverty and spirituality by groups of laymen and women like the Humiliati but also by the friars and by heretical groups like the Waldensians and the Cathars. This continued to be a response of pious lay people to the growth of materialism, as the development of the Beguines and Begh-ards in the thirteenth century testifies.

Scholars have laid great stress on poverty in discussing these move-ments but stress should also be laid on virginity, chastity, sexual abstinence, and sexual renunciation. As Peter Brown points out in his dazzling book *The Body and Society* (1988), celibacy was a lifestyle that was open to everyone, whatever their background, age, or status. It answered a deep need and it removed people from the community at large, concerned as it was with property and procreation. The Cathars institutionalized celibacy in their hatred of sex; the Waldensians prac-tised a life of moderation and moralism; the Humiliati adopted a life of voluntary chastity; the Franciscans took vows of celibacy. Heretics and mendicant preachers alike drew attention to the imminent end of the world and the need to reach a state of spiritual perfection before the return of Christ. The rejection of property and of sex was a powerful manifestation of the desire to attain the status of the apostles.

The counterpart of the adoption of such a lifestyle was the desire for greater direct access to spiritual power. Many ordinary people no longer had faith in the priesthood, saw the whole paraphernalia of church buildings and rituals as redundant, and so sought a new system based on meetings of the faithful, the priesthood of all believers, and the study of the translated Bible in order to come into direct and immediate contact with the word of God. It was therefore a combination of the continuing appeal of poverty, asceticism, and the *vita apostolica*

with specific circumstances related usually to change and upheaval –
economic, social, and political – that explains the pattern and progress
of heresy in the Middle Ages.

4

WITCHES

The term 'witch hunt' has come in our time to mean a search for scapegoats, the hounding to destruction of innocent people in a bid to uncover and eradicate some imagined conspiracy. Many of the minority groups described in this book were at one time or another victims of this kind of mentality; none more so than witches themselves.

Medieval people lived in a world of fear: fear of taxes, disease, war, famine, death, hell. It was a society that believed in the supernatural, in the power of dark forces and the operation of Satan and his demons in the world. It believed also in witchcraft, which was a convenient explanation both for sudden natural catastrophes (famine, epidemics, storms, floods, the destruction of crops and animals) and for such recurrent family problems as impotence, infertility, stillbirth, and infant death. The last explains why midwives were so often the target for witchcraft accusations. Sudden and unexplained deaths might well be attributed to witchcraft and the services of witches might actively be sought to induce or destroy love, to restore or undermine health. The stock-in-trade of the witch was made up of ointments, potions, philtres, incantations, amulets, and waxen images.

Western European witchcraft was different from all other kinds in one notable regard. In Europe witches came to be seen as servants of the Devil. By the end of the Middle Ages a luridly consistent picture had developed in which witches – often but not always women – signed pacts with the Devil, renouncing Christianity and enlisting in Satan's service. They sealed the agreement by copulating with the Devil. They met in regular sabbats, which involved cannibalism, sexual orgies, and blasphemous parodies of Christian services. Witches had animal 'familiars', enjoyed the power of flight, and sometimes the ability to change shape. They were empowered to commit evil. They were part of a world-wide Satanic conspiracy aimed at undermining Christianity.

Satanist witchcraft was thus the comprehensive mirror image of Christianity, an alternative faith. Satan and his demons were the counterparts of God and his angels. They exalted evil rather than good

74

and promoted the flesh above the spirit. Where Christianity most prized celibacy, Satanists exalted promiscuity. Their ceremonies parodied Christian ritual with Christian symbols openly reviled and the use of children's ashes in their bread and wine mocking the doctrine of Transubstantiation. Their customary practices were those regarded with the greatest horror by the Christian Church: murder, cannibalism, incest, infanticide, and orgiastic sex.

But what is perhaps most interesting from the point of view of this study is the centrality of sex. The witches' equivalent of Christian baptism was copulation with the Devil. Indiscriminate sexual orgies were integral to their rituals. This directly reflects Christianity's age-old fear of sex and it also highlights the suspicion and dislike of women integral to medieval culture.

The most extreme example of this attitude is to be found in one of the most notable works of demonology, *Malleus Maleficarum* (The Hammer of the Witches), published in 1486. It ran into fourteen editions in the next forty years. *The Hammer* was the work of two Dominican inquisitors, Heinrich Kramer and Jacob Sprenger, who, armed with authorization from Pope Innocent VIII, had conducted tireless witch-hunts in Germany and Austria. It was a compendium of what was by then the received wisdom about Devil-worshipping witches and it declared anyone who did not believe that witches existed to be guilty of heresy. It is also a work of pathological misogynism and sex-obsession, harping particularly on the ability of the Devil and his witches to remove the male organ by causing temporary or permanent castration. The authors viewed this with horror, not because it prevented the male indulging in sex but because it denied the male his masculinity and also the chance to conquer the sex impulse and attain a life of voluntary chastity, the highest state attainable on earth.

Kramer and Sprenger identified witchcraft squarely with the sex impulse: 'All witchcraft comes from carnal lust, which is in women insatiable.' They explained that women were much more prone to the evil of witchcraft and demon worship because they were more impressionable and credulous than men. Women were natural deceivers, inordinately vain, 'intellectually like children', and most important, 'more carnal than a man'. This was not an unusual view. It is in fact the 'official' medieval view of womankind; woman's inferiority decreed in perpetuity because of the Original Sin of her ancestress Eve. But in *The Hammer of the Witches* what was taken to be women's inherent weakness was seen as being harnessed to the active promotion of evil in the world. The alleged carnality of witches was already well established. The witch of Berkeley, for instance, whose death was related by the twelfth-century chronicler William of Malmesbury was described as 'excessively gluttonous, perfectly lascivious, setting no bounds to her debaucheries'. Free indulgence in sex certainly amounted to deliberate defiance and rejection of the Church's most solemn teachings on this most central of human activities. The additional idea of demons having sexual intercourse with mankind was of ancient origin. There was a legend first reported in the sixth century *Gothic History* of Jordanes and still current in the Middle Ages that it was male demons mating with outcast Gothic witch-women that created the race of the Huns. What was new was the idea of ritual intercourse with the Devil as part of the witches' initiation and the concept of sex orgies as part of a witchcraft cult. The development of such ideas highlights the extent to which witchcraft came to be seen by Christian fanatics as synonymous with sexual licence.

By the 1960s historians of witchcraft, influenced by scientific anthropology, had come to the view that Satanist witchcraft did indeed exist in the Middle Ages – a view nineteenth-century rationalists and Protestant polemicists had dismissed as mere Catholic propaganda. The anthropological view was classically outlined in Jeffrey Burton Russell's carefully documented study *Witchcraft in the Middle Ages* (1972). Russell argued that witchcraft existed in Europe long before Christianity. However, once Christianity took hold, it became increasingly allied in the minds both of its practitioners and its opponents with the evil spirit of Christian theology, the Devil, culminating in the fifteenth century in the development of the witches' sabbat. In Russell's view witchcraft in medieval Christian Europe merged elements of magic and pre-Christian pagan traditions with a spirit of opposition to, and rejection of, orthodox Christianity akin to that which inspired heresy. 'The essential element in Christian witchcraft is defiance of the church and society on behalf of the powers of evil,' Russell writes. The tendency of the authorities to regard witchcraft as a species of heresy actually confirmed the development of witchcraft as an alternative religious cult, while persecution ensured its transformation into a structured underground sect complete with secret meetings.

Christianity did its best to absorb paganism and to negate pagan magic, taking over pagan holy days and festivals, appropriating pagan holy places and building churches on them, transforming pagan deities into saints. Even the horned and hooved Devil of Christian mythology can be identified with the pagan god Pan or the Celtic Cernunnos, who is thus found a place in the Christian world-picture. The Church also had its own form of magic-miracles, efficacious holy relics, the power of prayer. In particular the mass stood at the heart of a system of belief about changes in nature induced through the operation of supernatural powers.

However, some elements of paganism defied Christian absorption, particularly fertility cults. Overt paganism with strong overtones of magic continued to exist and to be fought by Church and state until the ninth century. Indeed early medieval laws and penitentials contain regular references to folklore beliefs, witchcraft and sorcery, though not, it has to be said, as an organized cult, and not as Devil-worship.

The kind of paganism the Church was fighting in those days is described in the ninth-century *Canon Episcopi*, which appears in a compilation of regulations drawn up around 906 by Regino of Prüm. It was reproduced throughout the Middle Ages as the authoritative Church statement on the subject, being included notably in the *Decretum* of Gratian. In the earliest version of the *Canon*, bishops were asked to investigate their dioceses to discover if any women through incantations provoked love, hatred, or harm to persons or property, and to look into claims to the ability to change shape and to participation in the 'the wild ride' in which a host of women were believed to fly out at night, riding on beasts and accompanying the pagan goddess Diana. The author of the *Canon* suggested that both these phenomena were delusions planted in the minds of women by the Devil.

The *Canon Episcopi*, however, clearly detailed two separate phenomena: witchcraft and folklore. Russell believes that they merged after the ninth century to form medieval witchcraft and that also blended in was the belief in demons. Popular stories about demons inciting, misleading, tempting, and tormenting Christians go back to ancient times. Such stories were endlessly retold throughout the Middle Ages and featured regularly in the sermons of popular preachers. Demons were believed to be omnipresent, to be the emissaries of evil, but – *pace* Russell – no one worshipped them.

Russell locates witchcraft, along with heresy, mysticism, the crusades, and monastic reform, in that ferment of religious and intellectual discontent and desire for experiment that accompanied the expansion of towns, rapid population growth, and the dramatic changes in social and economic patterns characterizing the eleventh and twelfth centuries. This was the period, he claims, when the ancient paganism died out as an independent force and witchcraft emerged as a religious heresy like Catharism.

Russell argues that at the same time as some religious dissidents turned to Catharism, others turned to witchcraft. The pursuit of heretics and witches alike by the Papal Inquisition, established in 1227, is taken by Russell to mean that witchcraft had now come to be seen as a form of heresy. As such it flourished throughout the Middle Ages, drawing its adherents from all sections of society. He therefore takes at face value the accounts of Devil-worship uncovered by Catholic investigators and reported in the contemporary sources, believing, for example that the victims of the 1022 Orléans burnings and the persecutions of Conrad of Marburg in the 1230s were genuine witches. His principal underlying thesis is that Devil-worshipping witches evolved as part of popular culture and were only later recognized and defined as a major problem by intellectuals.

In his brilliant book *Europe's Inner Demons* (1975), Norman Cohn has comprehensively demolished this interpretation. He begins with the fact that medieval Catholics made allegations against heretics and witches which were substantially the same as those made by the classical pagan writers against the early Christians – incest, infanticide, canni- balism, and orgies. It was indeed standard practice to brand all dissident religious groups with the most unspeakable crimes in the calendar, and by the Middle Ages a common stock of slanders existed in the classical texts for monastic writers to plunder and redeploy. Such texts were regularly lifted verbatim and applied to the new dissident groups. Cohn claims that this familiar propaganda technique was taken further by Christian writers – thereby creating a convincing, but in fact deceptive image of a Christendom-wide Satanic conspiracy. Witches, who Cohn admits certainly existed as isolated individuals, were depicted as the foremost members of this conspiracy. Thus Christian propagandists and polemicists wove the old stories into a comprehensive pattern of belief and action, centred on the Devil and prominently featuring sexual activity, thus reflecting the horror it inspired in the minds of austere and fanatical celibates.

Cohn in fact takes a diametrically opposite view of the phenomenon of witchcraft from Russell's. In his contention, Devil-worshipping witches had no existence in popular culture, indeed no existence at all outside the fevered imaginations and paranoid delusions of a group of clerical intellectuals. Yet by the end of the Middle Ages the intellectuals' view was percolating down to the masses and would bear horrifying fruit in the witch hunts of the sixteenth and seventeenth centuries. (But it should be stressed that many intellectuals and theologians came genu- inely to believe in a Satanist threat because of the constant outbreaks of heresy, which they could interpret only as evidence of a demonic desire to destabilize Christian society.)

Cohn, then, locates the development of the Satanic witch cult in the cumulative process of propaganda by which religious dissidents were demonized, a process which began with the return of heresy to western Europe in the eleventh century, and specifically in 1022 when a group of pious ascetics and mystics, who denied various tenets of Christian belief, were burned as witches in Orléans. Contemporary and immedi- ately post-contemporary Christian writers branded them as worshippers of the Devil, who indulged in child murder and sex orgies. Within a century, this became the standard account of heretics. It is one of the many ironies with which this story abounds that many of the heretical groups branded as Devil-worshipping orgiasts were in fact pious puritans, who exalted a life of celibacy. Their persecutors were similarly extreme celibates but with a horror of religious dissidence which led them to insist that the heretics were hypocrites, who used their alleged celibacy as a mask for their more nefarious sexual activities.

Cohn's great achievement was to demonstrate how intellectuals created a new and wholly artificial construct out of four previously separate and distinct elements: folklore, witchcraft, ritual magic, and Devil-worship. The process of evolution was slow but by the end of the Middle Ages was complete. People had always believed in magic. The ancient world used the term *maleficium* to refer to harm caused by occult means and applied it equally to witchcraft and magic. It was condemned by Greek, Roman, and Germanic laws. But this concealed the real distinction between high and low magic, between magic used for good and for evil ends. Witchcraft was essentially low magic, the folk medicine of the local 'wise woman', skilled in herbs and midwifery, but also able to turn her hand to love potions, poisons, and abortifacients. It existed in the community, mainly among the lower classes, and was practised by individuals and not in cults. High magic was a science, practised by learned men, involving formal rituals, books of magic lore, and the summoning up of demons. But magicians invoked God and not the Devil and the demons were summoned as servants to do the bidding of the magicians and not as their masters instructing them in the Devil's work. Neither form of magic involved the worship of the Devil, orgies, infanticide, or cannibalism.

Cohn shows how on to the realities of witchcraft and magic were grafted the fantasies that were part of age-old peasant folklore. Since Roman times, there had been tales of women who could fly, night witches (*strigae*), who could change themselves into birds and were bent on sex, cannibalism, or murder. There was a long-established folk belief in the 'ladies of the night', beneficent, protective female spirits, for whom the peasants left out food and drink. They were an organized body, a host with a supernatural leader, variously known as Diana, Herodias, and Holda. Until the thirteenth century, the educated elite regarded these phenomena as delusions. John of Salisbury, for instance, expressed this view in the twelfth century. But in the later Middle Ages intellectuals came to believe that the stories were literally true and Kramer and Sprenger denounced the idea that they could be delusions. These stories, then, were blended with witchcraft, ritual magic, and the final, and wholly mythical, ingredient of Devil-worship to create the now familiar witch-stereotype.

Once the pattern of Satanist activities was established in the propaganda it could be regularly adduced. The recurrence of the same ideas in the accounts may be best explained not by the widespread occurrence of such practices but the standard set of questions that were put to prisoners under torture by Inquisitors and to which they freely confessed to end their torment. The pattern of persecution was set by the career of Conrad of Marburg.

A fanatical, ascetic priest, Conrad was appointed as the first Inquisitor of Germany in 1231. He initiated a reign of terror in which he claimed to have uncovered nests of Devil-worshippers. 'We would gladly burn a hundred if just one of them were guilty' was the dictum of Conrad and his associates. They were true to their word and the slaughter ended only with Conrad's murder in 1233, the first of several inquisitors to be eliminated by those they threatened or as a result of an increasing revulsion from their activities. But where Russell accepts that Conrad found witches, Cohn makes it clear that Conrad's victims were either innocent – and indeed many were subsequently exonerated by the authorities – or were members of the devout and ascetic Waldensian sect, who neither worshipped the Devil nor believed in promiscuity. Pope Gregory IX, however, accepted Conrad's reports as true, proclaimed him as champion of Christendom, and embodied his findings in a Papal Bull *Vox in Rama* (1233). The Papacy thus gave its official imprimatur not only to the whole Satanist paraphernalia of secret meetings, appearances by the Devil, obscene initiation rites, and bisexual orgies, but by so doing sanctioned the idea of a linkage between heresy, witchcraft, sodomy, promiscuity, and obscenity, rendering them more or less indistinguishable from each other.

The rise of Catharism, with its basic belief in two creators of the world, one good and one evil, the prominent role assigned to women in its priesthood, and its rejection of all Catholic sacraments, was particularly important in focusing attention on the idea of evil and sharpening the image of the Devil in Christian cosmology. Representations of the Devil had not been common until the ninth century but thereafter they increased in number. His presence and his personality grew in intensity with the tendency of the twelfth-century Renaissance to personalize and individualize, with the ubiquity of the Devil in sermons and folk-stories and with the rise of heresy. The gradual development in western art of the Devil as a distinct composite human/animal figure can be traced from the eleventh to the fifteenth century. He had become by the end of the Middle Ages a fearsome and familiar figure, ready for adoption as an alternative deity: tall, dark, thin, hairy, horned, hooved and winged. However, it should be noted that although they were often accused of being Devil-worshipping witches, the Cathars in fact hated and feared the Evil Spirit with greater fervour even than Catholics.

In the fourteenth century inquisitors claimed to have discovered a sect called Luciferans in Austria, Bohemia, and Switzerland, who were accused of rejecting the Catholic hierarchy, worshipping Lucifer, and practising sexual orgies. Over such an incident the basic difference of view between Russell and Cohn emerges clearly; whereas Russell believes they were Satanist witches, Cohn demonstrates that they were no such thing. They were either Waldensians or Cathars, tortured into admitting to Satanism, along with Cathar beliefs; the Cathar idea of light as the source of all good things being wilfully distorted into worship of Lucifer ('the bearer of light'). As actual Devil-worshippers, the 'Luciferans' in fact never existed, and were, according to Cohn, yet another variation of the Satanist witch cult conspiracy theory.

So regularly were the Waldensians accused of witchcraft that *Vauderie* (from Waldensians) became a term for witchcraft, while in Savoy witches were known as *Gazari*, a name derived from *Cathari*. Most heretical groups seem to have been accused of being Devil-worshipping witches almost as a matter of course. Russell notes that some areas were more susceptible to Satanism than others. Spain, though it had a strong tradition of magic, had little witchcraft. Portugal, southern Italy, Ireland, Scandinavia, and until the fourteenth century England, were also relatively untouched. Witchcraft was strongest, he says, in France, the Low Countries, northern Italy, and the Rhineland, exactly the regions where heresy was strongest. But this is not evidence that witchcraft existed there as a branch of heresy. It is evidence that heretics were regularly accused of witchcraft by their opponents.

The evidence for the existence of Satanist witches is further diminished by Cohn's demonstration that the alleged fourteenth-century witch hunts in Toulouse, Carcassonne, Como, and Novara, which all figure in the standard histories of witchcraft, never in fact took place. They are all based on forged evidence from much later periods.

The judicial process lent force to the idea of a witch-cult. There were few trials for witchcraft before 1300, in part because of the nature of the legal system. It was an accusatory system in which one person accused another, with the accuser providing the evidence and seeking to convince the judge. If this failed, the ordeal by fire, water, or combat might be invoked. But if in the end, the accuser failed to prove his case, he might suffer the penalty he had sought for the accused. Since it was so difficult to prove *maleficium*, few cases were therefore brought. Victims of witchcraft tended to take the law into their own hands and organize lynchings. The murders of alleged witches are recorded at various times in the earlier part of the Middle Ages: in 1074 (Cologne), 1090 (Vötting), and 1128 (Ghent). But the revival of Roman law in the twelfth century led to the introduction into the judicial process of the system of inquisition. This method, backed by torture, ensured more frequent confessions. The removal of the judicial penalty from unsuccessful accusers encouraged accusation. Roman law also promoted the introduction of harsher penalties. Law code after law code in the twelfth and thirteenth centuries prescribed burning for witches and sorcerers, a procedure that had a much-quoted scriptural warrant: 'Thou shalt not suffer a witch to live' (Exodus 22 v. 18). The inquisition method was used by both Church and state in its campaign to root out dissidents. It was the kind of judicial process into which preconceptions on the part of judges and prosecutors were easily fed.

Even so the inquisitorial procedure was aimed initially more at ritual magic than at witchcraft, as both Cohn and Edward Peters in his valuable book *The Magician, The Witch and the Law* (1978) have shown. Christianity identified all magical practices with paganism and condemned them. St Augustine in his treatise *de doctrina Christiana* listed the elements of magic to be avoided by Christians and these involved what would be classed both as witchcraft and magic: augury, astrology, amulets, charms, horoscopes, medical magic, and pacts with demons. These practices were regularly condemned by the Church fathers and Church councils, who saw the human race as particularly prone to demonic interference and saw all medical practices as the work of the Devil and his agents. But they continued to be practised.

This traditional hostility was maintained from the eighth to the twelfth centuries in a literature that was primarily monastic in its provenance and drew heavily on patristic traditions. This ensured that stories of powerful and wicked magicians continued to circulate. In that rarefied world in which scholarship and international politics overlapped, the charge of being a magician took on the same force as the accusation of being a Communist or Fascist in modern democratic societies. Such stories sometimes filtered out to a wider public. The Aquitanian scholar who became Pope Sylvester II (999–1003) was widely believed to have made a pact with demons to gain magical knowledge. Pope Gregory VII was denounced at the Synod of Brixen (1080) for having, like Sylvester, studied magic at Toledo and become a necromancer. Emperor Frederick II, nicknamed 'The Wonder of the World' (*Stupor Mundi*), who had a wide variety of intellectual interests, also earned himself a reputation for wizardry.

In the twelfth century clerical writers like John of Salisbury and Walter Map expressed worries about the craze for magic among the trend-conscious and fashionable young courtiers thronging the courts of the emerging national monarchies. But the Church was even more concerned about the revival of the study of magic, which had taken place as part of the twelfth-century intellectual renaissance. The ecclesiastical authorities moved to segregate it from approved areas of learning. Hugh of St Victor's *Didascalicon* (1141) included a powerful denunciation of all forms of magic:

Magic is not accepted as part of philosophy, but stands with a false claim outside it: the mistress of every form of iniquity and malice, lying about the truth and truly infecting men's minds, it seduces them from divine religion, prompts them from the cult of demons, fosters corruption of morals, and impels the minds of its devotees to every wicked and criminal indulgence.... Sorcerers are those who, with demonic incantations or amulets or any other execrable types of remedies, by the cooperation of the devils or by evil instinct, perform wicked things.

This view was regularly articulated throughout the twelfth and thirteenth centuries and formed a powerful prohibition on the study or practice of magic. Nevertheless, there continued to be great anxiety about the occult practices filtering into western Europe from the Arab world, from Byzantium, and from the rediscovered and eagerly studied Greek texts. This anxiety was intensified by the prevalence of millenarian ideas in the twelfth and thirteenth centuries. Central to these beliefs as they developed in the Middle Ages was the idea that the end of the world would be preceded by the appearance of Anti-Christ who would delude the Christian people until routed by the forces of the true Christ. The early Church fathers had developed the idea of Anti-Christ, a figure originating in the Book of Revelations, into a human born of Satanic union with a human woman or from a human union presided over by Satan. He was traditionally associated with magic and magicians, as the tenth-century writer Adso explained in his *Libellus de Anti-Christo* (Book of Anti-Christ):

Anti-Christ will have magicians, criminals, soothsayers and wizards, who, with the Devil's inspiration, will bring him up and instruct him in every iniquity, trickery and wicked art. And evil spirits will be his leaders and eternal friends and inseparable companions.

It was in this frame of mind that the Church's most influential theologian, St Thomas Aquinas, made in the thirteenth century a systematic exposition and denunciation of magical practices. He insisted that magicians became the servants rather than the masters of demons and thus fell under the influence of the demons' master, Satan. This effectively branded magic as the most pernicious form of heresy.

Despite the build-up of an intellectual synthesis linking magic with the Devil, much of the evidence cited in standard witchcraft histories as evidence of the existence of Satanic witches turns out on closer examination to be concerned with the practice of simple ritual magic. Indeed, there was initially even an official attempt to distinguish between harmful and harmless magic. Pope Alexander IV laid down in 1258 the principle that the Papal Inquisitors were not to concern themselves with cases of divination as such but only those which 'manifestly savoured of heresy'. The fourteenth-century inquisitor Nicholas Eymeric in his *Treatise against the invokers of demons* also discriminated between non-heretical forms of divination (palmistry, drawing lots) and the invocation of demons. But the Inquisition became more and more interested in both witchcraft and magic, blurring the distinctions between them and within them. This was particularly true after the decision of the theology faculty of the University of Paris, which in 1398 pronounced *maleficia* as necessarily entailing idolatry and apostacy and therefore tantamount to heresy. This justified the prosecution of all forms of magic by the Inquisition. Magic, it was argued, involved explicit or implicit pacts with the Devil. This was an important stage in the progressive demonization of witchcraft and magic.

The most spectacular prosecutions for ritual magic, however, were initially not instigated by the Church but by the state. There was a series of show trials staged by King Philip IV of France (1285–1314) as part of his bid to tame the Church and establish absolute mastery of his realm. The first person to be tried for ritual magic was Pope Boniface VIII (1294–1303), arch-opponent of Philip. He was posthumously arraigned for denying Christianity, practising magic, and sodomy. Bishop Guichard of Troyes was tried on the evidence of political and ecclesiastical rivals on charges of conjuring demons, summoning the Devil, consorting with witches, and practising *maleficium* against the royal family. Most spectacularly of all, the Knights Templar, though not accused of ritual magic, were accused of idolatry, sodomy, and Devil-worship. In the disturbed circumstances following the deaths of Philip IV in 1314 and his three sons, who followed each other in rapid succession on the throne, an atmosphere of fear and suspicion was engendered in which accusations of the use of dark forces were almost an inevitable part of the political process. The family of the unpopular *parvenu* chief minister of Philip IV, Enguerrand de Marigny, were accused of using image magic to destroy King Louis X; Countess Mahaut of Artois was accused of seeking to bewitch her son-in-law Philip V; and Count Robert of Artois of plotting to encompass the destruction by magic of Philip VI. It is not impossible that some of these figures did turn to magic in the hope of furthering their cause.

Similar in-fighting and factional strife in the Avignon Papacy formed the background to magical conspiracies against Pope John XXII, who regularly accused his opponents of heresy, idol-worship, and dealing with demons. Most notably, Bishop Hughes Geraud of Cahors was burned at the stake in 1317 for practising *maleficium*, consorting with a Jewish magician, and seeking to poison the Pope. The relationship of all these cases to the political circumstances can be shown by the fact

18 Suspect examined by torture at the witch trials at Bamberg in 1508. (Reproduced by kind permission of the Mansell Collection.)

19 The swimming of Mary Sutton, a suspected witch, in 1612. Those who survived the trial were acknowledged as witches. Here the victim's familiars help her to stay afloat. Title page of a pamphlet *Witches apprehended, examined and executed*, London 1613. (Reproduced by kind permission of the Mansell Collections.)

20 The hanging of three witches in Chelmsford in 1589. (Reproduced by kind permission of the Mansell Collection.)

21 The burning of a witch in Amsterdam in 1571. (Reproduced by kind permission of the Mansell Collection.)

22 Execution of English witches in the seventeenth century. The witchfinder is shown on the right receiving payment. (Reproduced by kind permission of the Mansell Collection.)

23 An Assembly of Witches, from Guazzo's *Compendium Maleficarum*, originally published in 1608. 'The devil is president of the Assembly and sits on the throne in some terrible shape, as of a goat or dog ... then they offer him pitch black candles or infants' navel cords and kiss him....' (Book I, Chapter 12, trans. Montague Summers 1912.) (Reproduced by kind permission of the British Library.)

24 and 25 Witches using human corpses to bring about the death of others. Infant corpses had their own particular uses. From Guazzo's *Compendium Maleficarum*, originally published in 1608. (Reproduced by kind permission of the British Library.)

26 Even on his wedding-day this Jewish bridegroom wore the 'rouelle', the wheel-shaped badge of infamy. Italy, *c.* 1477. (Reproduced by kind permission of the Hamburg Staats- und Universitatsbibliothek.)

27 Crucifixion of a Christian child by the Jews at Pontoise. From Schedel's *Nuremberg Chronicle*, 1493. (Reproduced by kind permission of the Mary Evans Picture Library.)

28 Brothel scene, German, fifteenth century. The shared bath and the figure of the fool were commonly used to signify prostitution. (Reproduced by kind permission of the Mary Evans Picture Library.)

29 Infidelity, lovers sharing a bath. From Johan Stumpf's *Schweizerchronik* c. 1550. (Reproduced by kind permission of the Mary Evans Picture Library.)

30 Prostitute with a young man, a German fifteenth-century woodcut. (Reproduced by kind permission of the Mary Evans Picture Library.)

31 Mercury taken as an anti-syphilitic. For those who contracted venereal disease as a result of their adventures, mercury offered a remedy. (Reproduced by kind permission of the Mary Evans Picture Library.)

32 Homosexuals consigned to Hell, from Dante's *Inferno*, Canto XV. Here Dante recognizes his old teacher Brunetto Latini and other Florentines condemned for their vice of sodomy. (Reproduced by kind permission of the Biblioteca Nazionale, Florence.)

33 Leper woman with a bell. English fourteenth century. (Reproduced by kind permission of the British Library.)

34 Leper with clapper and bowl, from the thirteenth-century *Miroir Historial* of Vincent de Beauvais. (Reproduced by kind permission of the Mary Evans Picture Library.)

that they petered out once Philip VI brought stable government to France and the controversial and embattled Pope John XXII died. But the trials and accusations focused attention on both magic and witchcraft and further advanced the intertwining of the two.

In his systematic study of European witchcraft trials, Richard Kieckhefer (1976) has noted that compared with the mass persecutions of the classic age of the witch hunts in the sixteenth and seventeenth centuries, there were comparatively few witch trials in the period 1300 to 1500 and almost never any sustained effort to eliminate witches *per se* from any particular locality. Before 1375 Satanism was rarely present in the accusations, the practising of magic and invocation of demons being the principal charges. Between 1375 and 1435 a two-fold change took place, with a steady increase in the number of trials for witchcraft and the intensification of concern about Satanism. With the rise of Satanism charges, there was a concomitant increase in references to sex with the Devil and accusations of sex orgies. It is particularly significant that Satanism arose in about 54 per cent of trials before ecclesiastical courts but in only 11 per cent of trials before secular judges. Kieckhefer therefore concludes, like Cohn, that Satanism charges were not grounded in popular belief but were introduced by ecclesiastical judges and jurists and confirmed by the accused under torture. What ordinary people believed in was witchcraft and folklore rather than Devil-worship. For instance, the records for Lucerne covering the period from the mid-fifteenth century to the mid-sixteenth century of accusations brought by 130 villagers against 32 alleged witches, the bulk of them women, omit all mention of the Devil. For the most part the charges seem to have been brought by disgruntled neighbours seeking to explain natural disasters that had befallen them.

In the thirteenth century Humbert of Romans, master-general of the Dominicans, complained that peasant women were

> normally much prone to magical practices ... they use them either on their own behalf or for some other reason; for their children when they are sick; or for their animals, so that wolves do not catch them, and so on.... Some use this kind of divination for personal profit ... some are so obstinate, nay even incorrigible, that they simply cannot be stopped, either by excommunication or by any other kind of threat.

In 1425 when St Bernardino of Siena was preaching in Arezzo, he learned of a grove once sacred to Apollo and containing healing springs used by witches and magicians to cure ailing babies. When he tried to have the grove destroyed, he was driven out by the locals, convinced of the efficacy of the springs. But fifteen years later, by planting a cross in the ground there and suffering no ill effect, St Bernardino demonstrated the superiority of his magic and persuaded the locals to drain the springs and abandon their belief in them.

The reason for the increasing number of charges of witchcraft may well be related to the climatic change around 1300 which ushered in the 'Little Ice Age' and unleashed a succession of harvest failures, floods, and famines, for which some supernatural cause might be sought, and to the atmosphere of hysteria and paranoia generated from mid-century by the plague pandemic. Certainly the pace of prosecutions was stepped up. There were 84 verified witch trials between 1365 and 1428 but 354 in the next 72 years, often involving large numbers of suspects. This coincides with the increasing involvement of intellectuals in the subject of witchcraft. 1430 marks the beginning of a period of great increase in the quantity of treatises dealing with witchcraft. The first printed book on the subject was issued in 1464.

Cohn singles out two trials as being of especial significance in demonstrating the process by which intellectuals created the witch composite. The idea of female copulation with the Devil received an important stimulus from the celebrated Kyteler trial. Lady Alice Kyteler, her son and associates in Kilkenny, Ireland, were tried in 1324–5, largely it seems as the outcome of internecine family feuds. The charges against Lady Alice and her circle were a familiar mixture of *maleficium*, poison, magic, and demon conjuration, but in addition Lady Alice was charged with copulating with demons in order to obtain magic powers, the first known example of such a criminal accusation. Although she escaped to England, some of her associates were burned at the stake. Since ancient times, there had been stories of humans mating with pagan deities and later demons; there had also been stories of pacts with demons. But this was the first time the ideas were linked.

Then in 1397–1406 a Swiss trial held at Boltigen before a secular judge, Peter of Grayerz, at which the accused confessed to a variety of *maleficia* linked with the summoning of demons, the use of infant corpses to concoct poisons, and the renunciation of Christ in church on Sunday mornings, provided the archetypal example of the existence of an anti-Christian sect of witches. Both trials, in Cohn's view, resulted from the elite imposing their ideas on the populace to confirm the fantasy of a Devil-worshipping cult.

On the basis of the work of Cohn, Kieckhefer, and Peters, we can conclusively reject the idea that Devil-worshipping witches really existed. Equally we can dismiss Russell's theory that witchcraft was a form of actual, organized heresy with its roots in pagan fertility cults, along with Margaret Murray's celebrated thesis of an underground witch religion surviving from ancient times into the seventeenth century. Her view was demonstrably based on misreading, mistranslating, and misunderstanding the sources. On the other hand, we can

86

accept the existence of folk tales about night witches and beneficent female spirits, but they have nothing to do with Devil-worship. We can accept the existence of witches, but as isolated women, not in sects and not worshippers of the Devil. Charges of witchcraft were usually brought by disaffected neighbours against particular women: the old, the solitary, the unpopular, the neurotic, the insane, the bad-tempered, the promiscuous, practitioners of folk-medicine or midwives; women who for various reasons had become targets of local hatred. Some old women may have believed they could fly or had magical powers, but most of them were harmless misfits or outsiders. There may have been a few stray eccentrics who did worship the Devil but the Satanic conspiracy was the creation of Catholic intellectuals, theologians, and jurists who merged ancient folk beliefs, learned magic, and rural witch-craft, emphasized the role of sex and postulated the aim of destroying Christendom.

The Satanist witches of the late Middle Ages were, then, the ultimate scapegoats, an invented minority, a composite image of evil, ready-made for application to anyone who disagreed with Church dogma and which by the use of torture and terror became a reality. The continuous propaganda about the danger, rooted as it was in recognizable images and ideas, fed into the popular consciousness until it bore horrific fruit in the witch hunts of the sixteenth and seventeenth centuries when the mass of the community accepted and encouraged the hunting out of Satan's servants.

5

JEWS

Although in the early Middle Ages, the Jews lived freely among Christians, wore the same clothes, and spoke the same language as their Christian neighbours, they were potentially vulnerable to persecution and scapegoatism. For they remained a distinct racial and religious minority who ate different food, obeyed different laws, held distinct religious services, and educated their children separately. They were closely associated with both medicine and magic, two practices open to fear and suspicion. It was a combination of circumstances that was to direct popular antagonism against them and inaugurate a long, bitter, and tragic chronicle in the annals of human hatred.

There is no evidence of any widespread popular hostility towards the Jews in the Roman Empire, though there were some cases of violent outbursts against them, notably in Alexandria where there was long-standing ill-feeling between Jews and Greeks. Jews – for example Paul of Tarsus – were able to become full citizens, and were free to practise their religion. There were some obviously distinguishing features about the Jews. They kept the Sabbath, practised circumcision, and refused to perform religious acts towards the Roman gods or the emperor. But they were given special exemptions from the latter, by praying for rather than to the emperor.

In educated circles, however, there were two major complaints made about the Jews: their exclusiveness and their proselytization. Tacitus wrote: 'The Jews ... reveal a stubborn attachment to one another.... They sit apart at meals, they sleep apart, and although, as a nation, they are singularly prone to debauchery, they abstain from intercourse with foreign women.' Their active propagation of their faith was also commented on disparagingly by Horace, Juvenal, and Seneca.

It was in part these two characteristics of the Jews, separation and proselytization, which brought them into conflict with the Christians. From the rise of Christianity in the first century, the new faith, like its parent, Judaism, was an actively missionary one, and competed with Judaism for converts throughout the Roman Empire. Further, the

Christians were anxious to be seen to be recruiting Jews and Gentiles equally into the Christian Church. But most seriously, the Jews came to be held responsible for the death of Christ. This was to be the basis of all the bitter anti-Semitism of the Christian centuries. From the third and fourth centuries on, writers and preachers were regularly accusing the Jews of deicide. This charge became the prime excuse for and explanation of the wave of medieval persecution.

Once Christianity became the state religion of the Roman Empire in the fourth century, Imperial laws began to restrict the Jews. First the law codes of Theodosius and later those of Justinian ordered that the Jew should be excluded from all political and military functions, forbidden to marry Christians, or to own Christian slaves. Under Justin I (518–27), Justinian's predecessor, the Jews were forbidden to make wills or receive inheritances, to give testimony in the courts of law, or perform any legal act. They became in effect second-class citizens. But throughout all this, they were permitted to practise their religion.

Under the post-Roman barbarian kingdoms, there is evidence that the Jews prospered. In Ostrogothic and Lombard Italy, Jewish privileges were protected by the crown and the law. In Merovingian Gaul, Jews were treated as Romans and enjoyed the same rights and obligations as non-Jews. The early Carolingian rulers, Pepin (752–68) and Charlemagne (768–814), allowed the Jews to own land and exercise authority over Christian labourers. They used Jews as settlers and soldiers, and encouraged Jewish merchants. The Frankish Emperor Louis the Pious (814–40) systematized and organized government institutions in his empire, creating the office of 'Master of the Jews' (*Magister Judaeorum*) to oversee Jewish rules and regulations. Louis also encouraged the Jews to be merchants, permitted the building of new synagogues, appointed Jews to government office with authority over Christians, issued charters of protection for Jewish merchants, and ordered that markets not be held on the Jewish sabbath. The extent to which the Jews became successfully integrated into Carolingian society is reflected in the campaigns mounted against them first by archbishop Agobard of Lyons (779–840) and later by archbishop Hincmar of Rheims (806–82).

As early as 538 the Council of Orléans decreed rules to eliminate Jewish proselytization. The Council condemned intermarriage, forbade Christians to eat with Jews, ordered Christians to cease celebrating the Jewish sabbath and to cease working on Sundays, and forbade Jews and Christians to mix in Holy Week. The recurrence of such regulations at subsequent Church councils powerfully testifies to the continuing fear of churchmen that Jews were winning Christians over to their faith.

Agobard of Lyons wrote a series of five anti-Jewish epistles, in which he sought to stop Christian slave-owners selling Christian slaves to Jews, to prevent Christians observing the Jewish sabbath, to order Christians to abstain from eating Jewish meat and wine, and to avoid feasting with Jews during Lent. Yet Agobard stressed that 'since they [the Jews] live among us, we should not be hostile to them or injure their life, health or wealth'. In a series of late ninth-century Frankish Church Councils a code of edicts having broadly similar aims was enacted by a faction headed by Hincmar of Rheims. The edicts included a ban on the building of new synagogues, an order ousting Jews from positions of authority over Christians, a prohibition against ownership of Christian slaves by Jews, and against Jewish proselytization. Penalties were imposed on Christians dining with or mixing too closely with Jews and mixed marriages were banned. Indeed such liaisons were to be considered adulterous. The Frankish clerics complained that they were compelled to act because 'now ... throughout the cities and towns ... so much [Jewish] arrogance and oppression have burst upon the scene'.

In Visigothic Spain savagely repressive laws were enacted against the Jews, inspired, as P. D. King points out, by 'the hatred of the Christian for the people who had betrayed God's trust'. But the Visigothic kings simply lacked the machinery necessary to implement these laws effectively.

However, in much of the barbarian west Jews were valued as merchants, doctors, diplomats, and soldiers. Many barbarian rulers seem to have treated the Jews as one of a number of different peoples under different law codes that made up their kingdoms. The Carolingian kings in particular encouraged immigration and the multiplication of Jewish communities. The Jews thus emerged from the Dark Ages as a distinct and recognizable minority, living under their own laws, increasingly prosperous, and reasonably secure. They were to reach a peak of numbers and prosperity in the twelfth and early thirteenth centuries but even before then attitudes towards them were to change dramatically.

The change in attitude came about in the eleventh century. Around the year 1010 rumours began to circulate in the west that at the instigation of the Jews, the Saracens had caused the destruction of the Holy Sepulchre and beheaded the patriarch of Jerusalem. Spontaneous massacres of the Jews took place in Orléans, Rouen, Limoges, the Rhineland, and Rome. The feeling against them subsided, but it was a harbinger of what was to come. Anti-Jewish feeling built up at the same time as anti-Islamic feeling did. As the millennium passed, Christendom moved into an expansionist phase and in its new mood of religious enthusiasm sought to Christianize the world, internally by reform and externally by crusade. In 1063 knights heading for Spain to participate in the advance of the Christian kingdoms against the Moslems attacked several Jewish communities en route, an action denounced by Pope Alexander II.

Then in the wake of the crusade proclaimed by Pope Urban II at the Council of Clermont in 1095, an atmosphere of religious hysteria was engendered by wandering preachers in which the promotion of the crusade was accompanied in some areas by massacres of the Jews. The main evidence of hostility towards the Jews comes not from the official armies of the crusade but from the unofficial armies of the poor which arose spontaneously to answer the call, and the independent bands of knights, similarly aroused, who desired to dip their swords in 'infidel' blood without waiting until they got to the Holy Land.

A group assembling in Normandy attacked the Jews of Rouen; a Saxon group under a priest Volkmar marched through Bohemia massacring the Jews of Prague; a group under the priest Gottschalk descended from the Rhineland to the Danube, massacring the Jews of Regensburg; a group from Flanders attacked the Jews of Cologne; a group from Lorraine attacked the Jews of Metz and most fearfully of all, Count Emicho of Leiningen and his band attacked the Jews of Speyer, Worms, and Mainz. Almost invariably, Jews were offered the choice of baptism or death. Many preferred suicide. Thousands died in one way or another as a result of these massacres. They set a grim precedent; as S. W. Baron notes: 'From the First Crusade on, anti-Jewish persecutions exercised a dangerously contagious appeal, which in periods of great emotional stress degenerated into a mass psychosis transcending national boundaries.'

In this first wave of medieval popular anti-Jewish violence, the reaction of both ecclesiastical and civil authorities was often to help the Jews. Bishop Johann of Speyer gave the Jews shelter in his castle and punished those guilty of attacking them. The city's burghers backed him because the policy of his predecessor, Bishop Rudiger, in initiating Jewish settlement had enriched Speyer. Survivors of the Worms massacre took refuge in the Bishop's palace but when Bishop Adalbert said he could protect them only if they accepted baptism, they committed suicide. Archbishop Ruthard of Mainz who tried to shelter the Jews was himself forced to flee from the angry mob. The burghers of Regensburg attempted to save the Jews from forcible baptism, but they were rounded up and herded into the Danube for mass immersion.

The Emperor Henry IV, when he learned what was happening, ordered the responsible authorities to protect the Jews and allowed those forcibly baptised to return to their faith. William II of England did the same. In 1103 Henry IV included the Jews along with the clergy and women as groups who were specially under his protection. But every time the crusade was preached the pattern of massacres resumed. Preachers promoting the Second Crusade in 1147 urged recruits to attack the Jews. Abbot Peter of Cluny, while not urging pogroms, focused attention on the Jews when he declared:

> What is the good of going to the end of the world at great loss of men and money to fight the Saracens when we permit among us other infidels who are a thousand times more guilty towards Christ than the Mohammedans.

A renegade monk Radulf, preaching the crusade in Germany, urged his audiences to avenge the death of Christ upon his murderers before marching against the Moslems. There were massacres at Cologne, Speyer, Mainz, and Würzburg in Germany, and at Carentan, Sully, and Ramerupt in France. Even so, the numbers of victims were smaller than in 1096 because the authorities were prepared for the disorder this time, and St Bernard of Clairvaux brought to bear his enormous prestige to denounce the massacres, urging that killing precluded the more desirable strategy of converting the Jews.

In 1190 mobs led by men being recruited for the Third Crusade attacked the Jews in Norwich, York, Lynn, and Bury St Edmund's. In 1239 as a crusade was being organized, the crusaders attacked Jews in western France and Pope Gregory IX wrote to the bishops of the area and to King Louis IX urging punishment on the perpetrators of the massacres:

> In an unheard-of and unprecedented outburst of cruelty, they have slaughtered in this mad hostility 2,500 of them; old and young as well as pregnant women. Some were mortally wounded and others trampled like mud under the feet of horses. They burned their books and for great shame and disgrace, they exposed the bodies of those thus killed, for food for the birds of heaven and their flesh to the beasts of the earth. After foully and shamefully treating those who remained alive after this massacre, they carried off their goods and consumed them.

Thus the period of the great crusades set a pattern for the remainder of the Middle Ages. Christian enthusiasm was accompanied by anti-Jewish violence.

This development had three consequences of long-term significance to the Jews. Their mobility was restricted and they turned increasingly from merchant activity to money-lending, remaining in ghetto areas for protection and using their capital in the only way possible. The Jews in the early Middle Ages had been notable merchants and traders but the growth of hostility and persecution made travel increasingly hazardous. The Catholic prohibition on money-lending by Christians opened up an occupation for Jews but it was one which only exacerbated their unpopularity and vulnerability. The insecurity which led them increasingly to be taken under the 'protection' of the European monarchies turned the Jews in effect into crown 'property' and kings continually used them as a convenient and regular source of money. But more significantly the Jews were now decisively identified as an alien group and their position was more and more circumscribed.

THE CHURCH AND THE JEWS

The Church's position on the Jews was based on the theology of St Augustine, who argued that they must be protected because they had a vital role to play in the divine plan for human salvation. They were the people of the Old Testament. They had played a part in spreading the word of God. Their stubborn refusal to accept the truth of Christ marked them down for the imposition of restrictions, which were duly imposed by the Imperial law codes. But it was believed that their repentance and conversion would signal the approach of the millennium. Without the Jews, there could be no salvation for the whole of mankind. So their conversion must be encouraged and facilitated.

The endorsement of Augustine's theology and the legal restrictions on Jewish freedom remained for a long time the Papacy's position. Pope Gregory the Great (590–604), whose letters were quoted in the Middle Ages as authoritative statements on the Papal attitude to the Jews, ordered that their legitimate rights be protected. They were not allowed to make converts, to marry non-Jews, to own Christian slaves, to hold office, to make bequests, or to build new synagogues. But they were not to be persecuted because of their religion nor were their synagogues to be destroyed or plundered.

The Gregorian principles were reaffirmed by the 1179 Lateran Council which added that no one should do feudal homage to a Jew but that Jews should not be forcibly converted. Successive popes regularly reissued a constitution *Sicut Judaeis Non*, first issued around 1120 by Pope Calixtus II. It contained a summary of the basic Papal principles regarding the Jews:

> Just as license ought not to be granted the Jews to presume to do in their synagogues more than the law permits them, just so ought they not to suffer curtailment in those [privileges] which have been conceded them. That is why ... we grant their petition and offer them the shield of our protection. We decree that no Christian shall use violence to force them to be baptized as long as they are unwilling and refuse, but that if anyone of them seeks refuge among the Christians of his own free will and by reason of his faith, after his willingness has become quite clear shall he be made a Christian without subjecting himself to any calumny....

Moreover, without the judgement of the authority of the land, no Christian shall presume to wound their persons or kill [them] or rob them of their money, or change the good customs which they have thus far enjoyed in the place where they live. Furthermore, while they celebrate their festivals, no one shall disturb them in any way by means of sticks or stones, nor exact from any of them forced service, except that which they have been accustomed to perform from ancient times.

Pope Innocent III duly reissued the constitution in 1199 but his pontificate saw a marked worsening of the Jews' position in the eyes of the Papacy. Innocent complained bitterly to King Philip Augustus of France about the 'insolence' and 'excesses' of the Jews, in particular their practice of usury, their employment of Christian maidservants, their building of new synagogues, their harbouring of and complicity with thieves, their blaspheming against Christ, and their ridiculing Christians at Easter. He denounced the protection extended to them by secular princes in a fierce letter to the Count of Nevers:

The Jews like the fratricide Cain are doomed to wander through the earth as fugitives and vagabonds, and their faces must be covered with shame. They are under no circumstances to be protected by Christian princes but are, on the contrary, to be condemned to serfdom. It is therefore discreditable of Christian princes to receive Jews into their towns and villages and to employ them as usurers in order to extort money from Christians.

It was Innocent whose 1215 Lateran Council decreed the introduction of a distinguishing badge for Jews so that they could be recognized as different from and separate from Christians. Innocent introduced into the relationship between Papacy and Jews a contractual element, creating the possibility of their expulsion for breach of the contract: 'Nevertheless we wish to protect by the buttress of this protection only those who do not presume to plot the subversion of the Christian faith'.

The context of the changing Papal attitude was the increasing equation of Judaism with heresy. When in the eleventh and twelfth centuries the crusading fervour arose to free the Holy Places from 'infidel' control and the Church undertook a mission to root out heresy, attention was inevitably focused on the Jews. Fanatical crusaders sought to eliminate the 'enemies of Christ' from western Europe before marching East; equally Christian theologians feared Judaism as a source of heresy and attention centred on the Jews' perceived responsibility for the Crucifixion as well as on their apparently stubborn refusal to accept the truth of the Christian gospels over their own holy books. An exasperated Peter the Venerable, Abbot of Cluny (1122–56), in his treatise against the unyielding obstinacy of the Jews (*Tractatus contra Judaeorum inveteratam duritiem*) declared: 'I don't know whether a Jew can be a human being for he will neither accede to human reasoning nor yield to authoritative statements that are divine and from his own tradition.'

Increasingly Jews and heretics were lumped together. The four-teenth-century Spanish monk Lucas of Tuy in his attack on the 'Albig-ensian errors' wrote:

Heretics simulate Jewish infidelity. Some of them with deliberate malice become circumcised and, under the guise of being Jews, come to Christians to ask heretical questions as if starting a disputation. Thus as apparent Jews they sow heresies more freely, while previously they had not dared to utter a word of heresy. The secular princes and city magistrates listen to these doctrines of heresy from Jews whom they number among their acquaint-ances and friends.

There was a concerted move to find heretical teachings in Jewish writings, and this further fuelled anti-Jewish feeling. A leading role in the hereticization of the Jews was played by the mendicant orders of friars, as Jeremy Cohen has shown in *The Friars and the Jews* (1982). Cohen argues convincingly that the Mendicants, as inquisitors, mission-aries, polemicists, disputants, scholars, and preachers, engaged in a systematic effort to undermine the religious freedom and physical security of the Jews. They succeeded in inculcating a new view of the Jews in Christendom.

It was Nicholas Donin, a convert from Judaism, who in 1236 approached Pope Gregory IX with a list of charges against the Talmud and other rabbinic literature. Gregory IX directed the rulers of Europe to investigate the Talmud as a possible source of heretical belief. St Louis ordered a great public debate in Paris in 1240 between Jewish scholars and Christian theologians. The Jews were deemed to have lost and the King ordered the Talmud to be burned. The Jews appealed to Pope Innocent IV who consented to a re-examination of the question. But a second commission, held in 1248, confirmed the original verdict.

The Paris debate of 1240 was only the first of a series of officially sponsored religious debates between Jews and Christians. The Jews were invariably held to have lost and this quickened the pace of official Jewish book-burnings. Successive kings of France, Louis IX, Philip III, and Philip IV, ordered the Talmud to be burned. Pope Clement IV ordered King Jaime I of Aragon to confiscate all copies of the Talmud, declaring 'in its huge volume ... are contained innumerable abuses and detestable blasphemies against the Lord Jesus Christ and his most blessed mother.'

It was only in the thirteenth century that the Church, with the friars in the forefront of the campaign, undertook a systematic study of contemporary Jewish literature and sought to demonstrate in public disputation that medieval Jewish traditions were incompatible with Christianity. Anti-Jewish polemic had hitherto been aimed at portraying the Jew as one whose obstinate adherence to a literalist interpretation of the Old Testament prevented his acceptance of Jesus as the Messiah. But having studied the Talmud and other Jewish writings, the Dominicans and Franciscans now attacked Judaism as a heresy, a perversion of and deviation from the Old Testament, and began the trend of awakening Christians to the discrepancy between the religion of contemporary Jews and that of the 'Biblical Jews' envisaged by St Augustine.

Jews were increasingly ordered to attend Mendicant sermons to learn the error of their ways. Jaime I of Aragon ordered it by law in 1242, Louis IX of France in 1263, and Edward I of England in 1280. In 1278 Pope Nicholas III formally made preaching to and missionizing among the Jews part of the apostolate of both the Dominican and Franciscan orders. But Pedro IV of Aragon found it necessary to censure Dominicans and Franciscans for delivering anti-Jewish sermons so inflammatory that they led to the murder of the Jews and the destruction of their property. Philip IV three times warned his bailiffs and seneschals not to co-operate with Mendicant inquisitors unlawfully seeking to deal with the Jews. Wherever they could, the friars encroached on the daily religious life of the Jews, burning books, invading synagogues, and using fear to induce Jews to convert.

A circle of prominent anti-Jewish polemicists gathered around St Raymond of Penaforte (c.1175–1275), Spanish Dominican Master-General and adviser to Gregory IX. They developed the charges of heresy against the Jews and called for their elimination by conversion. Among them was the Catalan Raymond Martini who gave the most thorough exposition of the Mendicant attitude to the Jews in his book *Pugio Fidei* (The Dagger of the Faith, c.1280). He argued that contemporary Jewish observance of Mosaic commandments was inherently degenerative, improper, and heretical. Pablo Christiani, a Jewish convert and Dominican friar, devoted his life to converting his former co-religionists, undertook extensive preaching missions to Aragon, and regularly argued that heresy was inherent in current Jewish practices. Raymond Lull, a Franciscan tertiary, wrote *The Book of Preaching Against the Jews* (1305) for use by missionaries, setting out the arguments to overcome the Jews' lack of belief in the Trinity and the Incarnation and expounding the Jews' 'misinterpretation' of key Mosaic commandments. According to Lull, there were only two options: conversion or expulsion. The Jew had no place in Christian society.

96

It was not just learned polemics that expounded these views but popular sermons. For instance, the acclaimed Franciscan preacher Berthold of Regensburg (d. 1272), who travelled Europe preaching from the 1240s to the 1270s, attracting huge audiences, presented the same basic message in accessible imagery and language. He aggressively attacked the Jews, regularly equating Jews, heathens, and heretics in undermining the Christian doctrine and Christendom: 'You Jews, you heathen, you heretics ... you say everything which is against Christian doctrine, like your lord the Devil.' He rejected medieval rabbinic teaching as a departure from Biblical Judaism, denounced the Talmud as 'completely heretical' and complained at the undermining of Christian morality by the usury of Jewish men and the immodest dress of Jewish women. The denunciations of the Jews by St Vincent Ferrer (1350–1419) and St John of Capistrano (1386–1456) were so continual and ferocious that both earned the nickname the 'Scourge of the Jews'.

Heretical imputation brought the Jews within the compass of the Inquisition. The Inquisition had no jurisdiction over Jews *per se* but it did over Jews promoting heretical ideas and helping heretics, over Jewish converts to Christianity who lapsed, and over Christians who converted to Judaism. In 1267 Pope Clement IV issued a bull ordering the Inquisition to proceed against Christians who converted and against Jews who converted them. The Bull was reissued in 1274, 1288 and 1290.

There was great fear still in the central Middle Ages of the proselytizing powers of the Jews and there is some evidence that medieval Christians could find Judaism attractive. According to Friedrich Heer, it was clerics who were drawn to Judaism, finding in the Old Testament God a closer approximation of their own idea of the Deity. In 1270 two Christian converts to Judaism were killed at Weissenberg in Alsace, one of them prior of a Mendicant order. But we know only of isolated individuals and there is certainly no evidence of mass conversions of entire populations. But such a prospect was feared. The papal legate at the Council of Breslau in 1267 voiced the fear:

> Since the Poles are a new plantation on the soil of Christendom, we must continually be on our guard lest the Christian population here, where the Christian religion has not as yet taken deep root in the hearts of believers, succumb to the influence of the counterfeit faith and the evil habits of the Jews living in their midst.

The medieval Papacy continued officially to advocate the protection of the Jews, but only Jews who conformed to the Augustinian concept of the 'bearers of the Old Testament', and that protection was increasingly ineffective. The friars were more in touch with the developing popular opinion and their rabble-rousing sermons accompanied changes in the artistic and folklore representations of the Jew and a rising tide of violence against Jews.

THE JEWS AND THE SECULAR AUTHORITIES

The principal centres of Jewish settlement in the central Middle Ages were Spain, France, and the Rhineland. There were over 200 Jewish communities in the kingdom of France. In England there were some 3,000 Jews; there were as yet few Jews in northern Italy. But the vulnerability of the Jews to attack, so cruelly highlighted by the massacres beginning in the late eleventh century, led to a new development in the twelfth century, the idea of Jews 'belonging' to Christian rulers. Charters were granted by kings, counts, and bishops defining the rights and role of the Jews and assuring them of protection. In return the Jews paid and it is clear that one of the main motives governing the actions of the authorities was the desire to tap Jewish wealth. In England the king 'owned' all the Jews. In France the king 'owned' only those on the royal demesne; elsewhere the barons 'owned' them. The German emperor claimed the ultimate jurisdiction over the Jews resident within his frontiers but he frequently surrendered the right to others because of his need for money. So Jews could be bought, sold, pawned or exchanged like any other property. The term 'Jewish serfdom' first appeared in decrees in the 1230s and effectively summarizes the position.

Paradoxically, this status was compatible with their being free citizens of the municipalities, which many were. Even so Jews could not hold municipal office and were subject to special Jewish taxes, though they enjoyed communal autonomy. They resembled one of a number of corporate bodies within the corporate structure of medieval society. Yet their legal position gradually deteriorated in all countries as the weight of prejudice grew.

In the first instance the issue of Jewish charters was positive and enlightened. In 1084, in order to promote the economic development of the city, Bishop Rudiger of Speyer invited the Jews in, envisaging a community of merchants engaged in local or general trade, with their own laws and customs, and the ability to employ Christians. Further, in clear recognition of the Jews' vulnerability, protection from the majority community and a walled quarter to live in were guaranteed. The Speyer charter was confirmed six years later by Emperor Henry IV, who issued a similar one to the Jews of Worms. In 1236 Emperor Frederick II applied protection to the whole of Germany, guaranteeing freedom of worship, travel, disposal of property, protection from unlawful exactions, and from the forcible conversion of their slaves and children to Christianity.

But between the thirteenth and fifteenth centuries control over the Jews of Germany gradually shifted from the crown to the various princes and cities. The Black Death led to extensive massacres, with an estimated 300 Jewish communities in the Holy Roman Empire annihilated. So essential were the Jews and their money-lending activities to the conduct of business that they were readmitted in the 1350s to Erfurt, Ulm, Nuremberg, Worms, Speyer and Trier. But they became pawns in the power politics of the city-states, aggravated by internal class struggle between patrician and artisan classes and envenomed by the continual stream of anti-Jewish propaganda. So the expulsions began again and the Jews left Saxony (1432), Speyer (1435), Mainz (1438), Augsburg (1439), Würzburg (1453), Brünn and Olmütz (1457), Salzburg and Württemberg (1498) and Ulm (1499).

In England, Jewish charters were issued by Kings Henry I, Richard I, and John. These charters, like those of the German rulers, envisaged a community of merchants. But also – significantly – they recognized the special needs of a class devoted to the lending of money. Richard I granted freedom of residence, freedom of passage, the right to possess and inherit land, loans, and property, and judicial rights. In England the Jews came to be exclusively identified with money-lending and were regularly exploited by the crown. But hostility to them grew and in 1290 Edward I expelled them; the Jews did not return to England until the protectorate of Oliver Cromwell.

In France, it seems that little was done to regulate the Jews' legal and communal privileges until popular hostility had reached a point at which it was necessary to take steps in order to preserve them as a source of profit. The Jewish community in northern France was small, cohesive, internally disciplined, intellectually creative, and economically prosperous. Its members tended to live in distinct streets or quarters and in the twelfth century they flourished, benefiting from the economic revival.

The Jews suffered some harm during the upheavals attending the First and Second Crusades. But their position began seriously to deteriorate after the accession of King Philip Augustus. Philip initiated a pattern of expulsion and recall of the Jews, which served a twofold purpose. It demonstrated the moral leadership of the crown in responding to popular hatred of Jewish money-lending activities and it served to fill the royal coffers. In 1180 Philip arrested all the Jews in his kingdom and forced them to pay a ransom of 15,000 silver marks for their release. In 1182 he expelled them and seized their property. But in 1198 Philip Augustus readmitted the Jews, setting up a department of the treasury to supervise their money-lending activities and concluding treaties with the counts of Champagne, St Paul, and Nevers to secure the forcible return of Jewish exiles who had found homes in adjacent provinces.

The earliest charter is that of 1315, granted by King Louis X when allowing the Jews to return following their expulsion in 1306, which had been carried out by Philip IV in order to help stave off bankruptcy. The Jews were to return for twelve years, to settle anywhere where there had previously been Jewish communities, to worship and to administer themselves, but not to practise usury. Even so, the public demand for them to resume their money-lending activities was so great that two years later King Philip V permitted it. But in 1322 the Jews were expelled again after implication in the 'Leper Plot' to poison the wells of France. In 1360 they were readmitted, mainly to help pay the enormous ransom demanded by the English for the release of the captive King John II. The Jews were promised protection and security but in 1394 they were expelled again, this time for good.

In the Spanish kingdoms charters made the Jews property of the crown, with permission to lend money and enjoy legal equality. Even so, Spanish Christian rulers were constantly petitioned to restrict or abolish the rights granted to the Jews. There were widespread massacres of the Jews in 1391, stirred up by the archdeacon Ferrant Martinez of Seville, who denounced the Jews for their usury and appealed to the Spanish national feeling against the alien group. Many converted; many more were slaughtered. In 1492 King Ferdinand and Queen Isabella of Spain, succumbing to and indeed capitalizing on popular prejudice, expelled the Jews from Spain. This was followed by their expulsion from Portugal in 1497.

For much of the Middle Ages the secular authorities, anxious to maintain their control of the Jews and their wealth, could be relied upon to keep them out of ecclesiastical courts and later out of the hands of the Inquisition, and to safeguard them from forcible baptism. But by the end of the fifteenth century the financial value of the Jews had been greatly reduced by successive massacres, expulsions, and mulctings. Furthermore the rising tide of anti-Jewish feeling, fed by rumour, slander, calumny and caricature, made defending them politically dangerous.

THE JEWS AND POPULAR CULTURE

The process by which the word 'Jew' became a term of abuse can be traced in the vast popular literature of the Middle Ages – mystery, miracle, and morality plays, legends and chronicles, poems and folktales. They all contributed to the development of the image of the Jew as 'the inveterate enemy of mankind'. Economic resentment and antialienism apart, a basis for Christian anti-Jewish feeling lay in growing acceptance of theories of diabolic conspiracy. Just as heretics were regularly accused of being witches, so Jews were increasingly accused of trafficking with the Devil. One popular and much-repeated story was that of Theophilus, a disgraced archdeacon, who, it was said, had sought through Jewish intermediaries to contact the Devil. One of the earliest dated sketches of a Jew, on the 1277 Forest Roll of Essex, bore the superscription 'Aaron, son of the Devil'. Caricatured hook-nosed, sinister and treacherous, Jews were depicted as encompassing the destruction of Christ in the Passion plays. These manifestations led to the cumulative view that fed into the image summed up in Shake-speare's *The Merchant of Venice*: 'The Jew is the very devil incarnal.'

In his definitive study *The Devil and the Jews*, Joshua Trachtenberg traces the growth of the stereotype of the demonic Jew. This grew from several sources. There was the legend of Anti-Christ. It was argued by theologians in the later Middle Ages that since the Messiah had arrived in the person of Jesus Christ, the Messiah that the Jews still awaited must of necessity be Anti-Christ. Both St Thomas Aquinas and St Albertus Magnus agreed that he would be a Jew, born in Babylon, who would persuade the Jews he was the Messiah, establish his rule and eventually be overthrown by the archangel Michael sent by Christ. Popular legends embellished the story with detail that made it parallel the life of Christ. So Anti-Christ is made the son of a union between the Devil and a Jewish harlot; he is raised in Galilee; trained by sorcerers and initiated in the black arts; he gains power and rules for three and a half years (thought to have been the length of Christ's ministry), sustained by his magic, force, and terror before being destroyed by the archangel. Plays, stories and engravings depicted the Jews as the followers of Anti-Christ. They were often shown wearing the badge and pointed hat of the Jew. R. K. Emmerson in his study of Anti-Christ in the Middle Ages notes 'one of the most pervasive beliefs concerning Anti-Christ is that he will be born a Jew'. It was argued that a secret Jewish horde in the east was awaiting the signal to pour out into Christendom and annihilate it. Rumours of the birth of Anti-Christ became increasingly frequent after the thirteenth century and kept Europe on edge.

A linked idea was that of Jews having horns and tails. The Vulgate version of the Bible mistranslated the Hebrew of Exodus 34 vv. 29, 35, so that 'and behold the skin of his face sent forth beams' became 'his face had horns'. Paintings and carvings of Jews showed them with horns, and the horned Jew was of course related immediately to the horned Devil. Philip III of France required the Jews of France to attach a horn-shaped figure to the customary Jewish badge. Other Devil-related imagery attached itself to the Jews. In the Middle Ages the

101

goat, the symbol of lechery, was portrayed as the Devil's favourite animal and Jews were commonly depicted riding on goats. Just as the Devil had a distinct odour of sulphur and brimstone, so, it was believed, Jews emitted a distinctive and unpleasant aroma (*foetor judaicus*), in contradistinction to Christian saints and holy men who emitted the 'odour of sanctity'. The *foetor judaicus* could be removed only by Christian baptism.

The Jews had been regarded as expert in magic since ancient times, and magic was increasingly associated with the Devil. Hebrew incantations were used in magic. Solomon was renowned as a master of demons and magic. Major works on sorcery were ascribed to Jews: Solomon, Adam, Enoch, Noah, Moses etc. In folklore sinister magicians were given Jewish or Jewish-sounding names: Zebulon, Zedekiah and Zambri. When Christian propaganda came to link magic with worship of the Devil, this tainted the Jews. Jews were said to have the evil eye and it was because of this that they were forbidden to witness the coronation of King Richard I of England in 1189. The traditional and customary acts of the Jews were viewed with suspicion and had sometimes to be abandoned. The practices of washing the hands after returning from cemeteries, of throwing a clod of earth behind one after a funeral, the ritual of cleansing ovens in preparation for Passover were all seen as magical. The *mezuzah*, a Biblical inscription attached to the front door post, became an object of suspicion. The Jews were also renowned as physicians; but this meant that they were vulnerable to charges of witchcraft if anything went wrong.

Poisoning was a charge regularly made against Jewish physicians who were powerless to refute it. In 1161 in Bohemia eighty-six Jews were burned as accomplices in an alleged plot of Jewish physicians to poison the population. The Vienna faculty of medicine reported that the private code of Jewish physicians required them to murder one patient in ten. In 1246 the Council of Béziers forbade Christians to resort to the medical care of Jews 'for it is better to die than to owe one's life to a Jew'. This injunction was repeated throughout the thirteenth, fourteenth and fifteenth centuries but widely ignored. Even some of the most vicious anti-Jewish rulers often had Jewish physicians.

Not just physicians but all Jews were in fact thought to be adept in the use of poisons. The Jew as poisoner was a stock figure of literature and legend, culminating in Christopher Marlowe's Barabbas in *The Jew of Malta* (c.1592). The frequently repeated legislation in secular and ecclesiastical codes forbidding Christians to purchase meat and other foodstuffs from Jews was motivated in part by the suspicion that they might have been poisoned, as the Vienna and Breslau Councils in 1261 and the statutes of Valladolid in 1412 expressly stated. A popular suspicion had it that Jews compelled their children to urinate on meat

102

before selling it to Christians. The fear of poisoning was part of a growing and more general horror of pollution. It came to be felt that anything a Jew touched was contaminated and by the fourteenth century this reached the point that the cities of Avignon and Bolzano decreed that Jews must buy anything which they touched.

Given the general state of rotten food, bad water, and poor hygiene, exacerbated by famine and shortage, it is small wonder that hysteria should periodically break out, attributing local epidemics to well-poisoning. The charge began early. Twenty-seven Jews were executed for well-poisoning in Troppau in Bohemia in 1163. Similar accusations were made at Breslau in 1226 and Vienna in 1267. There was a spectacular case in 1321 when the Jews were accused of co-operating with lepers and Moslems in a plot to poison all the wells of France. This took place against a background of prolonged famine and the ravages of the 'Shepherd's Crusade', whose participants had destroyed 120 Jewish communities in their violent progress across France. The 'Leper Plot' led the parlement of Paris to exact a huge fine of 150,000 *livres* from the Jews, who were subsequently expelled *en masse* by King Charles IV, but not before 160 had been burned at Chinon and 40 had committed suicide in Champagne.

This was but a forerunner of the anti-Jewish hysteria in the period of the Black Death. The catastrophe was so great that a search for scapegoats began at once. The French surgeon Guy de Chauliac, who fought the plague in Avignon, noted:

In some places they killed the Jews, believing them to have poisoned the world; in others they drove out paupers who were deformed; in others they drove out nobles. Things finally came to such a pass that guards were posted to see that no one who was not well known would enter a city or village. And if they found anyone carrying medicinal powders they would force him to swallow them to prove that they were not poisonous potions.

But by far the most common scapegoats were the Jews. The anti-Jewish movement began at Chillon on Lake Geneva where a Jewish surgeon alleged that several Jews in the south of France had concocted poison out of Christians' hearts, along with spiders, frogs, lizards, human flesh and sacred Hosts, and had distributed the powder to be deposited in wells and streams from Toulouse to Calabria. The story spread and similar plots were 'uncovered' elsewhere. One involved a plan to poison all the wells from Dassel in Westphalia to Lübeck and beyond into Prussia, Livonia and Sweden. Jews were arrested and tortured into confessing to their complicity. As if this was not bad enough, the Flagellants added to Jewish misery by regularly encouraging the inhabitants of towns and cities to exterminate the Jews as art of a strategy of placating God so as to avert the plague.

At Basel, the Jews were rounded up, herded on to an island in the Rhine and burned alive. All 2,000 Jews in Strasbourg were burned in February 1349. In the spring of 1349 the large Jewish settlements in Frankfurt, Mainz and Cologne were wiped out. Similar pogroms took place in Brussels, Stuttgart, Freiburg, Ulm, Gotha, Dresden, Worms, Baden, Erfurt and Speyer. As the fury of the inhabitants of the Rhineland died down, it flared up along the Baltic as the plague reached the Hanseatic towns and massacres of the Jews followed. According to Philip Ziegler, by 1351 60 major and 150 smaller Jewish communities had been wiped out and over 350 separate massacres had taken place. All this occurred despite the fact that the medical faculties of Paris and Montpellier Universities declared the Jews innocent of causing the plague and Pope Clement VI issued a Papal bull denying the Jews' guilt and urging the clergy to protect their local Jewish communities, as he himself successfully did in the Papal enclave of Avignon.

Even after the Black Death, the Jews were accused of poisoning the wells in Halle (1382), Magdeburg (1384), Durkheim and Colmar (1397) and Freiburg (1401). Pope Martin V issued a Papal bull in 1422 forbidding the dissemination of well-poisoning stories by 'all clerical and lay preachers of whatever rank, degree, order, religion or circumstance'. But accusations of well-poisoning continued (1448, 1472, 1475).

The Jews were believed capable of even more evil and blasphemous acts, which violated the basic tenets of Christianity. One of these was Host desecration. Transubstantiation was officially established as a doctrine of the Church by the Fourth Lateran Council of 1215, and it was after this that the idea of Jews' profaning the Host developed. The first occasion of Host desecration occurred near Berlin in 1243. As a result, all the local Jews were burned. These allegations did not become common until the end of the century and then continued for 200 years. The last serious case in Western Europe occurred in Berlin in 1510, when twenty-eight Jews were executed.

The charges occurred mainly in Germany and Austria, more rarely in France and the Netherlands. The aims behind Host desecration were supposed to be to re-enact the Crucifixion, piercing the wafer with knives and nails; to demonstrate that Christ was not present and thus undermine the Christian faith; or to use it as part of a witchcraft ritual or an offering to the Devil. The alleged discovery of bleeding wafers (e.g. at Wilsnack) both seemed to confirm Transubstantiation and to underline Jewish infamy. Needless to say 'bleeding' Hosts were often planted by Christians to foment trouble. Jewish apostates often played a part in stirring up such incidents. In 1338 a number of Jewish communities in Lower Austria and Moravia were exterminated when a 'bleeding' Host was found in the home of a Jew. But investigations by

Duke Albert of Austria revealed that it had been planted by a Christian. Jews were also accused of smashing, spitting on, stoning, or otherwise defiling crucifixes and holy images. A common story was that Jews dumped such sacred objects in latrines. These stories frequently led to violence. An alleged Host desecration by the Jews of Rottlingen in the spring of 1298 sparked off anti-Jewish violence in 146 communities.

But the longest-lasting, most notorious, and most damaging charge against the Jews was that of ritual murder. This allegation occurred for the first time in the twelfth century. In 1144 after a boy, William of Norwich, disappeared, a Jewish convert to Christianity, Theobald of Canterbury, came forward to say that Jews were required to crucify a Christian child annually at Easter and at a site selected by a yearly conference of rabbis. When the child was found murdered, there was an outbreak of violence against Jews. The child's grave became a site of pilgrimage and he was canonized.

Stories of the murder of Christian children by Jews now became a regular occurrence and similar charges were made at Gloucester in 1168, at Blois in 1171, at Bury St Edmunds in 1181, at Pontoise, Braisne, and Saragossa in 1182, at Winchester in 1192 and at Lincoln in 1255. There was no trial in any of these cases. But the stories were believed, became part of popular folklore, and were usually accompanied by violence against the Jews. Thirty-eight Jews were burned at the stake in Blois for instance. The earliest accusation of child murder in Germany occurred at Lauda in 1235 and regularly thereafter with horrific results. In 1285 Munich Jews were accused of the murder of a Christian child, and the mob forced them to take refuge in a synagogue and set it on fire. Sixty-eight Jews perished.

The most famous case was that of Hugh of Lincoln, a boy found dead in a cesspool. He was alleged to have been fattened up for ten days and then crucified before all the Jews of England. A hundred Jews were arrested; nineteen were hanged without trial but the rest were released when Richard, Earl of Cornwall, who held all the Jews in England in mortgage, intervened on their behalf. At about the same time, the blood element was introduced: the idea that the blood of Christian children was needed for Jewish ceremonies. It first cropped up in 1235. The recurrence of such charges led Emperor Frederick II to set up a commission of scholars to investigate the truth of the stories. The commission rejected the stories and the Emperor specifically acquitted the Jews of such charges in 1236. Pope Innocent IV issued a Bull in 1247 denouncing stories of Jewish child-killing and blood-use and in 1272 Pope Gregory X forbade the clergy to promote such ideas. But these interventions did no good. Throughout the Middle Ages the clergy denounced the Jews for their involvement in ritual murder.

In 1475 the leading preacher Fra Bernardino da Feltre delivered the

Lenten sermons at Trent in northern Italy, denouncing ritual murder by Jews. On Maundy Thursday a 2-year-old boy Simon disappeared. Jewish houses were searched and when the child's body was found floating in the river, Jews were arrested and tortured. The leading members of the community were executed and the rest expelled. The child's body was believed to perform miracles and locals revered him as a saint. Although the Papacy banned this, the pressure from the faithful was so great that Simon of Trent was eventually beatified.

Pictures of Simon and broadsheets telling of his murder and miracles circulated widely and sermons about him were given everywhere. Although the Venetian government and the Duke of Ferrara banned such sermons and put the Jews under their protection, Bernardino continued to preach his poisonous message and succeeded in bringing about expulsion of the Jews from Perugia, Brescia, and Gubbio as well as inspiring riots against the Jews at Florence and Forli and the burning down of the Ravenna synagogue. This regular charge of the 'violation of innocence' was one of the greatest burdens the Jews had to suffer. For it completed their demonization, bracketing them with heretics and witches as monsters capable of perpetrating the most heinous and revolting of crimes in cold blood.

SEGREGATION

The Christian perception of the danger from the Jews, 'the enemy within', can be seen in the desire to identify and isolate them, which became the dominant strategies towards the Jews from the thirteenth centuries onwards. The prohibitions on mixed marriage and inter-racial sex were strengthened. Indeed, there had long been an aversion to these practices. Intermarriage had been forbidden by the law codes of Theodosius and Justinian. The prohibition was repeated in many medieval lawcodes but with such ferocity that it is hard to see it just as the result of fear of Jewish proselytization of Christians. It looks suspiciously like the kind of sexual fear that white racists have of blacks – the idea of defilement and also jealousy of sexual potency. As it happens, the Jews were equally opposed to intermarriage but many Jews kept Christian concubines. King Juan I of Aragon (1387–95) prescribed the death penalty for sexual relations between Jews and Christians and the thirteenth-century English law code, *Fleta*, declared: 'Apostate Christians, witches and others of that kind are to be drawn and burned. Those cohabiting with Jews and Jewesses, those engaged in bestiality and sodomy are to be burned alive.' This clearly equates inter-racial sex with the most serious of sex crimes. The position was never straightforward and a complex interweaving of race, class, and gender can sometimes be seen at work in the regulations. In 1420 the city of Padua decreed a range of penalties from flogging to death for inter-racial sex, depending on whether a Jew had intercourse with a prostitute or a married lady of good standing; class distinction here moderating racial prejudice. But for a Christian male who had sex with a Jewess, the penalty was only flogging and prison or a fine. The inequality of the sexes here mitigated the racial feeling.

The Papacy was equally concerned about the sexual aspect of Jewish–Christian relations. This was the specific reason given for the imposition of distinctive clothing on Jews by the Lateran Council of 1215:

> In some provinces of the church a diversity of clothing distinguishes Jews or Saracens from Christians, but in certain others there has insinuated itself such confusion that no difference is noticeable. Hence it sometimes happens that by error Christians have intercourse with Jewish or Saracen women, and Jews and Saracens with Christian women. Lest therefore these (transgressors) advance the excuse of such error to cloak the sin of that condemned relationship, we decree that such persons of either sex be distinguished from other peoples by the kind of clothes worn in public in every Christian province and at all times.

In a letter to Philip Augustus in 1205 Pope Innocent III denounced the 'abominations' allegedly taking place between Jewish employers and Christian nursemaids; a fear echoed in the decision of the city of Regensburg in 1393 to prohibit Jews from keeping Christian nursemaids under 50.

Ever since Roman times there had been allegations of Jewish lechery. St John Chrysostom (c.347–407) had denounced the 'lewd' practices of Jews and equated the synagogue with a brothel. In western Europe, Jews were frequently banned from brothels. In 1289 Count Charles of Anjou justified the expulsion of the Jews from Anjou and Maine by their subversion of Christians, their reduction of people to poverty by usury. But he added also: 'What is most horrible to consider, they evilly cohabit with many Christian maidens.' It was because of their 'notorious sexual promiscuity' that in 1317 King Philip V ordered that the Jews wear the badges that distinguished them from Christians.

The most effective means of segregation was the ghetto. The term derives from the area to which the Jews of Venice were confined by decision of the Venetian senate in 1516. It is true that separate Jewish quarters had a long history, though their purpose – in medieval Spanish Christian cities, for instance – was to protect rather than to segregate Jews. Walls were certainly required around Jewish areas after the massacres attending the First Crusade.

However, the Papacy was anxious to assure the segregation of the Jews to prevent their 'contaminating' Christians. In 1179 the Lateran

Council ordered that throughout the west Christians who lived with Jews should be excommunicated because segregation was required. In 1339 Pope Benedict XII complained to King Pedro IV of Aragon that the required practice of segregating Jews and Saracens in separate quarters had been neglected in earlier years, and synagogues and mosques were being built in the midst of Christian populations. In 1442 Pope Eugenius IV declared: 'Jews shall not live among Christians but rather they ought to dwell among themselves, separated and segregated from Christians, within a certain distinction or place, outside of which they would by no means be allowed to own houses.' This had become the official policy.

However, in Spain it was not until 1391 that there were concerted efforts to establish ghettos or quarters for the Jews and to exclude non-Jews from those areas. King Juan II of Castile and Ferdinand I of Aragon in 1413 ordered Jews and Moors to be segregated in quarters, walled or entered by one gate only, but the ruling was widely ignored. In other medieval countries regulations varied. Jewish quarters tended to originate from custom and habit rather than legal requirement. The Jews in England had a quarter in London as early as 1115 but there was no Jewish quarter in York, where Jews lived dispersed through the community. In Germany, where the Speyer quarter was established in 1084 as a distinct privilege for the Jews, segregation was increasingly enforced by legal sanction, particularly after 1348. In Cologne in 1330 anti-Jewish riots forced the city elders to surround the Jewish quarter with a wall for better defence. There were few protests from Jewish communities about confinement in Jewish sectors for it served to protect them.

From the start of the thirteenth century the Jews were ordered to wear distinctive clothing, to prevent their mingling freely with Christian people. This was prescribed by the 1215 Lateran Council and bracketed the Jews with prostitutes, Moors, lepers, and reformed heretics. It did not specify the type of clothing but in France, Spain, and Italy the mark of the Jew was taken to be a round of cloth sewn into the clothes (the *rouelle*). This 'badge of infamy' originated in France and was in use in the diocese of Paris even before the Lateran Council. From the Council of Narbonne (1227) it was the sign specifically required by the Church. The requirement was regularly reiterated throughout the thirteenth and fourteenth centuries, at nine Church councils between 1215 and 1370, in nine royal decrees after King Louis IX ordered it adopted by the Jews in 1269, and increasingly in municipal statutes in towns like Avignon, Nice, and Marseilles.

In Spain the Jewish badge was introduced by King Jaime I of Aragon in 1228 and King Thibaut of Navarre in 1234. Alfonso X of Castile (1252–84) introduced the obligation to wear the *rouelle* into his law code and imposed a fine for delinquents. However, the rule was widely ignored and regularly had to be reiterated, with increasingly heavy fines for non-compliance.

In England the Jews were ordered in 1218 to wear two linen pieces sewn on their clothes. In the kingdom of Sicily Jews were ordered by Frederick II to wear distinctive clothing in 1221. In Germany, Austria, and Poland Jews traditionally wore a conical hat (*Judenhut*). The Holy Roman Empire was therefore reluctant to impose the *rouelle* and Pope Gregory IX complained about this in 1233 in a letter to the German bishops. But in the fifteenth century there was a concerted attempt to make Jews wear the *rouelle* and those of Cologne, Augsburg, and Nuremberg were compelled to adopt it.

The badge was common to both sexes and normally worn on the chest. The age of adoption varied (frequently it was the early teens). The material varied (felt, linen, silk). There were variations too in colour, but the most common was saffron yellow, the colour specified both by St Louis and Pope Gregory IX. It was thus the direct antecedent of the infamous Nazi yellow star. There were some changes of colour. King John II of France changed the colour to red and white in 1363. The reason for changes was frequently the desire to charge a fee for the new *rouelle*. The Papacy continued to prescribe yellow, as ordered by Pius II in 1459 and Alexander VI in 1494. The Church recommended no penalty for failing to wear the badge, but St Louis imposed a fine of 10 *livres tournois*, and his successors varied it up and down. Favoured individuals received special royal dispensations from wearing the badge. But the Jews were obliged to pay the royal treasury an annual fee for their *rouelles* and it became another way of exploiting them. Further revenue for authorities came from Jews paying for exemptions. Although the rules were often ignored, it is clear that the badge did make the Jew a target for attack. In 1273 the Jews of Provence pleaded that their badge made them objects of hostility, particularly on journeys, and Charles of Anjou, the ruler of Provence, granted them a blanket exemption on payment of an annual sum. Alfonso X of Castile also granted Jews permission to travel without the badge.

The imposition of the 'badge of infamy' was not uniform, and developed in different areas at different times. There were comparatively few Jews in northern Italy until the fourteenth century, probably because of the hostility of the emerging merchant class in the urban states. But after the Black Death, the Jews moved in to fill the gaps in the commercial world caused by the ravages of the plague and in some cases, to escape the hysterical massacres that elsewhere in Europe assailed the Jewish population in the wake of the rumours that they had caused the plague. By the beginning of the fifteenth century there were over 200 Jewish communities in northern Italy, twenty times the twelfth-century number, and peopled by refugees from Germany and Austria and by migrants from central and southern Italy. Jews entered fully into Italian urban life, lived intermingled with Christians, and some of them became full citizens, even holding office. By the mid-fifteenth century the Jews spoke the same language, dressed in similar clothes, and lived in houses similar to those of their Christian neighbours.

But pressure to enforce the Lateran Council's distinctive dress regulations in Italy began to be mounted by the friars. Their rabble-rousing sermons created an atmosphere of hysterical anti-Jewish feeling. Already the anti-Jewish campaign of the Dominican Inquisitor-General, Fra Bartolomeo de Aquila, had led to the destruction of Apulian Jewry by flight, massacre, or forcible conversion in 1292. St Bernardino of Siena and the Franciscans returned regularly to the theme of the Jews in their sermons in the fifteenth century. They regularly condemned the intermingling of Jews and Christians, linked the impurity of the Jew with the impurity of city life and continually urged the imposition of the badge and the introduction of segregation. St Bernardino confessed that while he could happily talk to thieves and murderers, he could not bring himself to eat or drink with a Jew. 'As to general love, we may love them but as to a particular love, we cannot.' It was directly due to Franciscan influence that the Jewish badge was introduced in Italian cities in the fifteenth century: Ancona in 1427, Padua in 1430, Perugia in 1432, Florence and Siena in 1439, Assisi in 1452. It was usually a red or yellow circle.

The circle was worn only by Jewish men. Diane Owen Hughes has demonstrated that the equivalent for Jewesses in Northern Italy was the imposition of the wearing of ear-rings, marking them as exotic outsiders. In the early Middle Ages, ear-rings had been worn by aristocrats and commoners alike. But by the twelfth century they had been largely abandoned. The Franciscan friar Giacomo della Marca said that ear-rings were jewels that 'Jewish women wear in place of circumcision, so that they can be distinguished from other women'. The ear-ring also enabled Franciscan rhetoric to identify Jews with vainglory and concupiscence, particularly at a time when sumptuary laws were restricting the amount of decoration Christian women could wear.

There was also a further identification that could be made – between Jewish women and prostitutes. In fourteenth-century Siena and Florence prostitutes were instructed to wear bells on their hats, similarly marking them out as exotic. In 1499 Jewish women in Recanti were forced to wear the yellow band of linen around the head that Pisan prostitutes in the fourteenth century and Bolognese prostitutes in the sixteenth century were condemned to wear. In 1494 Brescia expelled the Jews with a declaration:

> While the Christian Church may tolerate the Jews, it has in no way decreed that they should be tolerated in Brescia; they should be treated as public prostitutes, who because of their filth are tolerated (only) while they live in a *bordello*, even so should these Jews live their stinking life in some stinking place, separate from Christians.

The equation of Jews with prostitutes and the implication that Jewish women were the equivalent of whores is clear. The friars in their rhetoric continually linked all the ills of current Italian society with the Jews. Gambling, luxury, and sodomy were regularly castigated by the friars. Gambling and luxury were linked with Jewish usury, which financed it. Similarly sodomy was thought to be the result of the deferral of marriage, which could be attributed to men's reluctance to finance female extravagance, which was also funded by Jews.

CONCLUSION

By 1500, following 400 years of mounting hostility and rising violence, the Jews had been eliminated from much of western Europe. They were removed completely from England, Spain and France. Since Germany and Italy were not unified, Jews managed to hold on in some areas: Venice, Naples, the Papal States. The Holy Roman Empire never banned them entirely but the Jewish communities there suffered from regular outbursts of popular hostility. By the end of the Middle Ages, the bulk of Europe's Jewish population had been driven eastwards, to establish themselves chiefly in Poland and Russia.

What accounts for the persistent hostility towards the Jews throughout the Middle Ages? First, there was the continuing preoccupation with the imminence of the end of days. The works of Joachim of Fiore and the influential pseudo-Joachim corpus infused much of the Christian Europe with the expectation of an impending transition to the final perfect age of the spirit and focused attention on the need to purify and Christianize Europe in preparation for the Second Coming. The need to convert the Jews therefore became pressing and the view gradually developed that if they would not convert they must be physically removed from Christendom.

Second, there was the need to seek scapegoats for general disasters like the Black Death, for specific disasters like famine and harvest failure, and for the life of poverty and subsistence that many suffered in the Middle Ages. This was linked to a hostility to the Jews for both their money-lending and their wealth. When the biographer of Philip

Augustus gave the reasons for his expulsion of the Jews from France in 1182, he listed the habit of the Jews of sacrificing a Christian at Easter, the Judaizing of Christian servants by the Jews, and the desecration of holy vessels of the church, held as security for loans: a combination of popular prejudice and proselytization fears. But he added:

> When they had long made their sojourn there, they grew so rich that they claimed as their own almost half of the whole city ... and they took from the Christians their money in usury. And so heavily burdened in this wise were citizens and soldiers and peasants in the suburbs and in the various towns and villages, that many were constrained to part with their possessions. Others were bound under oath in the houses of the Jews in Paris, held as if captives in prison.

Greed for the wealth of the Jews and hatred of them for their economic success was a continuing element in anti-Jewish feeling. In 1233 Pope Gregory IX, appealed to by harassed French Jews, wrote to King Louis IX ordering him to extend protection to the Jews. They had complained that they were oppressed by various French lords 'cruelly raging in their midst and longing for their property, they torture them horribly by means of hunger and of thirst, by the privations of prison and by intolerable tortures of the body'. This feeling existed at almost every level of society. The pogromists of 1336 are described as 'poverty-stricken people' and there were references in accounts of the pogroms to the burning of the Jews' account books and financial records, so that information about debts owed by people of all classes would be lost. The hostility was initially not universal and burgesses in some towns sought to protect the Jews from attack. But the hostility grew as did the rivalry from Christian merchants and money-lenders, and in England, for instance, permission was obtained to expel the Jews from successive towns: Bury St Edmunds in 1190, Leicester in 1231, Newcastle in 1234, Southampton in 1236, Berkhamstead in 1242 and Derby in 1263.

At the heart of the Jewish predicament was usury, an avocation into which the Jews were forced but one which brought upon them unending obloquy. Usury, the lending of money at interest, was a sin. This was clearly stated in Leviticus 25 vv. 25–38 and Deuteronomy 23 vv. 19–21. It was reinforced by regular Papal pronouncements. Pope Urban III (1185–7), for instance, quoted Christ from Luke 6 v. 35: 'Lend without expecting any return.' Innocent IV (1243–54) condemned usury for producing evil consequences; in moral terms, avarice; in social terms, poverty. St Thomas Aquinas declared usury a logical impossibility, since it was selling something twice (the money and the use of the money). In 1179 the Lateran Council condemned the practice of usury and its prevalence and ordered usurers to be excluded from the community. It also rejected their alms and refused them Christian burial. For a hundred years the ban was reiterated by Church councils. The sin of usury was compared to homicide, perjury, sodomy, incest and parricide. It was not remittable by the local priest and needed to be referred to the bishop. In 1257 Alexander IV issued a bull officially identifying the practice of usury with heresy and placing it under the jurisdiction of the Inquisition, and in 1311 the Council of Vienne declared that anyone maintaining that usury was not sinful was a heretic.

Yet credit was essential in the emerging commercial and financial world of the Middle Ages. The very cathedrals were built using loans, and Jews moved in to fill the economic gap left by Christians. They became tainted with the sin but not punishable for it. The link of the Jew with usury and heresy was established. By the twelfth century the terms 'Jew' and 'usurer' were synonymous and in 1212 the Council of Paris declared: 'In almost every city, town and village of France the ingrained malice of the Devil has firmly established synagogues of usurers and extortioners.' All the malice attached to this was addressed to Jews.

Louis IX of France (1214–70), as part of his comprehensive programme for the moralization of his kingdom, sought to eliminate usury. He is reported as saying of the Jews: 'Let them abandon usury or they shall leave my land completely in order that it shall be no longer polluted with their filth.' In 1235 he banned the practice of usury by the Jews completely. On the evening of his departure on crusade in 1248 Louis ordered the general confiscation of all their funds and the obligations owed to the Jews, with the stated objective of restoring goods to those from whom 'the Jews had extorted them through usurious viciousness'. In the great General Reform of 1254 Louis ordered the Jews to desist from 'usury, blasphemy, magic and necromancy', threatened to expel those who disobeyed and ordered the Jews to live by light commerce and manual labour. This did not work and the Jews continued to be deeply involved in money-lending. Whatever regulations were enacted, the Jews practised lending at interest as long as it was needed. But in the thirteenth century Franciscan and Dominican theologians began to develop a justification for usury and general profit-taking which enabled Christians to participate with an easier conscience. Thus the Jewish domination of loan finance faded, though the legacy of economic resentment and stereotyping did not.

A third reason for the rise of anti-Jewish feeling was the growth of medieval nationalism, emphasizing the alien nature of the Jews, something which can be seen occurring in for instance the kingdoms of

France and England, from which the Jews were eventually expelled. This feeling was sharpened by the struggle against Islam which drew attention to the Jew as the 'ally of the Muslim'. The undoubted linkage between anti-Jewish and anti-Islamic feeling in western Europe has led Allan and Helen Cutler to claim in *The Jew as Ally of the Muslim* (1986) that medieval anti-Judaism was 'primarily a function of medieval anti-Muslimism'. They point to the association in the popular mind of the two groups. Jews were prominent in the service of the Moslem regimes in Spain; there had been a tradition of immigration of Jews to Europe from the Moslem Middle East; Jews and Moslems were associated by Pope Innocent III in his prescription of distinctive clothing. The original rumours provoking the early eleventh-century massacres hinged on collaboration between Jews and Moslems. The Jews, argue the Cutlers, were seen as a Moslem fifth column, the enemy within. There is some force in this argument. Jews and Moslems were clearly associated in the popular mind, as when both were implicated in the 'Leper Plot' of 1321. But this needs to be put into a broader context. Contemporary Hebrew chroniclers recalled the reasoning of the anti-Jewish mobs at the time of the First Crusade:

> We are marching a great distance to seek our Sanctuary and to take vengeance on the Moslems. Lo and Behold, there live among us Jews whose forefathers slew him [Jesus] and crucified him for no cause. Let us revenge ourselves on them first and eliminate them from among the nations, so that the name of Israel no longer be remembered, or else let them be like ourselves and believe in the son of [Mary].

This makes it clear that hostility to the Jews and to the Moslems were separate though linked phenomena, the outcome of the rise of Christian expansionism and religious fervour. The object was to eliminate all non-Christian elements either by conversion or extermination, so that at the Second Coming Christ would find a world of believers.

Fourth, the defensiveness of the thirteenth-century Church, manifesting itself in an attempt to regulate human thought and eliminate variation and dissidence, placed emphasis on the danger that ideas and beliefs not in accordance with orthodoxy might involve undermining the authority of the Church and threaten to destroy Christian unity. The crusade, the Inquisition, the missionary drive to convert Jews and heretics, 'the badge of infamy', the attack on the Talmud were all part of this general mindset. The Mendicant Orders in particular were prominent in all these movements, acting as the shocktroops of the Church.

All these developments led to the isolation of the Jews, their segregation, labelling and persecution. They were also decisively linked in

JEWS

the public mind with all the other dissident groups. The wearing of the badge linked them with lepers, prostitutes, Moslems and heretics. As presumed experts in magic and as acolytes of the Devil, they were linked with witches. They were tainted with 'heresy' by the practice of usury and by the intellectual campaign against the Talmud. They were seen in short as a religious, a moral, an economic and a sexual threat, and as such ready-made objects of popular hysteria and hatred for as long as their communities survived in medieval Europe.

6

PROSTITUTES

Prostitutes were an integral part of urban life in the Middle Ages, familiar figures in the surviving literature – poems, stories, songs, court records and chronicles. There was almost no town which did not have its 'good house' as the brothel was sometimes known. Ivan Bloch (1912–25) has identified seventy-five German towns and cities that contained brothels. One fifteenth-century observer estimated that there were 5–6,000 prostitutes in Paris, out of a population of 200,000. A hundred prostitutes have been identified in fifteenth-century Dijon out of a population of less than 10,000. The thirteenth-century chronicler Jacques de Vitry painted a vivid picture of the Parisian prostitutes of his day:

> Prostitutes were everywhere in the streets and neighbourhoods of the city, seeking to drag passing clerics by force into their brothels. If the clerics refused to enter, they immediately shouted after them 'Sodomite!' In one and the same building, there might be a school upstairs and a brothel downstairs. While in the upper part, the masters taught their pupils, in the lower part the prostitutes plied their nefarious trade. In one part, the prostitutes quarrelled with each other and their pimps; in the other part the scholars argued on scholarly matters.

Prostitutes solicited in taverns, squares, bath-houses, even churches. But there were also known 'red light' districts. To this day, many an old medieval town has a Rose Street, its fragrant horticultural association concealing a seamier past. 'To pluck a rose' was a common euphemism for 'to copulate with a prostitute' and Rose Street was usually a haunt of whores.

Women entered prostitution in the Middle Ages for much the same reasons as they do in any age: poverty, natural inclination, loss of status, a disturbed, violent or incestuous family background. The work of Jacques Rossiaud on prostitution in Burgundy gives us some precise statistics. In late medieval Dijon, four out of five prostitutes were from

116

the poorest section of the population, with seventeen as the commonest age of entry into the profession. A quarter of them had been put to prostitution by the family or had entered it to escape from an intolerable family situation. Only 15 per cent of prostitutes had taken up the life freely and of their own choice.

By the later Middle Ages, a hierarchy of activities had emerged in the prostitution business. At the top of the hierarchy was the full-scale municipal brothel, whose inmates took an oath to the authorities, paid a weekly rent to the madam, and often contributed to the costs of heating and protection by the watch. Then there were the smaller private houses (*bordelages*), usually run by women with a resident staff of 'servant girls'. There was widespread prostitution in bath-houses. The correlation of activities was such that the same term ('stews') came in English to be applied both to bath-houses and brothels. This was despite the fact that bath-house rules regularly excluded prostitutes. Finally there were freelance prostitutes operating in the open. In Paris, the ramparts, the open fields, public gardens, alleyways, river-banks, bridges and waste ground all served as sites of prostitution – anywhere, in short, where the prostitute could snatch a moment of privacy with the client. Privacy was not easily come by in the medieval urban world and the activities of prostitutes were often open to the public gaze. For instance, in a court case in Florence in 1400 when one Salvaza was being prosecuted for illegal prostitution, several eye-witnesses gave evidence about her lifestyle, one of them declaring 'she had frequently looked through a window of Salvaza's house and had seen her nude in bed with men, engaging in those indecent acts which are practised by prostitutes'.

Probably the largest group of clients served by the prostitutes of medieval Europe were young and unmarried men. Whatever the Church may have said about sex, there was widespread social tolerance of male pre-marital and extra-marital sexual activity in the medieval world. A fifteenth-century preacher complained to the fathers in his congregation: 'You give your sons money and permission to go to the brothel, to the bath-houses and to the taverns.' But prostitution was seen as a practical means of allowing young men of all classes to assert their masculinity and relieve their sexual needs while at the same time keeping them from consorting with respectable wives and daughters, deterring them from gang-rapes, and discouraging them from homosexuality. This was all the more important with the tendency of men to defer marriage until their late twenties. Apprentices, journeymen, and university students wanted to complete their training or establish their careers; other young men were deterred by the costs of dowries and wedding receptions. So young men were allowed to use the brothels from 16–18 years of age upwards. The need by young males for the

117

services provided by the brothel was explicitly recognized by King Charles VII of France when he authorized a brothel in Castelnaudary in 1445. He did so, he said, because of the presence in the town of so many young unmarried men.

Clerics, married men, Jews and lepers were not supposed to use the brothels and were often specifically excluded by the regulations governing them. But they did frequent them nevertheless. Humbert of Romans, Master-General of the Dominicans, observed of professional urban prostitutes that they 'take in not just a few, but very large numbers of men; now their own relatives; now even monks and friars'. Rossiaud estimates that clergy made up 20 per cent of the clientele of the bath-houses and private brothels of Dijon. But he suggests that this did not earn them particular disapproval because all unmarried men were expected to fornicate and husbands and fathers preferred handsome young clerics to use prostitutes rather than their women-folk. So the lecherous cleric became a source of humour in popular culture. Visiting farmers, merchants, pilgrims, migrant workers, soldiers, men in general away from home and family, were also among the regular clientele of the brothels.

There are few references to prostitution in the early medieval penitentials and it seems not to have been a problem at that time. Prostitution was essentially a product of the towns and as the towns grew and expanded from the eleventh and twelfth centuries, prostitution came increasingly to be seen as a social phenomenon that needed regulation. Not surprisingly, the Church, the emerging national monarchies, and the urban municipalities took steps to deal with it. The Church set the framework within which prostitution should be viewed and its attitudes reveal the extent of its realism with regard to the sexual drives of the faithful.

The fundamental definition of a prostitute, according to the Church, was that coined in the early fifth century by St Jerome: 'A whore is one who is available for the lusts of many men.' This was incorporated into canon law, which thus saw promiscuity as the key factor. Canon law distinguished prostitution (involving sex with many men) from concubinage (involving sex with one person but not within formal marriage). The canonists denounced prostitution but, following St Augustine, saw it as a necessary evil, something whose existence made it possible to maintain stable social and sexual patterns for the rest of society. Augustine wrote: 'If you expel prostitutes from society, you will unsettle everything on account of lusts.' A thirteenth-century glossator of Augustine added the colourful phrase: 'The prostitute in society is like the sewer in a palace. If you take away the sewer, the whole palace will be contaminated.' Leading theologians like St Thomas Aquinas and Thomas of Chobham repeated the analogy, arguing that prostitution prevented greater evils, such as sodomy and murder. Thomas of Chobham went so far as to argue that:

> prostitutes should be counted amongst wage earners. In effect they hire out their bodies and provide labour. If they repent, they may keep the profits from prostitution for charitable purposes. But if they prostitute themselves for pleasure and hire out their bodies so that they may gain enjoyment, then this is not work and the wage is as shameful as the act.

He was reiterating the fundamental Christian hostility to sexual activity viewed purely as a source of pleasure but he was acknowledging the existence of what had become a distinct socio-economic class in society.

Even so, the Church sought to deal with the prostitution problem by very carefully containing it. It used in fact some of the same means as it adopted for lepers. First, prostitutes had to be distinguished from the decent population by the prescription of a badge of infamy and second, they had to be segregated. Thirteenth-century canonists argued that prostitutes should be marked out by the wearing of distinctive dress and the Council of Paris (1213) decreed: 'We prohibit public prostitutes (frequent cohabitation with whom is more effective than the plague in bringing harm) from being permitted to live in the city or *bourg* but rather [they] should be set apart as is the custom with lepers.' This frame of mind led to the emergence from the mid-thirteenth century onwards of distinctive dress codes and 'red light' districts.

In many places the *aiguillette*, a knotted cord falling from the shoulder and of a different colour from the dress, was the badge of infamy. It was inspired by the red cord let down from her window by Rahab the harlot in the Book of Joshua. It thus became the direct equivalent of the *rouelle* of the Jews and the lepers' rattle. The red *aiguillette* was common in the kingdom of France, but the badge varied elsewhere. In Toulouse it was a white knot; in Vienna a yellow scarf; in Leipzig a yellow cloak trimmed with blue; in Berne and Zurich a red cap; in Dijon and Avignon a white badge four fingers wide on the arm. In Milan it was a black cloak; in Bergamo a yellow cloak; in Marseilles a striped tunic; in Bristol a striped hood. In Strasbourg it was a black and white sugarloaf hat; in Nîmes a sleeve of a different colour from the dress; in Florence gloves and a bell on the hat. Whatever form it took, some kind of distinctive dress was deemed crucial as a way of distinguishing the prostitute from respectable women and thus saving the latter from embarrassment. This objective also lay behind the ban on prostitutes wearing veils in Avignon, Arles, and Nîmes.

Beyond this, the Church laid stress on the prospect of reform and urged prostitutes to marry and abandon the trade. Pope Innocent III encouraged all true Christians to help reclaim prostitutes and offered remission of sins to those who married such women. Religious houses were set up for reformed prostitutes. The convent of Filles-Dieu was founded in Paris in 1226 for this purpose. Most towns in Languedoc had such an establishment by the late thirteenth century. In 1227 Pope Gregory IX approved the Order of St Mary Magdalene, set up to run houses for reformed prostitutes. There were also several saints whose cults were promoted as role models for reformed prostitutes: St Mary Magdalene, St Thais, St Pelagia, St Afra and St Mary the Egyptian in particular.

The emerging national monarchies began to take an interest in the regulation of prostitution as part of their gradual assumption of more and more responsibility for the lives of their subjects. One of the earliest rulers to take action was King Henry II of England who in 1161 laid down regulations for the brothels of Southwark. Southwark, outside the city walls, had developed into London's red light district; the extensive land-holdings of the Bishop of Winchester in the area led to prostitutes becoming known as 'Winchester Geese'. Henry saw a need to regulate the area after the disturbance to society and morals caused by the prolonged civil war, which had ended with his accession. There were to be no brothels opening on holy days or religious festivals, when parliament was sitting, or the King was holding council meetings. No pregnant women, married women or nuns were to be taken on as prostitutes. No woman was to take money from a man unless she had lain with him all night. No woman was to be prevented from giving up the profession if she wished to. There was to be no open soliciting for custom. No food or alcoholic drink was to be served to customers. Women were not to reside there but merely to work there. They were not to be charged more than 14 pence a week for a room. There were to be regular health checks on the women.

The aim was to create orderly, efficient centres for sexual release which as far as possible did not offend public decency. This became the consistent aim of both the crown and the municipal authorities. Initially it centred on a policy of keeping prostitutes outside the city walls and confined to known 'red light' districts. But court records reveal the inexorable tendency of prostitution to spread. New 'red light' districts sprang up to the north of the city of London in Moorgate and Cripplegate and to the west in Holborn, Fleet Street and Chancery Lane. These were tolerated because they were outside the city proper, though within the jurisdiction of the mayor and aldermen. But prostitution took root inside the city too. So in 1285 King Edward I ordered all prostitutes to reside outside the city walls on pain of forty days' imprisonment. The order was repeated in 1307, 1383 and 1483.

As well as seeking to maintain segregation, both crown and city council sought to enforce dress regulations. In 1345 Edward III re-enacted Henry II's regulatory decree of 1161, adding the stipulation that whores must wear a badge of distinction, which had not until then been the rule in London. In 1351 the city fathers amplified this, issuing an edict complaining that lewd women were adopting the dress of 'good and noble dames' and ordered them not to wear any vestment trimmed with fur and lined with silk or any rich stuff but to wear a hood of striped cloth and plain vestments. These rules were re-enacted in 1382 and 1437, when the prescribed hood was to be red.

But prostitutes and brothels were clearly seen as constituting a danger to public order as much as to public morals. With the backing of the crown, London city council imposed a curfew in 1393, forbidding any man to go about the city or suburbs after 9 p.m. No alien was to go about after 8 p.m. on pain of fine and imprisonment. No one was to go about masked. The ordinance went on to pinpoint brothels and prostitutes as a source of disorder:

> Whereas many and divers frays, broils and dissensions have arisen in times past, and many men have been slain and murdered, by reason of the frequent resort to, and consorting with, common harlots, at taverns, brew-houses of *huksters*, and other places of ill-fame, within the said city, and the suburbs thereof; and more especially through Flemish women, who profess and follow such shameful and dolorous life – we do by our command forbid, on behalf of our Lord the King, and the Mayor and Aldermen of the City of London, that any such women shall go about or lodge in the said city, or in the suburbs thereof, by night or by day; but they are to keep themselves in the places thereunto assigned, that is to say, the Stews on the other side of the Thames and Cokkeslane [Cock Lane, Smithfield].

The punishment for breach of the curfew was confiscation of the prostitute's clothing, the badge of her profession, thus in theory preventing her from working.

In 1417 the council was once again sufficiently exercised by the danger of public disorder to decree the closure of all brothels within the city, complaining that their presence led to 'many grievances, abominations, damages, disturbances, murders, homicides, larcenies and other common nuisances' and

> what is even worse, from one day to another, the wives, sons, daughters, apprentices and servants, of the reputable men of the City are oftentimes ... drawn and enticed thereto; and there they, as well as other persons, both regular and secular, are permitted

to do and carry on the illicit works of their lewd flesh, to the great abomination and displeasure of God and to the great dishonour and damage of all the City.

This was repeated in 1422.

In 1460 King Henry VI, concerned at the number of homicides, plunderings and improprieties occurring in Southwark due to the large concentration of prostitutes there, appointed a commission to remove all such prostitutes and their accomplices to prison. The recurrence of such orders at regular intervals throughout the Middle Ages shows that permanent firm control of the prostitution problem was largely a forlorn hope. Illicit copulation thrived inside and outside the city walls.

In France, King Louis IX (1226–70), as befitted a man who was to be canonized in 1297, took a highly elevated view of his duty to moralize his kingdom and sought to eliminate prostitution. This was in marked contrast to the realism of his grandfather, King Philip Augustus (1180–1223), who, it was said, had encouraged prostitution in Paris in order to discourage homosexuality among the students. Louis, however, initiated a grand programme of moral reform, including in his ordinance of 1254 a clear denunciation of prostitution and an order for public prostitutes to be expelled from the towns and the surrounding countryside. He also ordered the confiscation of the house of anyone who knowingly rented rooms to a prostitute. But this proved so unworkable that in 1256 Louis modified it. He ordered prostitutes simply to be put outside the walls and kept away from all holy places. But he returned to the question in a letter written in 1269 on the eve of his departure on crusade. As part of the purification of the realm in preparation for the holy enterprise, he ordered 'all notorious and manifest brothels' inside and outside towns to be closed down. He founded retreats for reformed prostitutes and promised a pension to all women of the streets who reformed; only 200 came forward to claim it.

Louis IX's son, Philip III (1270–85), following his father's lead, ordered royal bailiffs in 1272 to suppress blasphemy, gaming and brothels. Louis' grandson, Philip IV (1285–1314) put royal officials in Languedoc at the disposal of citizens wishing to expel prostitutes from respectable areas. But then there was no further royal initiative for nearly a century, perhaps because for much of this time the French kings were embroiled in the Hundred Years War. It was under King Charles V (1364–80) that a new policy was adopted. In 1367 the Provost of Paris, Hughes Aubriot, as part of a general policy of restoring order after the political and social upheavals of the war, ordered prostitutes to be limited to particular designated streets; if found elsewhere they were to be banished from the city. This became official royal policy for the next 150 years. The 1254 ordinance of St Louis was frequently cited to support the policy, but the wording was carefully modified to make it sanction 'red light' areas.

Attempts were made to restrict prostitution to eight particular streets and municipal decrees in the fourteenth and fifteenth centuries regularly reiterated the limits to be imposed on prostitution: the area in which it was to be practised, the times of day, the clothing to be worn, the behaviour expected. Prostitutes were to operate nowhere except for clearly identified brothels and they were to leave the brothels at dusk and not to practise the trade at home. But the rules were blithely ignored and prostitution went on everywhere in Paris. One area, the Clapier, became so notorious that it gave a nickname ('clap') to the sexually transmitted disease gonorrhea.

As with the monarchies, so too with the municipalities; the rising towns and cities began to interfere in the private lives of their citizens in the interests of public morality. In an exemplary study, Leah Lydia Otis has traced the regulation of prostitution in Languedoc and she sees a process of transformation from tolerance in the early Middle Ages to institutionalization in the later Middle Ages before repression in the sixteenth century.

The first reaction to what was seen as a growing problem of urban life was expulsion. In 1212 Simon de Montfort, legislating for the southern territories captured in the Albigensian crusade, in the Statutes of Pamiers, ordered that 'public prostitutes are to be placed outside the walls in all towns'. It has been suggested that he was applying to the south the convention prevalent in Northern France but if so, it was sympathetically received. The municipal laws of Carcassonne and Toulouse from the early thirteenth century ordered prostitutes to reside outside the city walls but made no designation of district. City statutes in Avignon, Arles and Marseilles merely banned prostitutes from respectable areas. In 1299 prostitutes and procurers were expelled from Narbonne. The last reference to this procedure in Languedoc came in 1321 when the charter of Bourg-Saint-Andéol confirmed the right of the town council to expel prostitutes. This policy inevitably led to the creation of brothels and 'red light' areas outside towns, in line with the segregation decreed by the Church and already in operation in London. The expulsion of prostitutes took place elsewhere too as the first stage in the action to control prostitution: Bologna in 1259, Venice in 1266 and 1314, York in 1301 and Modena in 1327.

But mere expulsion did not end the problem. The next step was the establishment of officially licensed 'red light' districts, a policy which made sense given the authorities' need to oversee areas which were frequent resorts of criminals, travellers, and spies, and regular sources of disorder. In Montpellier in 1285 it was decided to assign one suburban street, the 'Hot Street', as the official residence for prostitutes who had been expelled from respectable districts by the citizenry and the clergy. They were to be secure from expulsion as long as they stayed in the 'Hot Street'. Narbonne, which had expelled its prostitutes in 1299, went over to the 'red light' district policy in 1335, explicitly adopting the Montpellier model. Officially licensed 'red light' districts appeared in Toulouse in 1296, Uzès in 1326 and Lacaune in 1337.

A further step was the establishment of municipally owned brothels. Toulouse established one between 1363 and 1372. Castres established one in 1391 when the council took over an existing brothel in the suburbs, and then built a new municipal brothel within the city walls in 1398. In Albi a municipal brothel had been built by 1380. The municipalization of privately owned brothels continued throughout the fifteenth century in Languedoc – at Pézenas in 1399, Lodève in 1455 and Castelnaudary towards the end of the fifteenth century. Only Avignon and Arles retained whole streets of prostitutes, a practice which remained typical of Italian towns in the fifteenth century. Where there was not a large enough population or sufficient tolerance of prostitution for a municipal brothel, the 'once a week' custom was observed. Prostitutes were allowed to stay overnight in the town once a week, a custom which underlines the fact that their customary place was outside the walls. This policy received official approval. In 1425 King Charles VII placed the Toulouse brothel, which had been attacked and damaged, under royal protection and ordered the royal emblem of the fleur-de-lis placed on the house as a sign of this. In 1445 when the consuls of Castelnaudary asked the King's permission to build a municipal brothel, he ordered the royal judges to choose a suitable place and compel the town's prostitutes to live there, expelling those who would not do so.

Thus the principle of expelling prostitutes became one of defining 'red light' districts and then establishing single officially sanctioned houses. The same pattern that is to be seen in Languedoc seems to have been followed also in south-eastern France. The municipal brothel in Dijon was in operation by 1385 and a second one was opened at the start of the fifteenth century. The brothel in Pernes opened in 1430, in Sisteron in 1424, in Cavaillon in 1437, in St Flour in 1402, in Villefranche-sur-Saône in 1439, in Bourg-en-Bresse in 1439, in Tours in 1448, and in Amiens around the same period.

In central and northern France, prostitution fell under the control of a civic official, the King of Ribalds (*Le Roi des ribauds*). Such a figure is attested in Cambrai, Tournai, Arras, Lille, Noyon and Douai, as well as further south in Toulouse and Bordeaux. The duties of the official are defined in the oath taken by the King of Ribalds in Arras: 'To take note of girls and women of ill repute and to lead them and oblige them to live in public places and to also find out which of them are leprous and to bring them to trial and lead them outside our said city of Arras when they have been judged.' His duties were essentially segregatory and regulatory, requiring him to ensure that all prostitutes resided in the official brothel and to bring about the exclusion from the city of any who were diseased. The King of Ribalds frequently combined these responsibilities with duties relating to other malefactors. At Lille, he was put in charge of arresting, whipping, and expelling violent madmen; at Tournai arresting blasphemers; in Guyenne flogging thieves. In several places, he was the public executioner. From 1214 to 1449 there was a King of Ribalds in the royal household in Paris, supervising the prostitutes resident there for use by the palace staff and guests. He was a modest ranking official who took part in the great ceremonial events of the court. Many other noble and princely households had a similar official.

In 1403 a municipal brothel was set up in Florence and in 1360 Venice opened one. For Venice this marked a decisive change of policy, for the Grand Council had ordered prostitutes expelled from the city in 1266 and again in 1314. Since 1316 tavern-keepers had been forbidden to give food, drink, or lodgings for the night to prostitutes. But in 1358 the Grand Council declared prostitution 'absolutely indispensable to the world' (thus echoing the teaching of the canonists and theologians) and authorized an official house of prostitution to cater for the large number of men visiting the city. It was set up in a group of houses owned by two patrician families, Venier and Morosini, in an area called the Castelletto in the parish of San Matteo di Rialto. The Rialto had the greatest density of inns and was the traditional centre of prostitution.

The prostitutes were not to live in the brothel but only to work there. The brothels were run by registered matrons and the premises regularly inspected by the authorities. They were obliged to close by eleven at night. The proceeds of prostitution were placed in a chest which the authorities emptied at the start of each month, paying the salaries of the brothel staff and giving the prostitutes their share. The state officials in charge of visiting brothels were forbidden to receive presents from or to sleep with the prostitutes on pain of loss of office, fine, and imprisonment. The prostitutes were authorized to leave the Rialto only on Saturday mornings and they were obliged to dress in a short cloak with a yellow scarf knotted around their neck.

However it is clear from the legal records that the prostitutes con-tinually broke the rules and could be found operating in bath-houses, in porticoes, and outside churches. By the fifteenth century the entire Rialto, not just the Castelletto, was a stamping ground of prostitutes. The legal records also allow us to trace the spread of prostitution and they show the authorities continually having to give way and recognize the fact. By 1421 prostitution was established in Cà Rampani. The prostitutes there were frequently threatened with the confiscation of their clothes unless they either entered the official brothel or quit Venice altogether. But by 1480 a brothel had appeared in the area, run on similar lines to the official Rialto establishment. Prostitutes were ordered out of the district of San Samuele in 1421 and again in 1444. But in 1468 the state conceded permission to establish brothels in the parish though not near to the church. The brothels were closed in 1485 when a large number of houses was acquired in order to build a new monastery. Prostitutes were also reported in the Piazza San Marco and ordered out in 1448, 1489 and 1490. But they continued to frequent the area.

The municipal brothels took three forms. They could be farmed out to the highest bidder and revenue from them used to repair them and to benefit the town coffers. They could be run by a municipal charitable organization with profits going to charity. Where they were too small to turn a profit, they could be run on a non-profit-making basis as a public service. In any event the town was responsible for protection and security.

There were profits to be made from brothel-keeping, as can be seen in the virtual domination of private brothel-keeping by the nobility and *haute bourgeoisie*. It was the ownership of the Southwark brothels by prominent aldermen that led Wat Tyler and his rebels to burn them down in 1381. The Church also profitably leased property to brothel-keepers and towards the end of the Middle Ages, the Papacy netted 28,000 ducats a year from its premises leased for this purpose.

Why did this municipalization of the brothels, which peaked in the period 1350–1450, take place? Richard Trexler, in his study of prostitution in Florence, suggests that it was part of an official bid to combat the incidence of homosexuality by introducing young men to the delights of heterosexuality. Homosexuality was certainly perceived as a problem by the authorities in fifteenth-century Florence in the context of a population decline, which can be attributed both to the effects of the plague and to the practice of young men deferring marriage. Popular opinion, reinforced by preachers like St Bernardino of Siena and Savonarola, believed that such young men found sexual release in homosexuality.

In 1403 therefore the government of Florence set up the Office of Decency (*Onestà*) to oversee public morals and instituted a series of measures designed to promote marriage and childbirth. Bachelors over 30 were subjected to taxation. Sumptuary laws were introduced to restrain female extravagance, which was seen as a deterrent to marriage. Fathers were encouraged to invest so as to allow sons to have enough capital to marry by 25 and daughters to be dowried by 18. Punitive measures were taken against homosexuality and in 1432 the Office of the Night was established to pursue homosexuals.

As a corollary, in 1403 the government sought to build or buy a suitable building for use as a bordello and to recruit foreign prostitutes to staff it. Their motivation was explained when in 1415 they authorized two more municipal brothels. They were, they said, 'desiring to eliminate a worse evil by means of a lesser one'. In the context of Florentine concerns, that 'worse evil' seems to be interpretable as sodomy. But there was also a concern to maintain public decorum. For the locations were to be chosen 'in places where the exercise of such scandalous activity can best be concealed for the honour of the city and of those who live in the neighbourhood in which the prostitutes must stay'. These two further brothels seem not to have been built. But in the event it may well be that the Florentines simply replaced one problem with another. For while in the fifteenth century preachers regularly complained at the shortage of married men and blamed the Florentine propensity to sodomy, in the sixteenth century they were complaining about the surplus of unmarried women being corrupted and seduced into prostitution (young widows and their daughters, orphans, servants, slaves). In 1498 the parishioners of San Remigio formed bands to drive out prostitutes from the area around the church.

The problem of homosexuality among young males seems not to have been one which worried the authorities in Burgundy. From his study of prostitution there, Jacques Rossiaud attributes the municipalization phenomenon to the need to cater for the sexual needs of the large unmarried male population and to protect respectable wives and daughters from molestation. It is clear too that the authorities were concerned about the general question of law and order when it came to policing prostitution. The London regulations indicate that prostitutes and brothels were a focus for potential violence. Eighty-three per cent of the court cases involving prostitutes in fifteenth-century Florence were for violence.

This concern for public order can certainly be seen to lie behind the detailed regulations the authorities drew up to govern their brothels. Prostitutes were to be kept away from respectable areas, churches, main streets and schools. Prostitutes were forbidden to operate outside 'red light' districts and frequently forbidden to go into taverns. In the brothels themselves the women were supposed to remain cloistered, often under a manageress known as the abbess. Arms were to be surrendered by customers on entry, though many Italian towns authorized the brothel-keeper to carry arms to maintain order. Customers were often recommended to leave jewellery and money with the abbess. Admission was selective and could be refused. Many brothel regulations banned gaming.

127

From her study of Languedoc, Leah Lydia Otis says that municipalization was due partly to the profits to be made, partly to the need to
regularize the supply of prostitutes with the population fall after the
Black Death but was mainly a response to increasing moral rigour. The
classic formula in Languedocian documents justifying an authorized
centre of prostitution was that a place was needed to 'avoid greater
evil'. This greater evil was the bad example prostitution set and the
danger of women being seduced into the life because of their natural
frivolity and sensuality. The idea of having them closeted in brothels,
run by 'abbesses', had a certain symmetry. At one end of the scale
celibate women in nunneries lived lives in imitation of the Virgin; at
the other end, public women in cloisters expiated the sin of Eve by
catering to male lust. So public brothels were a response not to moral
laxity but to moral rigour.

Further evidence of the moral spur to municipalization can be seen
in the general closure of brothels during Holy Week and the ferocity
with which unauthorized brothels, freelance brothel keepers and stray-
ing prostitutes were pursued. Prostitutes operating outside the authorized area were penalized by flogging in fourteenth-century Nîmes,
Bologna, Lunel, and Uzès, and by branding in Florence. Freelance
brothel keepers were also often flogged. Procuring was particularly
heavily punished. In London in 1383 male and female procurers were
ordered to be pilloried for a first offence, pilloried and imprisoned for
ten days for a second, and pilloried, jailed and expelled from the
city for the third. In Paris in 1416 a decree was issued threatening procurers with pillory, branding and banishment. Procurers were regularly
threatened with beating and banishment in southern France and various
Italian towns.

Similarly, the deliberate recruitment by the city fathers of foreign
prostitutes suggests that they were seeking to leave their local women
undefiled. Two thirds of the prostitutes about whom anything is known
in Dijon between 1440 and 1540 were local women from the city or its
immediate surroundings. But the bulk of the inmates of the municipal
brothel were foreign. Out of sixty-six in the brothel whose origins are
known, fifty-three are foreign. All the public brothels in the Rhone
Valley were staffed mainly by northern French women or women from
the Low Countries. The authorities in Florence specifically set out to
find foreign prostitutes for their municipal brothel and 70 per cent of
the prostitutes cited in the Florentine court rolls were foreign (from
Flanders, Rhineland, and northern France). Only 28 per cent are known
to have been Tuscan. We know too that Flemish women were an
important element in the London brothel population.

The counterpart of the introduction of municipal brothels was the
growth of municipally financed institutions to support and house retired

or repentant prostitutes. For instance, they can be found in Abbeville, Amiens, Lyons, Avignon and Paris. They also suggest a desire to provide a limit to the extent and duration of the prostitute's working life.

Despite their difference of emphasis, there is no substantive difference between the reasons for municipalization advanced by Trexler, Rossiaud or Otis. All can be seen as aspects of a desire to create a moral atmosphere in society and to regulate the sexual conduct of the population, in particular the young. Along with the sacralization of marriage, the increased persecution of homosexuals and the enhanced concern of the Church with masturbation, went the desire to channel the impulse to fornication into an acceptable haven – the officially run, controlled, and inspected brothel, staffed by foreign women and kept out of sight of the respectable citizens.

The prostitutes' official position thus resembled that of the Jews or the lepers. All three groups were required to wear special clothing. All three were increasingly segregated. All three were urged to repent and reform. It was no coincidence that St Thomas Aquinas included his defence of the necessity of prostitution in a chapter in his *Summa* dealing with toleration of the Jews. Like the Jews, they defy the teaching of the Church but are to be tolerated because they perform a necessary if distasteful function: usury (the Jews) and sex (prostitutes). Avignon city regulations of 1243 prohibited Jews and prostitutes alike from touching fruit or bread in the market, obliging them to buy whatever they touched. A similar statute from 1293 for Salon included lepers. A regulation from Bagnol links prostitutes and lepers. A thirteenth-century Marseilles statute forbade bath-house keepers to allow Jews or prostitutes to enter public baths except on specified days. In Paris from the thirteenth century onwards prostitutes and lepers were specifically forbidden to use bath-houses. In Perpignan, the town prostitutes were traditionally confined in the local leper-house during Holy Week. Jews and prostitutes alike were forbidden to go out into towns during Holy Week.

As with lepers, the Church sought to deprive prostitutes of their civil rights. Canon law debarred prostitutes from accusing others of crimes except simony and from appearing in court. Prostitutes were debarred from inheriting property. They were deemed incapable of being victims of rape. Sex with a prostitute against her will, therefore, was not punishable by canon law. But the Church did not demand punishment for a prostitute plying her trade.

However, despite canon law, there is clear evidence of an improvement in their legal position. Otis has found examples of prostitutes being called as witnesses and bringing accusations in court. They can be found making wills and contracting marriages. The legal restrictions

appear to have become non-functional by the end of the fourteenth
century. There was a moderation too in the penalties for infractions of
municipal statutes. In the thirteenth century this was met by whipping
or loss of clothing; by the fourteenth and fifteenth centuries merely by
a fine. There is also evidence of increasing legal provision of protection
from rape. Emperor Frederick II, in advance of his time in this respect
as in others, decreed in his Constitutions of Melfi (1231) that rapists of
prostitutes should be executed. The local legislation of Germany and
Italy varied from town to town. Some towns (Parma, Bologna, Ems)
did not consider the rape of a prostitute to be an offence. Others imposed
a penalty, but usually a lighter one than that for the rape of an honest
woman. It was a fine in Rome, Pisa and Perpignan. In Vienna the
position moved from one of no punishment for rape in 1221 to the
imposition of punishment by 1244. The municipal laws of France
normally imposed a fine for the rape of a prostitute.

Rossiaud suggests that this legal amelioration of the position of
prostitutes was part of a change of attitude towards prostitutes characterizing the fifteenth century. They were becoming more integrated
into society. The use of the *aiguillette* was abandoned, the office of *Roi
des ribauds* was phased out and prostitutes subjected instead to the
ordinary courts, and prostitutes are to be found participating in civic
festivals, weddings, funerals and baptisms. In addition their days and
hours of work were being extended as the tradition of closure on
religious festivals declined. Yet it may be that Rossiaud exaggerates
the significance of this change of attitude. The dress, time and location
regulations for prostitutes had been continually flouted since they were
introduced. Young men at the end of the Middle Ages held the same
view about fornication that they had held at the beginning. The position
of the prostitute had improved steadily over time and it may be that
after the Black Death, prostitutes, like labourers, enjoyed something
of a seller's market with the all-round labour shortage and that this led
to a general improvement of their conditions. Nevertheless, there was
greater emphasis than ever on marriage and childbirth after the Black
Death, and a philosophy of moderation and temperance in all things
emerged to balance the attitude of 'eat, drink, and be merry, for
tomorrow we die' that in some produced a 'cult of the good time'.

The stimulus to morality provided by the Black Death gave a fresh
lease of life to movements exalting asceticism and self-denial and these
provided a potent counterbalance to the 'good time' boys in society.
The decisive change, however, came in the sixteenth century. In 1561
the Ordinance of Orléans closed all the brothels. But by this time almost
all the municipal brothels in Languedoc had already closed. Otis rules
out the popular view that this was due to reaction to the syphilis
epidemic that swept Europe in the early sixteenth century. She says

the closure would have happened earlier than 1561 if this were the cause. But one should not rule out the cumulative effect of the disease, the gradual acceptance of the link, and the reinforcement that this gave to the moral pressure building up on the brothels. The moral pressure came from Protestantism, which demanded chastity before marriage and envisaged an active sexuality within marriage but was not willing to countenance youthful fornication at all. Lutheran preachers were instrumental in the closure of the public brothels in Augsburg (1532), Ulm (1537), Regensburg (1553) and Nuremberg (1562). The Protestant influence in Languedoc was strong and eventually even more so that of the Counter-Reformation, the Catholic response to the Reformation which sought to match it in moral rigour and the repression of sexual immorality. For both Protestant and Catholic, then, prostitution became something to be repressed and not encouraged even within strictly defined limits. The reaction to prostitution can be seen, despite the changes of strategy towards it, to have remained fundamentally the same throughout the Middle Ages. The authorities moved to control it in the early thirteenth century as part of their general imposition of regulation and direction that can be seen in many other areas of life and there was a second round of regulation and direction in the aftermath of the Black Death. For all that, it was consistently seen as a necessary if distasteful aspect of society that had to be tolerated for fear of something worse.

7

HOMOSEXUALS

In discussing the role of homosexuality in the Christian world, it is necessary to engage with the work of John Boswell, whose book *Christianity, Social Tolerance and Homosexuality* (1980) is the main scholarly study of the subject. It is a brilliant, detailed and indispensable work, which has stimulated a lively and continuing debate. But it seems to me seriously to overstate its case and at times positively to mislead in a desire to prove that Christianity is not fundamentally hostile to homosexuality and that during the course of the Middle Ages an early tolerance gave way to a later intolerance for reasons not connected with basic Christian teachings.

There can be little real argument about the basic stance of Christianity. Since sex, according to Christian teaching, was given to man solely for the purposes of reproduction and for no other reason, any form of sexual activity which did not lead or could not lead to procreation was a sin against nature. Sins against nature specifically included bestiality, homosexuality and masturbation. As St Augustine, the most important of the Church fathers in defining the Church's attitude to sex, wrote in his *Confessions* (III.8):

> Sins against nature, therefore, like the sin of Sodom, are abominable and deserve punishment wherever and whenever they are committed. If all nations committed them, all alike would be held guilty of the same charge in God's law, for our Maker did not prescribe that we should use each other in this way. In fact the relationship which we ought to have with God is itself violated when our nature, of which he is the Author, is desecrated by perverted lust.

Augustine was simply expanding on what was implicit and sometimes explicit in earlier Christian teaching. The Old Testament (Leviticus 18 v. 22 and 20 v. 13) declared homosexuality an abomination punishable by death, bracketing it with incest, bestiality and adultery, and Judaism was the matrix of Christianity. Jesus himself says nothing

132

about homosexuality. Boswell claims that St Paul says little and he tries to explain it away but not convincingly. St Paul in I Corinthians 6 v. 9, I Timothy I v. 10, and Romans I vv. 26–7 clearly condemns homosexuality. The Corinthians passage in the Authorized Version of the Bible reads: 'Know ye not that the unrighteous shall not inherit the kingdom of God? Be not deceived; neither fornicators, nor idolators, not adulterers, nor the effeminate, nor abusers of themselves with mankind ... shall inherit the kingdom of God.' The Jerusalem translation of the Bible renders the last two categories as 'catamites and sodomites'. Boswell suggests that the word used by St Paul ἀρσε-νοκοῖται meant specifically male prostitutes but David Wright in a carefully argued etymological analysis has refuted this, demonstrating that it meant unambiguously those who commit homosexual acts.

Boswell claims that in the similar passage in Romans, St Paul is not stigmatizing homosexual acts in themselves and when committed by homosexual people, but is condemning homosexual acts committed by heterosexual people. But this will not do. For as Boswell himself admits, it is inherently unlikely that St Paul had any concept of someone who was homosexual by nature. He could conceive only of homosexual acts committed by heterosexual people. In these circumstances, it is not surprising that St Paul laid out a catalogue of sexual misdemeanours which were sins whoever committed them. It is equally comprehensible that he should have attacked homosexual relations between males, given that he, like Christ, disapproved of promiscuity, lust and fornication, placed the greatest value on celibacy and believed that life-long indissoluble, heterosexual marriage was the best alternative to celibacy. In I Corinthians 7 vv. 1–9 he was quite explicit:

Now concerning the things whereof ye wrote to me; it is good for a man not to touch a woman [i.e. celibacy is best]. Nevertheless to avoid fornication, let every man have his own wife, and let every woman have her own husband [i.e. the only alternative to fornication is heterosexual marriage]. I would that all men were even as I myself.... But if they cannot contain, let them marry; for it is better to marry than to burn.

There can be no doubt in this context that all other forms of sex are illicit and that includes homosexual relations.

St Paul's views were to some extent formulated as a rejection of the moral values of the pagan Ancient World. This was particularly true of his attitude to homosexuality. The very different standpoint on this matter in the Ancient World demonstrates conclusively that such things are relative and culturally determined; not moral absolutes. Sir Kenneth Dover in his definitive study of Greek homosexuality concluded that in Ancient Greece homosexual relationships supplied the need for personal relations of an intensity not found in marriage or with parents and children. Women were regarded as inferior intellectually, physically and emotionally; males tended to congregate in groups where pair-bonding took place. In some places (Sparta, Crete), the men were physically segregated and in others (Thebes, Sparta), male lovers were encouraged as part of military training and discipline, an early acknowledgement of the close links between Ares and Eros. However – and this is crucial – homosexuality in Greece related closely to masculinity and it is important to grasp this perspective in order to understand its social role. The basic Greek homosexual relationship was between an older man (*erastes*) and a youth (*eromenos*). The older man admired the younger for his male qualities (beauty, strength, speed, skill, endurance) and the younger man respected the older for his experience, wisdom and command. The older man was expected to train, educate and protect the younger, and in due course the young man grew up and became the friend rather than the lover-pupil and sought out his own *eromenos*. In sex, the older man was expected to be the active partner, the youth the passive partner. Both males were expected in due course to marry females and father children.

Greek society was then genuinely bisexual but within strictly defined limits. Greek law permitted male prostitution but prohibited its practitioners from holding office. But Greek society very strongly disapproved of sexual relationships between men of the same age. This was deemed unnatural because it meant one of the men adopting a passive position, thereby betraying the masculinity which required him to take the active role. The equation of women, slaves and youths in the application of legal protection from sexual assault also indicates that these are the passive partners in sexual relationships. So long as a man retained the active role and his sexual partner was a woman (naturally inferior), a slave (unfree) or a youth (not yet a fully grown man), his masculinity was preserved. But the Greeks also developed a philosophy to regulate the sex drive. It was based on the ideas of moderation, decorum and self-mastery and involved what Michel Foucault called 'the principle of stylization of conduct for those who wished to give their existence the most graceful and accomplished form possible'.

In the Roman Empire, as in Greece, people were not categorized as heterosexual or homosexual. Male prostitution flourished, licensed by the state, and men might have sex with women, slaves, youths, or prostitutes without exciting adverse comment. What was crucial here was the maintenance of the culturally defined and socially sanctioned roles and characteristics of masculinity and femininity. This is why there was such disapproval of those emperors like Caligula and Nero who dressed up as women and took a passive role in homosexual relations and no such disapproval of the emperor Hadrian who enjoyed an idealized Greek-style teacher-pupil love affair with the youth Antinous, after whose death the grieving emperor named cities in his honour. There was hostility to the prostitution of youths of good family (for reasons of status and snobbery), to lesbianism (which involved women adopting the dominant male role), to the practice of *fellatio* (which involved total passivity), to promiscuity (which involved lack of decorum), and to effeminacy (which was a denial of virility).

The coming of Christianity changed all this, though there were in the Middle Ages distorted echoes of past practice in the tendency to equate homosexuality with effeminacy and to see homosexuality exclusively in terms of pederasty. There is a problem over terminology. The term 'homosexual' was unknown in the Middle Ages. The condition itself was not seen as innate. It was seen as an acquired habit. The terms used in the Middle Ages were sodomy and sodomite. Although this was often used to mean anal sex, it could also be applied to masturbation, bestiality and non-procreative sex in general, further evidence that the medieval mind understood only sexual practices as distinct from sexual orientation.

The question that we need to address is not what was the attitude of Christianity to homosexuality in principle – since it was clearly opposed to it – but how did Christianity believe that offenders should be dealt with. Christ had not outlined a comprehensive set of sexual ethics and is not recorded as encountering any homosexuals. But when he came upon an adulteress being stoned – and adultery was like homosexuality a capital offence in Old Testament law – he said: 'Let him who is without sin amongst you cast the first stone', and to the woman: 'Go thou and sin no more.' Forgiveness and understanding, then, rather than punishment was the message of Christ. But his attitude does not mean that he does not regard adultery as a sin. The abandonment of the sin is what he seeks. It seems reasonable to assume that his attitude to homosexuality would have been similar.

The early Church fathers developed the comprehensive code of sexual ethics that Christ himself had not provided. Clement, Jerome, Origen and Augustine laid down the principle that sex for any other purpose than procreation was a violation of nature. Such views were enshrined in the law once the Roman Empire adopted Christianity as its official religion. The great Byzantine law-maker, the Emperor Justinian (527–65), who viewed himself as God's vicegerent on earth, presided over the imposition of a far more rigorously moral law code than the pagan empire had enjoyed. Divorce by consent was banned, for instance, and as part of this moral clampdown the death penalty was imposed for homosexual acts. Justinian took a literal view of homosexual acts as a violation of nature which provoked nature to retaliate: 'because of such

135

nes there are famines, earthquakes and pestilences' he declared. This
ain was to return in the later Middle Ages when the succession
lisasters which overtook Christianity was attributed by popular
preachers and theologians directly to the prevalence of sodomy. Jean
Gerson (1363–1429), for instance, declared of sodomy:

> on account of this detested sin the world was once destroyed with
> a universal flood and the five cities of Sodom and Gomorrah were
> burned with a celestial fire so that their inhabitants descended
> live into hell. Likewise on account of this sin – which calls forth
> divine vengeance – famines, wars, plagues, epidemics, floods,
> betrayals of kingdoms, and many other disasters come more fre-
> quently as Holy Scripture testifies.

When the west was overrun by barbarian tribes, it passed out of the
jurisdiction of the Roman Empire. Their kingdoms were not on the
whole interested in legislating on moral matters and their attitude
to homosexuality remains somewhat obscure. The Carolingian rulers,
particularly the Emperor Charlemagne (771–814), who saw himself as
a western Justinian, were anxious to see the Church's moral rulings
implemented and so regularly issued denunciations of sins which they
defined as sacrilege and which included homosexuality, adultery, incest
and perjury. Such sins came under the jurisdiction of the Church, which
was regularly besought by the Carolingian rulers to raise the moral tone
of Christendom.

The Church's attitude to homosexuality in the early Middle Ages can
best be seen in the penitentials, the handbooks for confessors. The
penitential system was an institutionalization of Christ's commandment to 'go and sin no more'. It provided for penitent sinners a
chance to expiate their sin by mortifying the flesh, reflecting upon its
gravity and resolving not to commit it again. The penances varied
according to the age, status and sex of the offender and whether the
penitent was lay or clerical. Boswell maintains that the penitentials
suggest 'a relatively indulgent attitude towards homosexual behaviour'.
But Pierre Payer has demonstrated that every penitential has at least
one and frequently many canons censuring homosexual acts and with
striking consistency they impose their heaviest penance on sodomy.

One of the most influential of these works was the *Decretum* of
Burchard of Worms (*d*.1025), which drew on a number of previous
penitentials and on his own experience as a confessor. In the *Decretum*,
Burchard attempted to keep as close as possible to ordinary morality.
He imposed his highest penalty on sodomy and bestiality. There are
variations in different parts of the work reflecting the different sources
he was using. But in one place, in a section circulated separately, he
equated bestiality and sodomy. He declared that if it had been com-

mitted once or twice and the penitent was single, the excuse being 'that you had no wife to enable you to expend your lust', the penance was seven years of fasting and abstinence. If the penitent was married, the penance was ten years; if the offence was habitual, fifteen years. If the offender was a youth, the penance was a hundred days on bread and water. Elsewhere Burchard specifically distinguished between homosexual sodomy (ten years for a first offence, twelve years if habitual) and heterosexual sodomy (three years for adults, two years for boys). It is clear then that he regards homosexual sodomy as by far the most serious of sexual sins. But interestingly – and here he is in line with other penitentials – he regards other homosexual acts as far less serious. Mutual masturbation carried a penance of thirty days and interfemoral intercourse forty days, the same as challenging someone to a drinking bout or having sex with the wife during Lent. The most likely explanation of this discrepancy is that the act of penetration, the perverse imitation of procreative coitus, is what was being punished. The other activities were seen as variations of masturbation which at this time was very lightly punished and seems to have been seen as an inevitable boyish indiscretion or part of the sexual rough-and-tumble of randy unmarried young men.

The age of ecclesiastical reform and the upsurge of ascetic spirituality coupled with the revival of towns and of urban life heightened the general awareness of homosexuality and created the perception of a 'homosexual problem'. A distinctive gay subculture emerged in the towns and cities, with recognized meeting places like bath-houses and barber's shops and gay slang (a homosexual youth was known as a 'Ganymede'; homosexual activity was called 'The Game'; 'hunting' was the term applied to the activity now known as 'cruising'). The revival of interest in and study of classical texts as part of the twelfth-century renaissance inspired a flourishing genre of erotic love poetry addressed by males to other males and defences of boy-love, modelled on pagan Greek works. There is evidence of male prostitution in Italian cities and references to male brothels in Chartres, Orléans, Sens and Paris. Some Italian cities, particularly Venice and Florence, became notorious homosexual centres, so much so that in Germany pederasts were known as *Florenzer* (Florentines). By comparison, there was little evidence of homosexuality in the countryside.

Three groups were regularly said to be involved in homosexual activity. First, there was the nobility, particularly the young nobility. In the mid-eleventh century there were regular accusations of sexual misconduct against noble and royal circles, and homosexuality was one of the vices alleged to flourish at the courts of Robert, Duke of Normandy, and King William II of England, the sons of William the Conqueror. The same charge was made against the circle of friends of

William, son of Henry I, who went down in the White Ship disaster, thus, according to the chronicler Henry of Huntingdon, paying the price of sodomy. In the twelfth century John of Salisbury complained at the effeminacy of young courtiers, but he seems to have been influenced more by their long hair and peacock finery than anything else. There is evidence to suggest that Richard the Lionheart was homosexual.

The clergy, both secular and regular, were accused of indulging in homosexuality. The chronicler Fra Salimbene in the thirteenth century and St Catherine of Siena and Benvenuto of Imola in the fourteenth century claimed that the sin was common amongst clerics and scholars. There was gossip about what went on in monasteries and Walter Map preserves an authentic medieval 'saloon bar' joke. Hearing a story of St Bernard throwing himself on a dead boy and praying over him but failing to revive him, Walter quipped: 'Then he was the most unlucky of monks. I have never heard before now of a monk throwing himself upon a boy but always when the monk got up, the boy promptly got up too.' Sexual contact between monks was a very real fear for the authorities, close friendships between individual monks were frequently discouraged, and regulations introduced to reduce the danger of nocturnal encounters. *The Rule of the Master*, for instance, contained the provision that all monks were to sleep in the same room, with the abbot's bed in the middle, and *The Rule of St Benedict* prescribed that monks should sleep with their clothes on and a light should be kept burning in the dormitory.

Students were regularly accused of homosexuality. Paris University students were notorious for their involvement and the detailed evidence which has survived in the case of Arnaud of Verniolles, a priest accused of heresy and sodomy in 1323–4, shows that he had a succession of affairs with compliant teenage students. What is striking about these three groups is that they were, in the case of students and nobles, young men who were deferring marriage either for the sake of their studies or because of primogeniture, and in the case of clerics, taking a vow of celibacy. This suggests that the medieval popular perception of homosexuality was that it was something that occurred in the absence of women or marriage and that it was not an autonomous inclination. In some of these cases that analysis may well have been true. Homosexuality was also seen almost exclusively as a sin of the city, the court, and the upper and professional classes; but that is probably because it was most visible in those places and those classes. The court records of late medieval Venice show homosexuals existing in every age-group and every class: clerics and nobles, barbers and heralds, boatmen and servants, men and boys.

The twelfth and thirteenth centuries witnessed a number of crucial developments in the Church that were to lead to the introduction of more restrictive moral rules. As with the cases of prostitutes and lepers, Church, crown and urban communities took action to deal with the perceived problem of homosexuality against a background of general moral and spiritual reform. The Church initiated a drive to reform the lives of the priesthood, waging war on the sins of simony and marriage of clergy. Homosexuality among priests was inescapably a prime target of this campaign. Alongside this there was the Church's bid to take control of and promote the sacralized institution of marriage as the central lay institution in a civilized society. Homosexuality would be seen as a threat to that long-running campaign.

There was then an inevitable impulse towards tackling the problem of homosexuality and a number of developments in the twelfth and thirteenth centuries provided the means. Under the stimulus of the rediscovery of Roman law, a systematic and coherent code of Church law emerged to replace the fragmentary and sometimes contradictory set-up that had previously existed. Church courts and canon lawyers were able to turn with confidence to an authoritative body of legislation. The Fourth Lateran Council of 1215 established the machinery of the Inquisition for investigating moral offences and authorized the handing over of clerics and laymen, once condemned, to the secular authorities for punishment. It tightened the regulations for moral guidance and instruction, imposed an obligation of annual confession, and ordered regular investigations.

The thirteenth century also saw the development of the *Summae*, the systematic handbooks for confessors which superseded the sometimes contradictory and negotiable penitentials of the early Middle Ages. All of these developments pointed to the emergence of a harsher policy towards homosexuals and a move away from the philosophy underlying the early medieval treatment of the subject. The Papacy in the eleventh century had not given the highest priority to the pursuit of homo-sexuals, though the reform movement had produced a classic anti-homosexual text. *Liber Gomorrhianus* (The Book of Gomorrah), written between 1048 and 1054, was the first of St Peter Damian's works concerning clerical sexual abuses. Damian was a key figure in the reform movement and his book is unique in medieval Christian literature as 'the only continuous prose treatment of the various forms of homo-sexuality, the circumstances of clerical offences and the proposed meas-ures against such behaviour'. Peter saw it as a terrible and heinous sin:

> Truly this vice is never to be compared with any other vice because
> it surpasses the enormity of all vices. Indeed this vice is the
> death of bodies, the destruction of souls. It pollutes the flesh; it
> extinguishes the light of the mind. It evicts the Holy Spirit from

the temple of the human heart; it introduces the Devil who incites to lust. It casts into error; it completely removes the truth from the mind that has been deceived.... It opens hell, it closes the door of heaven.... This vice tries to overthrow the walls of the heavenly homeland and is busy repairing the renewed bulwarks of Sodom. For it is this which violates sobriety, kills modesty, strangles chastity and butchers irreparable virginity with the dagger of unclean contagion. It defiles everything, staining everything, polluting everything. And as for itself, it permits nothing pure, nothing clean, nothing other than filth.

Peter was concerned about the spread of homosexuality among the priesthood. He listed four variations: masturbation, mutual masturbation, interfemoral and anal intercourse. He specifically condemned priests who after engaging in homosexual activities confessed to each other in order to get minimal penance and priests who sinned with male penitents who had confessed their homosexuality. He advocated barring homosexual offenders from ever being priests and wanted the wholesale deposition of offenders from the priesthood.

Damian establishes a direct linkage between homosexuality, heresy, leprosy and the Devil. Like the Council of Ancyra (314), much quoted in the Middle Ages, he compares sodomy to leprosy. He likens himself to Ambrose denouncing the Arians, Augustine the Donatists and Manichaeans, and Jerome other heretical sects. He sees homosexuality as the result of demonic impulse.

But as interesting as Damian's writing of the book is the reaction of its dedicatee, Pope Leo IX. The Pope is careful to distance himself from its rigour. He declares that he would act 'more humanely' than Peter demands. He says that those guilty of solitary or mutual masturbation or interfemoral intercourse, if not long-term or promiscuous, could, if they curbed their desires and did appropriate penance, be readmitted to ecclesiastical rank. Those who could not be admitted were long-time and promiscuous sinners and those guilty of anal intercourse.

Archbishop Anselm of Canterbury took a similar view to that of Pope Leo in 1102. The Council of London, perhaps responding to the louche atmosphere of the Anglo-Norman court, sought to anathematize all homosexuals until they had confessed and done penance, and it imposed penalties; demotion for clerics, loss of civil rights for laymen. But Anselm suppressed this decree and wrote to the Archdeacon William advocating a gentler approach. He wanted the traditional policy of penance awarded according to age, marital status and the duration of the sin and urged that clerical sodomites be warned to desist from the practice and that sodomites not be admitted in future to the priesthood. The reason he gives for his policy is that hitherto 'the sin

has been so public that hardly anyone has blushed for it and many ...
have plunged into it without realizing its gravity'. It would be wrong
to interpret the view of St Anselm and Pope Leo as tolerance of
homosexuality. They were simply adopting a different strategy from
the rigorists for eradicating it. Theirs was a policy of differentiating
between occasional and habitual offenders and proceeding in a cautious
and traditional way rather than launching a punitive blitzkrieg. They
were in fact endorsing the viewpoint underlying Burchard's *Decretum*
which had distinguished sharply between sodomy and lesser homosexual offences and between minor and major offenders.

But if there were people unaware of the gravity of homosexuality in
the eleventh century, they would be left in little doubt about it by the
thirteenth century, as a wealth of literature appeared providing chapter
and verse from the Church fathers, Church councils, the New Testament
and the Old, to underline its heinousness. Gratian's *Decretum*, the
cornerstone of the new legal developments, took up Augustine's definition of sexual sins, distinguishing between natural sins (fornication,
adultery) and unnatural sins (homosexuality, bestiality). The *Summae*
elaborated on this basic position. Alain of Lille in his *Liber Poenitentialis*
(1199–1202) defined the sin against nature as expending one's seed
outside the proper vessel and proscribed masturbation, oral and anal
intercourse, bestiality, rape, incest and adultery as coming into this
category. In his *Sermons on Capital Sins* he equated sodomy and
homicide as the two most serious crimes and in his poem *The Complaint
of Nature* he defined happiness as the fulfilment of one's natural purpose
(procreation); since sodomy frustrated the conception of children, it
was therefore unnatural, sinful and conducive of unhappiness.

The Dominican and law professor Paul of Hungary in his *Liber
Poenitentialis* (1220) similarly defined the sin against nature as the
wasting of one's seed outside its normal vessel. It was worse than incest
because it violated Man's relationship with God. The sin against nature
(homosexuality, bestiality, unnatural heterosexual intercourse) caused
the destruction of Sodom and Gomorrah and the Great Flood. It
brought about starvation, pestilence and natural disasters because it
upset the natural order in sexual matters. It denied God's injunction
to be fruitful and multiply. The punishment was unequivocal. The
sodomite was consigned irredeemably to Hell. The causes of the sin
against nature, Paul thought, were too much food, too much drink,
and too much leisure, which led to luxury and self-indulgence. The
answer was prayer and fasting. This interpretation once again gives the
impression that homosexuality was regarded not as something innate
and inescapable but rather a habit deliberately taken up as an act of
defiance and wickedness. Indeed theologians reasoned that homosexuality would have to be voluntarily perverse since God would not

have given men unnatural leanings. William of Auvergne (*c.*1180–1249) in his *Summa de Poenitentia* declared that homosexuality led to leprosy and insanity, that it was linked with paganism and idolatry and that its practitioners were guilty of homicide (spilling their seed unproductively) and sodomy (placing it in an improper vessel). Caesarius of Heisterbach in his *Dialogue on Miracles* (1220–35) added a further warning about the dangers of wasting the seed. He claimed that demons regularly collected up the wasted human seed and fashioned it into the male and female bodies in which they appeared to torment and harass humankind.

St Albertus Magnus (1206–80) considered sodomy the worst sin against nature and he defined it as sex between man and man or between woman and woman. He demanded special punishment for it for four reasons: it proceeded from a burning frenzy that subverted the order of nature; the sin was distinguished by its disgusting foulness and was yet more likely to be found among persons of high degree than low; those who became addicted to such vices seldom succeeded in escaping them; such vices were as contagious as any disease.

The most systematic treatment of homosexuality was in St Thomas Aquinas' *Summa Theologiae* (*c.*1266). He saw it as an unnatural form of lechery because it could not lead to procreation. He agreed with St Augustine that the crime against nature was the worst sin, so that even unnatural sexual acts performed by mutual consent and harming no one were doing an injury to God. They violated the natural order prescribed by God. In ascending order of seriousness, the sins against nature were masturbation, unnatural intercourse with the opposite sex, homosexual intercourse and bestiality. These views were widely disseminated and if literature is any reflection of popular opinion, they prevailed in secular society. Chaucer regarded homosexuality as a primary sin and Dante consigned homosexuals to the Seventh Level of Hell along with the violent because they had violated the laws of Nature.

The twelfth and thirteenth centuries saw a decisive move away from the position outlined by Pope Leo IX for dealing with homosexuals as a much harsher and more rigorous policy was adopted by successive Church councils. The Council of Nablus held in the crusading kingdom of Jerusalem in 1120 made the ruling that the persistent adult male sodomite was to be burned by the civil authorities. This was the first time that this penalty had been invoked since the fall of the Roman Empire and it put homosexuals on a par with murderers, heretics, and traitors. Michael Goodich has plausibly suggested that the reason for this new severity was the fear of an upsurge of homosexuality because of the shortage of Christian women, contact with the Moslems (who were – according to Christian propaganda – addicted to pederasty), and the presence in the Holy Land of large numbers of Normans (already said to be tainted with the sin).

The Third Lateran Council of 1179 also dealt with homosexuality, and while it did not follow the harsh lead of the Council of Nablus, it gave clear evidence of a tightening of regulation by decreeing deposition and penance in monasteries for clerical sodomites, and excommunication for laymen. The Councils of Paris (1212) and Rouen (1214) repeated the canon and the 1215 Lateran Council ordered its strict enforcement. It was incorporated into the new collection of Papal decretals *Liber Extra*, produced for Pope Gregory IX in 1234. It was also Gregory IX who sent Dominican inquisitors to root out homosexuality in Germany, which he described as 'so ridden with unnatural vice ... that some parts, especially Austria, are thought of as if infected with the foulness of leprosy'. Further evidence of the seriousness with which it was regarded is the fact that by the late twelfth century homosexuality had been removed from the jurisdiction of the parish priests and had become a reserved crime, which only the bishop or his representative could deal with. In 1221 the Cistercians decreed the expulsion of convicted sodomites from the order and the Dominicans, the Carthusians, and the Cistercians all required the building of prisons to hold sodomites along with thieves, forgers, murderers, and incendiaries. Homosexuality became an inevitable concomitant of accusations of heresy and witchcraft. When Pope Gregory IX included in his bull *Vox in Rama* (1233) a description of the obscene initiation ceremonies of the heretics and witches discovered by Conrad of Marburg, he went on: 'When this ceremony is over the lights are put out and those present indulge in the most loathsome sensuality, having no regard to sex. If there are more men than women, men satisfy one another's depraved appetites, women do the same for each other.' Sodomy, bestiality and other unnatural crimes became an increasing part of witchcraft accusations from the fourteenth century onwards.

The next step was for secular law to take an interest in these matters. Until the twelfth century tribal and customary law prevailed in this area, though this tradition in fact left moral matters in the hands of the Church. By the thirteenth century the rediscovery of Roman law, envisaging a moral role for monarchical law-makers and imposing capital sentences, had made a marked impact on legislators. Roman law was seen by centralizing monarchs as an ideal way of imposing national uniformity and emphasizing the role of the monarch as the fount of justice by referring capital crimes to royal courts. Justinian's law code had prescribed public burning for homosexuals and this formed the model for the law codes introduced by the national monarchies. King Edward I of England (1272–1307) and King Louis IX of France (1226–70) decreed death by burning for homosexuals, and Alfonso X of Castile (1252–84), castration followed by hanging by the legs until dead. The Spanish punishment was changed to burning by King Ferdinand and Queen Isabella at the end of the fifteenth century. The exception to this general move was the Holy Roman Emperor Frederick II, whose Constitutions of Melfi (1231) banned heresy but were notable for the absence of restrictions on Jews, Moslems and homosexuals. Since his kingdom depended on the first two groups for its administration and since pederasty was popularly believed to be a feature of Moslem life, political considerations may have dictated the legal course.

The use of deviancy charges to dispose of enemies was a regular part of medieval politics, and sodomy was frequently linked with witchcraft and Devil-worship. In the first political trial to involve magic charges, Pope Boniface VIII was posthumously accused of heresy, simony, communion with demons and sodomy in 1310–11. But perhaps the most spectacular case involving sodomy charges was the trial of the Knights Templar. The Templars, a monastic order of knighthood founded shortly after the First Crusade, had retreated to France after the loss of the Holy Land in 1291. Owing obedience only to the Pope and based in their great fortress headquarters, the Temple in Paris, the Templars became 'a state within a state', wealthy, powerful, arrogant and increasingly unpopular. It was probably the order's wealth that attracted King Philip IV of France. Facing bankruptcy from the cost of his wars with England and Flanders, he had already debased the coinage, taxed the Church, milked his wealthiest subjects by forced loans, seized the assets of the Lombards and expropriated and expelled the Jews.

In 1307 Philip arrested the Templars and charged them with the grossest crimes imaginable – rejecting Christ and spitting on the cross, making false offerings to idols, adoring a cat (the usual image of the Devil), having obscene initiation rites that involved kissing the penis or anus of the Grand Master, and indulging in homosexual acts with each other on demand and with no possibility of refusal. So here we get the familiar equation of Devil-worship, heresy and sodomy. Thirty-six Templars died under torture; at least seventy-two more (including the Grand Master) who either refused to confess or, having confessed, recanted, were burned. Only three ever admitted to taking part in homosexual acts. Philip adroitly mobilized public opinion against the Templars and demanded that Pope Clement V suppress the order. The Council of Vienne (1311) voted against the dissolution of the order on the grounds that the charges were unproven but Clement, fearful of repercussions from France, went ahead and suppressed it anyway. Tribunals appointed to investigate the guilt of the Templars in countries outside France – England, Scotland, Portugal, Castile, Aragon, Cyprus and Germany – found them innocent or the case not proven. But the case contributed to the demonization of homosexuals.

Finally, the towns, coming under the puritanical and moralistic influence of the Mendicant Orders, moved to suppress homosexuality. The Mendicants campaigned consistently in the towns for the implementation of Christian morality and this involved the denunciation of gambling, drinking, prostitution and sodomy. These principles became an integral part of an emerging bourgeois mentality. Humbert of Romans, Master-General of the Dominicans, wrote to the brethren at Bologna, Mantua and Faenza in the mid-thirteenth century, urging them to concern themselves with heresy and 'that evil filth' sodomy. Town after town in the thirteenth and fourteenth centuries decreed death by burning or sometimes beheading and confiscation of property for habitual sodomites: Ancona, Belluno, Bergamo, Bologna, Cremona, Faenza, Florence, Lucca, Modena, Orvieto, Parma, Perugia, Reggio Emilia, Siena, Spoleto, Todi, Urbino. There were frequently lesser penalties for underage and irregular offenders, in order to encourage them to repent before it was too late. Perugia imposed heavy fines for the first two convictions and burning alive for the third. Todi fined offenders under 33 but burned those over 33. In Florence boy offenders under 16 were beaten and fined. This probably reflects the judgement that the young were naturally lustful and that marriage and maturity should settle them down. If they persisted in the offence as adults, they were then beyond redemption. But the extent of the desire to pursue homosexuals can be seen in the resolutions of the Siena Council in 1324 to appoint men to hunt out sodomites 'in order to honour the Lord, ensure true peace, maintain good morals and praiseworthy life of the people of Siena'. By the middle of the hirteenth century the instruments of sexual repression had been firmly established. The Inquisition and the lay confraternities associated with the Mendicant Orders became a means of persecuting heretics and sodomites.

Concern in the towns with the problem of homosexuality was exacerbated by the plague pandemic and the consequent decline in population. This was certainly the case in Florence where the problem was compounded by the fashion for men to marry late or not at all, partly because of the high cost of dowries and weddings, and where, according to contemporary commentators, young men were becoming feminized by virtue of being raised by their mothers or within exclusively female environments. There also seems to have been a fashionable affectation of homosexual conduct, inspired by admiration for Greek classical texts which was a feature of the burgeoning Florentine Renaissance. Popular poetry satirized the alleged propensity for sodomy of Florentine youth and it became a recurrent theme of preachers.

In 1415 a series of treatises condemning the Florentine addiction to sodomy was published by clerics and the Office of Decorum was set up to police public morals. One of its tasks was the establishment and staffing of a municipal brothel, which would wean young Florentine males away from sodomitic practices. In 1432 the Office of the Night was set up to suppress 'the vice which cannot be named'. A rising scale of fines from 50 to 500 florins was instituted for the first four offences, followed by burning for the fifth. A qualitative transformation has also been observed in the nature of Florentine court cases involving homosexuality. In the fourteenth century, a sampling of cases has revealed that they are exclusively concerned with homosexual rape. But after 1432 homosexual lovers are being arrested. Court documents list the duration of homosexual relationships and the cases show habitual offenders naming their lovers. In 1461–2 a silk weaver and a ragman respectively named nine and eight of their lovers. The same offenders were also regularly being rounded up and the evidence suggests a definite drive to extirpate the sin.

All this activity needs to be set firmly against the background of continual preaching against sodomy by the leading preachers of the day. The most notable was St Bernardino of Siena (1380–1444), the Franciscan who regularly drew huge crowds and who, with the encouragement of the government, thundered against the practice of homosexuality. He claimed that Florence was worse than Sodom and Gomorrah, that Tuscany had the lowest population in the world because of it and that the stench of homosexuality caused the plague that Florence suffered from. He took up the same refrain in Siena, declaring that if he had sons he would send them abroad from the time they were three until they were at least forty because this was the age of vulnerability to homosexuality. He blamed parental indulgence, provocative fashions, failure to go to confession or communion and the study of the classics, exalting eroticism, paganism, and pederasty, for the prevalence of the sin:

> I have heard of some boys who paint their cheeks and go about boasting of their sodomy and practice it for gain.... It is largely their mothers' and fathers' fault for not punishing them, but especially the mothers, who empty their purses without asking where the money came from. And it is a grave sin to make them a doublet that reaches only to the numbril and hose with one small patch in front and one behind, so that they show enough flesh to the sodomites. You spare the cloth and expend the flesh!

Sodomy made its practitioners prone to envy, jealousy and discontent. It destroyed their energy and moral fibre:

> He may be a young man of rare talents, one of great intelligence, fit to perform marvels, but once he has been corrupted by sodomy,

146

he turns into the Devil's creature. He rejects all natural good things, all thoughts of God, of the state, of his family, his business, his honour, his very soul ... he thinks only about evil matters.

Sodomites must be removed from society. 'As refuse is taken out of the houses, so as not to infect it, so wicked men should be removed from human commerce by prison or by death.' The sin must be burned out of society. 'To the fire!' thundered St Bernardino at this congregation. 'They are all sodomites!' And you are in mortal sin if you seek to help them.' Adult and adolescent confraternities were established in Florence to combat civic decline and disorder, with homosexuality as a cause for expulsion and St Bernardino helped both Siena and Perugia in 1425 to frame new and harsher law codes to deal with moral failings, including death at the stake for persistent sodomites.

A similarly serious view of the threat from sodomy was taken in Venice. There it was deemed to be a practice which could undermine the basic organization of society – the family, male/female bonding and reproduction. According to Venetian rhetoric, it was the sin which had caused God to destroy Sodom and Gomorrah and bring down the Great Flood. Preachers inevitably blamed the onset of the Black Death on it.

There was a recognizable and well-defined homosexual subculture in Venice, centred on apothecary shops, gymnasia, pastry shops, schools, indeed anywhere that young men gathered and where there was gaming, drinking and all-male company. The clergy were also implicated. In 1408 the authorities complained to the Pope that efforts to eliminate sodomy were hampered by the clergy who either escaped punishment altogether or were leniently dealt with by the courts. There is clear evidence of extensive involvement by clerics and monks in homosexual activity. The Augustinians apparently presented a particular problem and in 1422 their Vicar-General decreed life-time imprisonment on bread and water for Augustinian sodomites.

Masturbation was not prosecuted in Venice and was seen as fairly normal among males, though not of course approved of. Sodomy was defined as homosexual acts, anal intercourse with women and bestiality. By the mid-fifteenth century anal penetration of boys and women was regarded as so serious that a regulation was passed in 1467 insisting that doctors, barbers and other healers report anal injuries to the authorities so as 'to eliminate the vice of sodomy from this our city'.

Venice took the view that the passive partner was less guilty and so the active partner was punished. The passive partner was often younger and male children under 14 were below the legal age of prosecution. The active partner was deemed the most responsible and the most culpable in part because he retained his masculinity, whereas the passive partner forfeited his by virtue of his playing the female role in sex.

Sometimes male lovers claimed to have forced themselves on their partners in order to save the partner from the rigours of the law: a touching echo of a devotion reaching out to us from the surviving court records.

There was a dramatic rise in sodomy prosecutions in Venice in the fifteenth century. There were nine convictions in the period 1348–68 but this had risen to 110 in the period 1448–69. Venetians outside Venetian territory had previously been beyond the reach of the law. But from 1420 it was declared that anyone committing sodomy on a Venetian ship was to be punished as if committing the offence on Venetian soil. In the 1450s a sodomy census was held with two nobles from each parish detailed to spend a year investigating the incidence of sodomy in their neighbourhoods. In 1444 the authorities ruled that no masters of arts were to hold classes after sunset for fear of homosexual activities, a decree repeated in 1477 with the aim of 'eliminating this abominable vice that we are told is committed daily and publicly in this our city'. In Venice as in Florence, homosexuals had become scapegoats for both the plague and population decline and were clearly seen to be outraging the newly established Mendicant-influenced code of bourgeois respectability. How far homosexuals were prosecuted in other areas is not as yet entirely clear. London court records, for instance, show a remarkably low incidence of cases. Only one out of 21,000 defendants before the London Church courts was charged with sodomy between 1420 and 1518.

What caused the rise of anti-homosexual feeling from the twelfth century onwards? Boswell points to two related phenomena. First, there was the xenophobia stirred up by the crusades. Anti-Moslem propaganda stressed the prevalence of homosexuality among the Moslems and highlighted stories of homosexual atrocities against Christians, children, and clerics. The forged 'Appeal of the Eastern Emperor' for aid to save the Holy Land, circulating in the west to whip up support for the First Crusade, stressed the ravishing of Christian virgins and the sodomizing of men and boys of every rank. Jacques de Vitry in his *Oriental History* even alleged that the prophet Mohammed had popularized sodomy among his people. Sodomy was also associated with heresy and this seems equally significant. The celibacy of the Cathar *perfects* gave rise to persistent rumours that they refrained only from sex with women and had sex with each other instead. The Cathar maxim 'if all things are forbidden, then all things are permissible' was taken as a justification for promiscuity and sodomy. Other heretical groups were subject to similar accusations and in some cases the accusations stuck. Since the two greatest threats to Christendom were perceived to be Islam without and heresy within and since both were associated with sodomy, homophobia received a powerful boost.

Equally important is the puritanism of the evangelical revival of the eleventh and twelfth centuries, which inspired systematic attempts to define and deal with sins and increased concern to police the moral lives of both clergy and laity. As a homosexual subculture became more visible in the expanding cities, so Church, crown and municipal authorities, strongly influenced both by Roman law and the spirituality preached by the Mendicant Orders, moved in to suppress it. These attempts were intensified by the onset of the plague in the mid-fourteenth century, both for the practical reason of population decline and the moral reason that God was punishing people for the prominence of sodomy.

For all the invaluable illumination that Boswell's book throws on the subject of attitudes to and the practice of homosexuality in the Middle Ages, his two principal theses seem to me to be contrary to the evidence. Christianity was fundamentally hostile to homosexuality. What changed in the Middle Ages was not a move from tolerance to intolerance for reasons not intrinsic to Christian belief but an alteration in the means of dealing with it. In the early Middle Ages, the punishment was penance; in the later Middle Ages, burning. But there was never any question of homosexuals being allowed to carry on with homosexual activity unpunished. They were obliged to give it up or risk damnation.

8

LEPERS

There is perhaps no disease in history which has given rise to such fear
and loathing as leprosy. The very term 'leper' has become a synonym
for outcast. In the Middle Ages this reaction arose in part from the
physical deformities, suppurating sores and noxious odour caused by
the disease. But even more it derived from the certain knowledge that
leprosy was the outward and visible sign of a soul corroded by sin and
in particular by sexual sin.

It is now known that leprosy is a contagious disease caused by the
bacillus *Mycobacterium Leprae*, which is related to the tuberculosis
bacterium. It is spread through personal contact, abrasions and insect
bites. It has a lengthy incubation period, sometimes running into years,
and there is a high natural resistance to it. This natural resistance can
be seriously undermined by poor diet, bad housing and unhealthy living
conditions; hence the incidence of the disease in under-developed areas
like medieval Europe and the present-day Third World. The disease
emerged in both high and low resistance forms. Low resistance leprosy
is characterized by lumps and patches on the skin, which develop into
sores; damage to the eyes, resulting in blindness; hoarseness of the voice
as the throat is affected. High resistance means that the skin is not
seriously disfigured but the nervous system is damaged, muscles are
paralysed and feeling is lost. Limbs become deformed and the mutilation of fingers and toes frequently occurs.

Today leprosy can be cured; in the Middle Ages it was incurable. The
influential fourteenth-century physician and medical writer Guy de
Chauliac recorded: 'It is agreed by all that leprosy is a very injurious
disease ... and is almost impossible to eradicate.' Although there was
an attempt to divide leprosy into types, based on an imbalance of the
humours, earth, air, fire and water, this did not relate to the variations
in the disease now recognized and for the most part 'leprosy' was one
of the Middle Ages' catch-all terms like 'scrofula' and 'putrid fever',
covering a multitude of conditions. It was difficult in the early stages
to distinguish between genuine leprosy and a wide variety of other skin

conditions, notably impetigo, psoriasis, dermatitis, Raynaud's disease, scabies and fungal infections. Given the poor hygiene and diet endemic in the period, skin infections were quite common. But usually they did not lead to the physical deformities characteristic of leprosy proper.

Medieval medical writers relied far more on tradition than on observation, drawing principally on the work of the great Arab physicians who in their turn borrowed from the Greeks. So it was often antique wisdom that was being handed on from generation to generation, a set of medical and physiological principles unquestioned until the sixteenth century. Nevertheless, it did contain elements of truth and individual details were modified by medical experience. When, for instance, Bartholomaeus Anglicus lists as the causes of leprosy association with other lepers, the bite of a venomous worm, rotten food and drink, hereditary infection, sexual intercourse with infected women and polluted air, he touches on some of the means of infection identified by modern knowledge (prolonged physical contact with other lepers, insect bites, poor diet).

For someone to be identified as a leper, the normal procedure was formal denunciation, usually by neighbours, and then an investigation. In the early Middle Ages, this was undertaken under the auspices of the Church authorities. But as the towns and cities grew and developed the machinery for self-regulation in the Central Middle Ages, the procedure was often taken over by local magistrates. In the early Middle Ages there was no guarantee that a doctor would be involved. Sometimes it was clergymen, at other times gatekeepers and policemen who were familiar with a wide variety of travellers. In a few places the inmates of the local leper hospital were called on to pronounce on the case. But increasingly it became a matter for doctors. They would look for the signs.

Guy de Chauliac listed the infallible signs of leprosy: a rounding of the eyes; loss of hair, particularly of eyebrows and eyelashes; growth of patches and pustules on the head; dilation of the nostrils; thickening of the lips; a raucousness of voice; fetid breath and horrible body odour; and the fixed look and horrible leer of the satyr. Equivocal signs, which might also apply to other diseases included muscle wasting, insensitivity to pain, retraction of limbs.

Because there was great danger of committing someone wrongly to a leper hospital and doctors wanted to be certain their diagnosis was correct, Guy de Chauliac prescribed four alternative procedures for investigators: to clear the subject and issue a certificate to that effect; to admonish them to live a healthier life because of the danger of contracting the disease; to confine them to their houses if showing early symptoms; or to separate them from society in a leper hospital if the signs were indisputable. Both Bernard of Gordon and John of Gaddesden also exhorted doctors to defer the seclusion of patients in hospitals until the evidence of the leprous distortion of limbs and appearance was clear and indisputable.

There is some evidence to suggest that most of the lepers in the hospitals were genuine leprosy sufferers. The vast majority of the skeletons buried in the leper cemetery at Naestved in Denmark, excavated in 1957, reveal the characteristic deformations of the bones whereas excavations in general cemeteries have revealed few such skeletons. The much smaller South Acre leper cemetery in Norfolk similarly yielded an overwhelming preponderance of genuine leper skeletons.

Leprosy was no respecter of persons and it could strike down the highest in the land as well as the lowest. King Baldwin IV of Jerusalem and King Magnus II of Norway, Abbot Richard of St Albans and Bishop Aelfweard of London, Count Thibaut VI of Chartres, and Count Raoul of Vermandois are all said to have died lepers, though it is possible that some of them suffered from venereal disease rather than leprosy proper. The chivalric order of St Lazarus was founded in 1120 in the Holy Land to accommodate leper knights and to look after other lepers. They attended the leper King Baldwin IV (1160–84).

It used to be believed that leprosy was introduced into western Europe at the time of the Crusades as a result of increased contact with the east, where it was endemic. But there is clear evidence of its existence in western Europe before the Crusades. Leper skeletons dating from the seventh century have been found in the Scilly Isles and Cambridgeshire. The disease is referred to in seventh-century Lombard laws, eighth-century Frankish laws, tenth-century Irish chronicles and Welsh laws, and eleventh-century Norwegian laws. They almost all include provisions for the segregation of victims of the disease, a procedure that goes back to the Bible.

Chapters 13 and 14 of Leviticus were devoted entirely to the identification of the disease and its ritual treatment. Sufferers from the disease were deemed to be ritually 'unclean' and could not therefore enter holy places. Although it is making a ritual distinction between cleanliness and uncleanliness, there is a clear implication of the fear of infection in the Biblical pronouncement (Leviticus 13 vv. 45–6):

> The leper, in whom the plague is, his clothes shall be rent, and his head bare, And he shall put a covering upon his upper lip, and shall cry, unclean, unclean. And the days wherein the plague shall be in him he shall be defiled; he is unclean; he shall dwell alone; without the camp shall be his habitation.

The segregation from others and the covering of the mouth to prevent the emission of the infected breath which was believed to spread the disease are hygienic as much as religious procedures. The washing and cleansing procedures also have a hygienic value. Only when the priest can presume the disease gone and appropriate sacrifices and rituals have been performed can the sufferer rejoin the community. These basic ideas (segregation, infected breath) remained standard throughout the Middle Ages.

The fear of the disease was based in particular on its contagion. The idea, once held, that medieval man had no idea of infection is wrong. He may not have understood how it worked, but the passage of infection from one person to another by handling items touched by the sick person, by sexual contact, by breathing in infected breath were all well-established ideas. The very precise nature of the regulations governing leper colonies attached to healthy monasteries demonstrates how far-reaching were the fears. The lepers were not permitted to touch food supplies intended for the monks. They were not allowed to walk about bare-foot with their ulcerated feet touching the places where monks would tread. They were not allowed to boil their dressings during the preparation of food. They were not allowed to draw water from the wells because of fear of their infecting the well-ropes with their hands.

The conventional view of the disease is that the incidence of leprosy increased to epidemic proportions from the eleventh century onwards and continued at a high level until the fourteenth century when it declined again. But this view is based almost entirely on the increased expressions of concern in the sources and the evidence of the foundation of leper hospitals. In the areas which have been studied in detail, England, Paris, Normandy, the Pas-de-Calais for instance, there is a similar pattern of rapid rise in foundations in the twelfth and thirteenth centuries and dramatic decline in the fourteenth century. But all this may have been due to changing social circumstances and altered perceptions rather than a response to an epidemic.

It has been estimated from the number of leprosaria in England that there were no more than 2,000 lepers in institutions at any one time out of a population of around three million. There will have been lepers not in institutions too. But W. H. McNeill in his book *Plagues and Peoples* estimates that there were something in the order of 19,000 leprosy sufferers in Europe in the Central Middle Ages out of a population of some 60–70 million. It is on nothing like the scale of the Black Death for instance, which killed off at least a third of the population of Europe.

So what accounts for the increased concern? In the late twelfth century three leprosaria were founded in Toulouse, the first such institutions seen in the city. Four more were founded in the early thirteenth century, making seven in all. They were mainly the result of charitable action by individuals. The average number of inmates of such houses was around ten, suggesting facilities for some seventy lepers at a time when the population of Toulouse was 20–25,000.

The growth in the number of leprosaria was matched by the growth in the number of general hospitals – five new ones added in the early thirteenth century to the existing seven. J. H. Mundy suggests that the growth of facilities matched the growth in population, the increase in the power and independence of the city, and the development of religious sentiments which encouraged charitable foundation. It seems not unlikely that these reasons could be applied generally.

There probably was an increase in the number of lepers in society proportionate with the rise in population. But with increased social mobility and the growth of towns and cities, which served as magnets for the deracinated, they will also have become more visible. The growth of charitable foundations to cater for them can be seen as an aspect of the development of religious individualism, allowing for a potent personal expression of piety, and as a positive response to the newly articulated teaching of the Church on wealth. Its acquisition was justified if it was spent on charitable activity.

The perception of a problem caused those authorities which were developing enhanced regulatory instincts and practices – the Church, the crown, the municipalities – to step in to deal with it. The Church moved first at the Third Lateran Council in 1179, presided over by Pope Alexander III. It is often said that this Council ordered the segregation of lepers. But this is an over-simplification. It was authorizing the provision for lepers of special chapels, chaplains, and cemeteries at their places of seclusion and exempting them from paying tithes on their produce and animals. But it assumed rather than introducing the process of segregation. 'Lepers cannot live with those not so afflicted and cannot assemble with them in the church' said the decree of the Council, merely repeating a statement of fact long enshrined in law and custom. But the necessity of making special provision for the excluded signals a recognition by the Church that increasing numbers of lepers were being segregated and were in need of facilities for worship.

Thereafter the Church developed a coherent and continuous programme of action to ensure effective segregation. A Church council held in southern France in 1368 summarized its teachings in these matters:

Because the illness is contagious, wishing to prevent danger, we command that lepers be sequestered from the rest of the faithful; that they do not enter any public place – churches, markets, public squares, inns; that their clothing be uniform, their beards and hair shaved; they shall have a special burial place and shall always carry a signal by which one can recognize them.

The requirement of distinctive dress brought lepers into line with Jews, prostitutes, and reformed heretics. But the nature of the distinctive clothing varied from place to place. In some places they were expected to dress in white, in others to wear a piece of red material on their clothing. In France, they were supposed to wear grey or black embroidered with the letter L. Individual leper hospitals sometimes had distinctive uniforms for their inmates. In illustrations, lepers are frequently seen wearing ankle-length tunics and cowled hoods. They were often required to wear gloves, further evidence of the fear of contagion. But more significant and universal than their dress was the signal, the rattle, bell or horn, with which they were required to announce their approach. All of this symbolized the leper as a member of a distinctive minority group, a person apart.

Even more symbolic of their separation from society was the formal ceremony of seclusion, by which they wee pronounced dead to the world. This developed in the twelfth and thirteenth centuries. Initially the ceremony involved the leper actually standing in an open grave and having three shovels of earth thrown at him. But this became more symbolic in most places. It was an awesome occasion. The leper would be led by the priest to the church. He would be sprinkled with holy water and would make his confession. He would kneel beneath a black cloth supported by trestles while the priest said mass. Then either inside the church or outside, the priest would sprinkle three spades full of earth, either on his feet or on his head, declaring: 'Be thou dead to the world, but alive again unto God.' Then the leper would be led out into the fields and the priest would conclude with the set of prohibitions:

I forbid you ever to enter churches or go into a market, or a mill, or a bakehouse, or into any assemblies of people. Also I forbid you ever to wash your hands or even any of your belongings in spring or stream of water of any kind; and if you are thirsty you must drink water from your cup or some other vessel. Also I forbid you ever henceforth to go out without your leper's dress, that you may be recognized by others; and you must not go outside your house unshod. Also I forbid you, wherever you may be, to touch anything which you wish to buy, otherwise than with a rod or staff to show what you want. Also I forbid you ever henceforth to enter taverns or other houses if you wish to buy wine; and take care even that what they give you they put into your cup. Also I forbid you to have intercourse with any woman except your own wife. Also I command you when you are on a journey not to return an answer to anyone who questions you, till you have gone off the road to leeward, so that he may take no harm from you; and that you never go through a narrow lane lest you should meet someone.

Also I charge you if need require you to pass over some toll-way ... or elsewhere, that you touch no posts or things whereby you cross, till you have first put on your gloves. Also I forbid you to touch infants or young folk, whosoever they may be, or to give to them or to others any of your possessions. Also I forbid you henceforth to eat or drink in any company except that of lepers. And know that when you die you will be buried in your own house, unless it be, by favour obtained beforehand, in the church.

This set of prohibitions applied whether the leper was retiring to his own house in seclusion or a house outside the community or a leper hospital. It clearly recognizes that he may have to emerge in order to obtain supplies and in some places lepers were allowed into towns on special purposes. In Paris they were allowed out of the hospitals once a week to beg. But the ritual is seeking to minimize the danger to the public of such appearances. The formal exclusion from society deprived the leper of his civil rights. He became a non-person, unable to bequeath or inherit property, to bring court cases etc., though the church regularly reiterated that leprosy was not a cause for the dissolution of marriage.

Lepers could not be admitted to ordinary hospitals and funding leper hospitals therefore came to be seen as a notable act of charity. They were under the control of the Church, which ran them on monastic lines. The aim was for the leper to prepare himself spiritually for the next world. Many of the leper hospitals were dedicated to St Lazarus, hence the terms lazar and lazar-house for leper and leper hospital. The Biblical Lazarus, raised from the dead by Christ, had come traditionally to be seen as a leper, though there was no scriptural authority for the view. In Scandinavia and Germany, many hospitals were dedicated to St George, his dragon being symbolically interpreted as the disease.

In England, over 200 leper houses were founded in the Central Middle Ages. They were – following Leviticus – always outside towns and away from centres of activity. They ranged in size from large ones, holding a hundred inmates, to small ones, holding about ten. The two earliest in England were St Bartholomew's in Rochester and St Nicholas' at Harbledown, founded before 1100. By 1150 there were leper hospitals at Lincoln, Norwich, Colchester, Newark, Oxford, Northampton, Newcastle, Warwick, Peterborough, Lancaster, Dover, Whitby, St Alban's, Bury St Edmunds, York and Wilton. The will of King Louis VIII of France, who died in 1226, bequeathed a hundred *solidi* to each of 2,000 leper hospitals in his kingdom. The population of France was four times that of England but whether the discrepancy in numbers of leper-houses between England and France represents a difference in size of the leper population or merely the fact that there were more charitably disposed people in France is impossible to say. Most of the cities in Italy founded leper hospitals outside the walls in the twelfth and thirteenth centuries.

Rules in hospitals varied and the provision for the inmates did also. The leper hospital at Sherburn, founded in 1181 by the Bishop of Durham, provided for up to sixty-five lepers. Males and females were to be kept separate. Each inmate was to receive one loaf of bread and one gallon of beer a day. They were to have meat three days a week, fish four days a week. They were to be given fuel for fires, an uninterrupted water supply, and cloth for clothing, either white or rust-coloured. At various times of the year, according to the season, they were to have eggs, butter, cheese, apples, and beans. They were to have a chaplain to minister to them; friends and servants were permitted to visit them. They were to have their clothes washed twice a week and utensils once a week. Disobedience or breaking of the rules would be met by beating, confinement on bread and water, or ultimately expulsion from the house. The well-endowed leper-houses generally supplied food, clothing, baths, and fires; but many were small with insecure incomes and the provision was less generous. There was also class distinction in the treatment of lepers. The wealthy could arrange seclusion in their own houses or in buildings in the grounds of the leprosaria. Some leper hospitals, Walsingham and Noyon for instance, were reserved for the lepers of good family.

Although it presided over their exclusion from society, the Church taught that lepers should be treated with compassion. It promoted the idea that lepers were in a sense specially favoured by God because he was enabling them to suffer in this life as Christ had suffered. One of the rituals of separation included the words: 'Our Lord gives you a great gift when he wishes to punish you for the evil you have done in this world.' Lepers were therefore sometimes referred to as 'the poor of Christ' (*pauperes Christi*) or just 'the Christians' (*Christiani*) in reference to this emulation of Jesus.

But the Church was never able to overcome the instinctive loathing of lepers that most people carried with them. One of the special marks of sanctity that the Church recognized was love for and care of lepers. Stories of saints tending, washing and kissing lepers are part of the hagiographic folklore of the Middle Ages. Particularly associated with the care of lepers were St Catherine of Siena, St Francis of Assisi, St Elizabeth of Thuringia, St Hedwig of Neumarkt, St Hugh of Lincoln and the Blessed Mary of Oignies, many of them, interestingly, twelfth-century saints. But this is a backhanded recognition of the popular sentiment of fear and revulsion. It is the very loathsomeness of the disease that confirms the sanctity of the saint in tackling it.

The compassion of the saint for the leper was a recurrent theme in

157

medieval art. Fifteenth-century Italian paintings highlight the charity of St Martin, St Peter and St John to lepers and German paintings celebrate the involvement of St Elizabeth of Thuringia with lepers. The painters show complete familiarity with the classic symptoms of leprosy: the deformation and ulceration of the bodies, the loss of noses, fingers, and eyesight and the rounded condition of the eyes.

Like the Church, the secular authorities took steps to ensure the seclusion of lepers from the midst of society. Municipal records show regular orders excluding lepers from towns and cities. Italian city-states took powers to exclude lepers and instructed gatekeepers to watch out for them. During the thirteenth century Padua, Bologna, Modena, Vicentia, Ferrara, Treviso and Ivrea all took such action. In 1300 Venice ordered all the lepers who were 'hanging about in churches, on bridges and in public thoroughfares and infecting air' to be rounded up and placed in hospitals.

The crown also intervened at a time when the monarchy was becoming increasingly conscious of its role as enforcer of public order, public health and public decency. In England a writ *de leproso amovendo* appeared as early as 1220, authorizing the expulsion of lepers on account of the danger of contagion. This could be applied for in the courts. In 1346 King Edward III issued an order excluding lepers from London, stressing not only the danger of contagion in general but of sexual contagion specifically:

> Forasmuch, as we have been given to understand, that many persons, as well of the city aforesaid, as others coming to the said city, being smitten with the blemish of leprosy, do publicly dwell among the other citizens and sound persons, and there continually abide; and do not hesitate to communicate with them, as well in public places as in private; and that some of them, endeavouring to contaminate others with that abominable blemish (that so, to their own wretched solace, they may have the more fellows in suffering) as well as in the way of mutual communications, and by the contagion of their polluted breath, as by carnal intercourse with women in stews and other secret places, detestably frequenting the same, do so taint persons who are sound, both male and female, to the great injury of people dwelling in the city aforesaid and the manifest peril of other persons to the same city resorting.

They are ordered out within fifteen days and commissions are to be set up to examine suspects for signs of the disease.

But in 1375 the gatekeepers of London were being instructed by the city council to forbid entry to the city to lepers and to arrest them if they tried to enter. In 1376 lepers were forbidden to beg in the streets and a date was fixed for the departure of lepers and beggars alike. The recurrence of the instructions suggests widespread ignoring of the regulations about the presence of lepers. The same situation seems to have obtained in Paris. In 1371 King Charles V of France complained about the number of lepers roaming freely in the capital. King Charles VI ordered lepers to stay out of Paris in 1404 and again in 1413. The Provost of Paris issued orders forbidding lepers to enter the city in 1388, 1394, 1402, 1403, 1488 and 1502. All this evidence makes it perfectly clear that all the lepers were not confined in leper-houses and many wandered about begging for their subsistence. In France there was a category of people known as *cagots*, who were officially classed as lepers but not confined to institutions. They were, however, deemed to be outcasts. There is some debate about the meaning of the term but the most likely interpretation is that *cagot* is a slang word meaning dirty or unclean. It seems likely that these were people suffering either from the early stages of milder forms of the disease or from other leprosy-like complaints, none of which presented the symptoms in sufficiently convincing a way to enable physicians to commit them. It is a term also that was applied both to vagabonds and to remote rural populations. In either case they were supposed to keep away from healthy people.

Church, crown, and municipalities were equally concerned with the problem of contagion. But it is also clear that this contagion had a moral as well as a medical connotation. The link between leprosy and sin was as old as the disease. But this is likely to have been understood. For elsewhere in the Bible, leprosy is sent as a punishment for sin to Uzziah, Miriam, Azariah and Gehazi. Hebrew commentators on Leviticus gave a variety of causes for leprosy: idol worship, gross unchastity, bloodshed, profanity, blasphemy, robbing the public, illegally usurping a dignity, overweening pride, evil speech, the evil eye. So they made it clear that the disease resulted from sin. The Hebrew tradition carried over into Christianity and when the Bible was translated into Greek and Latin, the words used for 'unclean' – *akathartos* and *immundus* – did have moral connotations.

The excessive desire for sex had been associated with the disease by the ancient writers. It could be seen in lepers' faces; hence Guy de Chauliac's reference to the look of the satyr as one of the signs. Medieval writers made no distinction between leprosy and venereal disease, regarding the two as interchangeable, and although syphilis was unknown in medieval Europe, other sexually transmitted diseases, involving skin conditions, were known. It is understandable then that sexual intercourse should be seen as one of the causes of leprosy. 'If you have sex with lepers you will be leprous' stated an anonymous fifteenth-century treatise flatly, summing up the conventional medical wisdom. It was for this reason that lepers were generally banned from brothels and bath-houses.

This link between leprosy and sex had the effect of reinforcing the generally held view of the inferiority and potential immorality of women. Even more it labelled women as a potential source of infection. For it was generally held that sexual intercourse with a menstruating woman could lead to leprosy and that if a woman had intercourse with a leper, she would be spared the disease but would pass it on to the next man with whom she had sex. These beliefs served to reinforce the Church's prohibitions on certain forms of sexual activity.

Medieval commentators and popular preachers regularly defined leprosy as the punishment for moral failure and in particular sexual sin. The poets regularly, though not invariably, linked leprosy with lust. Pride and vainglory, defiance of the laws of God and the Church, were also invoked as causes. In Harmann von Aue's poem *Poor Heinrich* (*c.*1195), the knight Heinrich is punished for his pride with leprosy sent by God. But more typical were Eilhart von Oberge's *Tristram and Isolde* and Béroul's *The Romance of Tristram*, two twelfth-century romances. In them the leader of a band of lepers suggests handing the adulterous Isolde to them for punishment, so that they can all rape her and thus destroy her with sex. 'Give us Iseult and let us have her in common. The sickness arouses our lust,' says the leper leader in Béroul. Here destruction by leper lust is seen as a symbolic punishment for the breaking of vows.

The association of leprosy with lust became deeply ingrained in the public consciousness. As Saul Brody, who has made the most thorough study of leprosy in medieval society, writes:

> The Jewish exegetes state that leprosy can be a punishment for gross unchastity, public edicts warn that lepers frequent houses of prostitution and medical writers observe both that the disease can be venereal in origin and that it excites sexual desire. Thus the connection between leprosy and carnality is ubiquitous in medieval culture and the religious, medical and popular understandings of leprosy influence and reinforce each other.

The segregation and exclusion of lepers by the authorities then must also be seen in terms of a desire to isolate a living symbol of lust and promiscuity from society at large and to prevent it infecting that society with its rampant sexuality.

Whatever the scale of the disease in the twelfth and thirteenth centuries, there does seem to have been a decline in its incidence in the fourteenth century. This decline can most probably be explained by an improvement in bodily resistance by the population and by an increase in the frequency of tubercular infection, driving out the leprosy bacillus, after the Black Death. The Black Death itself is likely to have wiped out the most unhealthy elements in the population, thus improving the stock. There may have been some improvement in diet with greater intake of vitamin C. The Black Death also led to improvements in public health provision, the establishment of public health boards with sweeping powers, and the greater professionalization of medicine.

As early as 1342 the leper hospital at Ripon reported that no more inmates were being admitted and the funds were being diverted to provide dole for the general poor. In 1348 the large leper hospital at St Alban's had only two or three inmates. The number of inmates at Harbledown fell from a hundred in 1276 to only a handful in 1371. By 1361 the leper hospitals of St John and St Leonard at Aylesbury were in ruins. At Rheims, in the twelfth and thirteenth centuries the hospital of St Lazarus had beds for eight lepers. By 1336 only one was occupied; in the fifteenth and sixteenth centuries it was frequently completely empty. In 1351 the number of lepers interned in the fifty-nine leper hospitals in the diocese of Paris was only thirty-five. From the early fifteenth century to the mid-sixteenth the leper hospital at Namur had only an average of four to five inmates. The reduction in the number of new hospitals being founded and the evidence of decay in the existing hospitals is reinforced by specific references in medical works to a decline in the number of lepers and by the reduced number of references to the disease in general works. By the seventeenth century the disease was more or less extinct in western Europe, though it lingered in northern Europe until the nineteenth century.

Despite the Church's encouragement of compassionate attitudes, popular fear of lepers laid them open to the same sort of scapegoatism that dogged other minority groups. This occurred spectacularly in 1321 when the lepers found themselves at the centre of one of those irrational outbursts that convulsed medieval society from time to time. The inquisitor Bernard Gui described what happened:

In 1321 there was detected and prevented an evil plan of the lepers against the healthy persons in the kingdom of France. Indeed, plotting against the safety of the people, these persons, unhealthy in body and insane in mind, had arranged to infect the waters of the rivers and fountains and wells everywhere, by placing poison and infected matter in them and by mixing (into the water) prepared powders, so that healthy men drinking from them or using the water thus infected, would become lepers or die, or almost die, and thus the numbers of lepers would be increased and the healthy decreased. And what seems incredible to say, they aspired to the lordship of towns and castles, and had already divided among themselves the lordship or places, and given them-

selves the name of potentate, count or baron in various lands, if
what they planned should come about.

This belief sparked a spring and summer of hysteria and violence in
much of France. It seems to have begun in Périgueux in the spring of
1321 when the rumour of the poisoning of the wells by lepers spread,
probably occasioned by some minor outbreak of ill-health in the area.
The local lepers were rounded up, tortured into confessing their guilt,
and burned at the stake.

The story, however, spread like wildfire and in many other places,
lepers were arrested. In some places, the authorities acted against the
perceived threat; but in many other places, the enraged populace rose
up and burned the lepers in their houses. The ramifications of the plot
spread. A leper from near Poitiers confessed to the involvement of the
Jews in the plot and his confession was forwarded to King Philip V.
The leader of the leper colony at Estang in Pamiers was arrested and
tortured. He confirmed that there was a plot by lepers to poison all the
wells in Christendom and kill the healthy people or turn them into
lepers. The Jews were involved. But even more significantly the whole
plot was being backed and financed by the Moslem King of Granada
and Sultan of Babylon who promised the lepers wealth, honours, and
lordship of the places they lived in when the plot was successfully
accomplished. The lepers held secret meetings which involved the rejection of Christ and his Church, secret oaths, and the distribution of the
potion sent them by the Moslems. A hundred and fifty lepers were said
to be involved in the plot. Two letters, purporting to be from the
Moslem Kings of Granada and Tunis, confirming the whole story,
turned up, making special provision for the poisoning of the King of
France. They were undoubtedly forged.

Faced with this evidence, Philip V ordered the arrest of all the lepers
in France. He issued detailed instructions, which applied equally to
men and women. Those lepers who had confessed or did confess in
future to involvement in the plot were to be burned alive. Those who
did not confess spontaneously were to be tortured. Those lepers who
despite torture did not confess, all future lepers, and lepers under 14
were to be imprisoned in their places of origin. The goods of all convicted
lepers were to be confiscated by the crown. But there were protests
from various bishops, barons, and local communities who claimed to
possess proprietary rights over their local leprosaria, forcing the King
to order the restoration of the property he had seized.

The action taken in response to the King's ordinance was clearly
widespread and references to it are found in the provinces of Flanders,
Anjou, Vermandois, Touraine and Aquitaine and in the towns of
Paris, Amiens, Rouen, Caen, Avranches and Coutances in the north,

Chaumont, Vitry and Mâcon in the east, Tours, Ouches, Limoges, Poitiers and Périgueux in the centre, and Toulouse, Carcassonne, Albi, Narbonne, Pamiers and Lyons in the south. The King took no action initially against the Jews but the people did and there were widespread massacres. A hundred and sixty Jews were burned at Chinon, for instance, and forty committed suicide at Vitry to avoid a similar fate.

As the panic died down and the hysteria exhausted itself, further action was taken. In 1322, King Charles IV ordered that all surviving lepers be permanently immured, a procedure of which Bernard Gui approved:

> At last more mature advice and consultation having been taken, the rest, all and individually, who had remained alive and were not found guilty, circumspectly providing for the future, were enclosed in places from which they could never come out, but wither away and languish in perpetuity, so that they would not do harm or multiply, men being completely separated from women.

In the same year, the Jews were expelled from France.

The speed with which the rumours spread and the extension of the conspiracy to include the most hated and feared elements of society reflects the disturbed state of France. The country had been racked by famine and disease in successive years from 1315 onwards and had further been considerably destabilized by the violence and disorder attending the so-called Shepherd's Crusade in 1320. In such circumstances popular fears crystallized and the fury turned on groups who were seen to be threatening the life and health of the country. The Jews and the Moslems were the usual sources of such paranoia, the enemy within and without. But this time they were joined by another outcast group, the lepers, in a conspiracy whose alleged intention to infect the healthy population created a peculiar frisson of horror. The involvement of heretical, anti-Christian rituals and the manufacture of potions and poisons completes the picture. Nothing could be more calculated than this unholy brew of prejudice and paranoia to stir up fear and hatred and put Europe's minority groups at the most serious risk.

FURTHER READING

1 THE MEDIEVAL CONTEXT

Bartlett, R. J. (1986) *Trial by Fire and Water*, Oxford.

Benson, R. L. and Constable, G. (eds) (1982) *Renaissance and Renewal in the 12th Century*, Oxford.

Bolton, Brenda (1983) *The Medieval Reformation*, London.

Bossy, John (1985) *Christianity in the West 1400–1700*, Oxford.

Bowsky, William (ed.) (1971) *The Black Death: a turning point in history?*, New York.

Brown, Peter (1975) 'Society and the Supernatural: a medieval change', *Daedalus* 104: 135–51.

Chenu, M-D. (1957) *Nature, Man and Society in the 12th Century*, Chicago.

Cohn, Norman (1975) *The Pursuit of the Millennium*, London.

Douglas, Mary (1966) *Purity and Danger*, London.

Duby, Georges (1978) *The Three Orders: Feudal Society Imagined*, Chicago.

——(1981) *The Age of the Cathedrals: Art and Society 980–1420*, London.

Ennen, E. (1979) *The Medieval Town*, Amsterdam.

Focillon, Henri (1969) *The Year 1000*, New York.

Gilman, Sander L. (1985) *Difference and Pathology: the stereotypes of sexuality, race and madness*, New York.

Gottfried, Robert (1986) *The Black Death*, London.

Gurevich, Aron (1988) *Medieval Popular Culture*, Cambridge.

Hamilton, Bernard (1986) *Religion in the Medieval West*, London.

Haskins, C. H. (1927) *The Renaissance of the Twelfth Century*, Harvard.

Huizinga, Johan (1955) *The Waning of the Middle Ages*, Harmondsworth.

Le Goff, Jacques (1988) *Medieval Civilization*, Oxford.

——(1988) *The Medieval Imagination*, Chicago.

Le Roy Ladurie, Emmanuel (1980) *Montaillou*, Harmondsworth.

Lucas, Henry S. (1930) 'The Great European Famine of 1315, 1316 and 1317' in *Speculum* 5: 343–77.

McCall, Andrew (1979) *The Medieval Underworld*, London.

Moore, R. I. (1987) *The Formation of a Persecuting Society*, Oxford.

Morris, Colin (1972) *The Discovery of the Individual*, London.

Mullett, Michael (1987) *Popular Culture and Popular Protest in Late Medieval and Early Modern Europe*, London.

Mundy, J. H. (1973) *Europe in the High Middle Ages 1150–1309*, London.

Murray, Alexander (1978) *Reason and Society*, Oxford.

Origo, Iris (1963) *The World of San Bernardino*, London.

Peters, Edward (1985) *Torture*, Oxford.

Robert, Ulysse (1891) *Les Signes d'infamie au moyen age*, Paris.

Rörig, F. (1967) *The Medieval Town*, London.

Southern, R. W. (1953) *The Making of the Middle Ages*, London.

—(1970) *Western Society and the Church in the Middle Ages*, Harmondsworth.

Thrupp, Sylvia (ed.) (1965) *Change in Medieval Society*, London.

Tillmann, Helene (1978) *Pope Innocent III*, Amsterdam.

White, Jr., Lynn (1974) 'Death and the Devil' in Robert S. Kinsman (ed.) *The Darker Vision of the Renaissance*, Berkeley.

Wolff, Philippe (1968) *The Awakening of Europe*, Harmondsworth.

Ziegler, Philip (1988) *The Black Death*, Harmondsworth.

2 SEX IN THE MIDDLE AGES

Andreas Capellanus (1941) *The Art of Courtly Love*, trans. and introduced by J. J. Parry, New York.

Ariès, Philippe and Béjin, André (eds) (1985) *Western Sexuality: practice and precept in past and present times*, Oxford.

Biller, P. A. (1982) 'Birth Control in the Medieval West in the 13th and early 14th Centuries' in *Past and Present* 94:3–26.

Boswell, John (1980) *Christianity, Homosexuality and Social Tolerance*, Chicago.

Brown, Peter (1989) *The Body and Society*, London.

Brundage, James A. (1987) *Law, Sex and Christian Society in Medieval Europe*, London.

—and Bullough, Vern L. (1981) *Sexual Practises and the Medieval Church*, Buffalo.

Bugge, John (1975) *Virginitas*, Hague.

Duby, Georges (1984) *The Knight, the Lady and the Priest; the making of modern marriage in Medieval France*, London.

—— (1968) 'The "Youth" in 12th century Aristocratic Society' in F. L. Cheyette (ed.) *Lordship and Community in Medieval Europe*, 198–209, London.

Flandrin, J-L. (1975) 'Contraception, Marriage and Sexual Relations in the Christian West' in R. Forster and O. Ranum (eds) *The Biology of Man in History* 23–47, Baltimore.

Goody, Jack (1983) *The Development of the Family and Marriage in Europe*, Cambridge.

Jacquart, Danielle and Thomasset, Claude (1988) *Sexuality and Medicine in the Middle Ages*, London.

Le Roy Ladurie, Emmanuel (1980) *Montaillou*, Harmondsworth.

Noonan, Jr., John T. (1965) *Contraception*, Cambridge, Massachusetts.

Payer, Pierre (1984) *Sex and the Penitentials*, Toronto.

Rossiaud, Jacques (1988) *Medieval Prostitution*, Oxford.

Ruggiero, Guido (1985) *The Boundaries of Eros*, Oxford.

Shahar, Shulamith (1983) *The Fourth Estate; a History of Women in the Middle Ages*, London.

Shapiro, Norman (1971) *The Comedy of Eros*, Illinois.

Tentler, Thomas N. (1977) *Sin and Confession on the Eve of the Reformation*, Princeton.

3 HERETICS

Bolton, Brenda (1972) 'Tradition and Temerity: Papal attitudes to deviants 1159–1216', *Studies in Church History* 9: 79–91.

Brooke, C. N. L. (1971) *Medieval Church and Society*, London.

Brown, Peter (1988) *The Body and Society*, London.

Cohn, Norman (1975) *The Pursuit of the Millennium*, London.

Evans, A. P. (1958) 'Hunting Subversion in the Middle Ages' in *Speculum* 33: 1–22.

Hamilton, Bernard (1981) *The Medieval Inquisition*, London.

Haskins, C. H. (1929) 'Robert le Bougre and the Beginnings of the Inquisition in Northern France', *Studies in Medieval Culture* 193–244, Oxford.

Kieckhefer, Richard (1979) *Repression of Heresy in Medieval Germany*, Liverpool.
Lambert, M. D. (1977) *Medieval Heresy*, London.
Leff, Gordon (1967) *Heresy in the Later Middle Ages* 2 vols, Manchester.
Lerner, Robert E. (1972) *The Heresy of the Free Spirit*, Berkeley.
Little, Lester K. (1978) *Religious Poverty and the Profit Economy in Medieval Europe*, London.
——and Rosenwein, Barbara (1974) 'Social Meaning in Monastic and Mendicant Spiritualities' in *Past and Present* 63: 4–32.
McDonnell, E. W. (1954) *The Beguines and Beghards in Medieval Culture*, New Brunswick.
Moore, R. I. (1975) *The Birth of Popular Heresy*, London.
——(1977) *The Origins of European Dissent*, London.
——(1983) 'Heresy as Disease' in D. W. Lourdaux and D. Verhelst (eds) *The Concept of Heresy* 1–11, Leuven.
——(1987) *The Formation of a Persecuting Society*, Oxford.
Murray, Alexander (1972) 'Piety and Impiety in 13th century Italy', in *Studies in Church History* 8: 83–106.
——(1974) 'Religion among the Poor in 13th century France' in *Traditio* 30: 285–324.
Nelson, Janet L. (1972) 'Society, theodicy and the origins of Medieval Heresy', in *Studies in Church History* 9: 65–77.
Peters, Edward (1980) *Heresy and Authority in Medieval Europe*, London.
Russell, Jeffrey B. (1965) *Dissent and Reform in the Early Middle Ages*, Berkeley.
Wakefield, W. L. and Evans, A. P. (eds) (1969) *Heresies of the High Middle Ages*, New York.
Wakefield, W. L. (1974) *Heresy, Crusade and Inquisition in Southern France 1100–1250*, Berkeley.

4   WITCHES

Anglo, Sydney (ed.) (1977) *The Damned Art*, London.
Baroja, J-C. (1971) *The World of the Witches*, Chicago.
Cohn, Norman (1976) *Europe's Inner Demons*, St Albans.
Emmerson, R. K. (1981) *Anti-Christ in the Middle Ages*, Manchester.
Jones, William R. (1972) 'The Political Uses of Sorcery in Medieval Europe' in *The Historian* 34: 670–87.
Kieckhefer, Richard (1976) *European Witch Trials*, London.
Klaits, Joseph (1985) *Servants of Satan*, Indiana.
Kors, Alan C. and Peters, Edward (1973) *Witchcraft in Europe 1100–1700*, London.
Kramer H. and Sprenger, J. (1971) *The Hammer of the Witches*, London.
Peters, Edward (1978) *The Magician, the Witch and the Law*, Hassocks.
Russell, Jeffrey B. (1972) *Witchcraft in the Middle Ages*, Ithaca.
——(1984) *Lucifer: the Devil in the Middle Ages*, Ithaca.

5   JEWS

Bachrach, Bernard S. (1977) *Early Medieval Jewish Policy in Western Europe*, Minneapolis.
Baron, S. W. (1967) *A Social and Religious History of the Jews* vols. 4–12, New York.
Chazan, Robert (1973) *Medieval Jewry in Northern France*, Baltimore.
——(ed.) (1980) *Church, State and Jew in the Middle Ages*, New York.
Cohen, Jeremy (1982) *The Friars and the Jews*, Ithaca.
Cutler, Allan and Helen (1986) *The Jew as Ally of the Muslim*, Notre Dame.
Eidelberg, Schlomo (ed.) (1977) *The Jews and the Crusades*, Madison, Wisconsin.

FURTHER READING

Emmerson, R. K. (1981) *Antichrist in the Middle Ages*, Manchester.
Guerchberg, Séraphine (1965) 'The Controversy Over the Alleged Sowers of the Black Death in the Contemporary Treatises on Plague' in Sylvia Thrupp (ed.) *Change in Medieval Society* 208–24, London.
Heer, Friedrich (1961) *The Medieval World*, London.
Hughes, Diane Owen (1986) 'Distinguishing Signs: Earrings, Jews and Franciscan Rhetoric in the Italian Renaissance City' in *Past and Present* 112: 3–59.
Katz, Jacob (1961) *Exclusiveness and Tolerance: Studies in Jewish-Gentile Relations in Medieval and Modern Times*, Oxford.
King, P. D. (1972) *Law and Society in the Visigothic Kingdom*, Cambridge.
Kisch, Guido (1949) *The Jews in Medieval Germany*, Chicago.
Lowenthal, Marvin (1970) *The Jews of Germany*, London.
Marcus, Jacob R. (ed.) (1973) *The Jew in the Medieval World*, New York.
Parkes, James (1938) *The Jew in the Medieval Community*, London.
Poliakov, Léon (1965) *A History of Anti-Semitism* 2 vols., London.
Roth, Cecil (1969) *History of the Jews of Italy*, Philadelphia.
Synan, Edward A. (1965) *The Popes and the Jews in the Middle Ages*, New York.
Trachtenberg, Joshua (1943) *The Devil and the Jews*, Yale.
Williams, A. Lukyn (1935) *Adversus Judaeos*, Cambridge.

6 PROSTITUTES

Basserman, Lujo (1967) *The Oldest Profession*, London.
Bloch, Ivan (1912–25) *Die Prostitution* 2 vols., Berlin.
Brucker, Gene (ed.) (1971) *The Society of Renaissance Florence*, New York.
Brundage, James A. (1987) *Law, Sex and Christian Society in Medieval Europe*, Chicago.
Burford, E. J. (1973) *The Orrible Synne*, London.
Bullough, Vern L. (1964) *The History of Prostitution*, New York.
——and Brundage, James A. (1981) *Sexual Practices and the Medieval Church*, Buffalo.
Geremek, Bronislaw (1987) *The Margins of Society in Late Medieval Paris*, Cambridge.
Muchembled, Robert (1985) *Popular Culture and Elite Culture in France 1400–1750*, Baton Rouge.
Otis, Leah Lydia (1985) *Prostitution in Medieval Society*, Chicago.
Pavan, Elisabeth (1980) 'Police des moeurs, societé et politique à Venise à la fin du Moyen âge' in *Revue Historique* 264: 241–58.
Rossiaud, Jacques (1988) *Medieval Prostitution*, Oxford.
Ruggiero, Guido (1985) *The Boundaries of Eros*, Oxford.
Salusbury, G. T. (1948) *Street Life in Medieval England*, London.
Terroine, Anne (1978) 'Le Roi des Ribauds de l'Hôtel du roi et les prostitutées Parisiennes' in *Revue d'Histoire de Droit Française et Etranger*, 4th series, vol. 56: 253–67.
Trexler, Richard (1981) 'La Prostitution Florentine au XVe siècle: patronages et clientèles' in *Annales* 36: 983–1015.
Weiner, Merry E. (1988) 'Paternalism and Practice: the control of servants and prostitutes in early modern German cities' in P. N. Bebb and S. Marshall (eds) *The Process of Change in Early Modern Europe* 179–200, Athens.

7 HOMOSEXUALS

Bailey, Derrick Sherwin (1955) *Homosexuality and the Western Christian Tradition*, London.
Barber, Malcolm (1987) *The Trial of the Templars*, Cambridge.

Boswell, John (1980) *Christianity, Social Tolerance and Homosexuality*, Chicago.

Brundage, James A. (1987) *Law, Sex and Christian Society in Medieval Europe*, Chicago.

Bullough, Vern L. and Brundage, James A. (1981) *Sexual Practices and the Medieval Church*, Buffalo.

Bullough, Vern L. (1976) *Sexual Variance in Society and History*, Chicago.

Cohen Jr., Samuel Kline (1980) *The Labouring Classes in Renaissance Florence*, New York.

Dover, Kenneth (1978) *Greek Homosexuality*, London.

Foucault, Michel (1986) *The Use of Pleasure*, London.

——(1988) *The Care of the Self*, London.

Goodich, Michael (1979) *The Unmentionable Vice*, Santa Barbara.

Karlen, Arno (1971–2) 'The Homosexual Heresy' in *The Chaucer Review* 6: 44–63.

Kuster, H. and Cornier, R. (1984) 'Old Views and New Trends: Observations on the Problem of Homosexuality in the Middle Ages' in *Studi Medievali* series 3 vol. 25: 587–610.

MacMullen, Ramsay (1982) 'Roman Attitudes to Greek Love' in *Historia* 31: 484–502.

Olsen, Glenn W. (Summer 1981) 'The Gay Middle Ages' in *Communio* 119–38.

Origo, Iris (1963) *The World of San Bernardino*, London.

Partner, Peter (1987) *The Murdered Magicians*, London.

Payer, Pierre (1984) *Sex and the Penitentials*, Toronto.

St Peter Damian, *The Book of Gomorrah*, ed. and trans. Pierre Payer (1982), Waterloo, Ontario.

Ruggiero, Guido (1985) *The Boundaries of Eros*, Oxford.

Trexler, Richard (1980) *Public Life in Renaissance Florence*, New York.

Wright, David F. (1984) 'Homosexuals or Prostitutes? The meaning of *Arsenokoitai*' in *Vigiliae Christianae* 38: 125–53.

Veyne, Paul (1985) 'Homosexuality in Ancient Rome', in P. Ariès andA. Béjin (eds) *Western Sexuality: practice and precept in past and present times* 26–35, Oxford.

8 LEPERS

Anderson, J. G. (1969) 'Studies in the Medieval Diagnosis of Leprosy in Denmark' in *Danish Medical Bulletin* 16 supplement 9.

Barber, Malcolm (1981) 'Lepers, Jews and Moslems: the Plot to overthrow Christendom in 1321', *History* 66: 1–17.

Brody, Saul N. (1974) *The Disease of the Soul: Leprosy in Medieval Literature*, Ithaca.

Cougoul, Jacques-Guy (1943) *La Lèpre dans l'Ancienne France*, Bordeaux.

Clay, Rotha Mary (1909) *The Medieval Hospitals of England*, London.

DeMaitre, Luke (1985) 'The Description and Diagnosis of Leprosy by 14th century Physicians' in *Bulletin of the History of Medicine* 59: 237–44.

Fay, H. M. (1910) *Histoire de La Lèpre en France: lepreux et cagots du Sud-Ouest*, Paris.

Gordon, Benjamin L. (1960) *Medieval and Renaissance Medicine*, London.

Gron, K. (1973) 'Leprosy in Literature and Art' in *International Journal of Leprosy* 41: 249–83.

Jeanselme, E. (1931) 'Comment l'Europe au Moyen Age se protégea contre La Lèpre' in *Bulletin de la Societé française de l'Histoire de Médecine* 25: 1–155.

MacArthur, Lt. Gen. Sir William (1953) 'Medieval Leprosy in the British Isles' in *Leprosy Review* 24: 8–29.

McNeill, W. H. (1977) *Plagues and Peoples*, Oxford.

Mercier, Charles (1915) *Leper Houses and Medieval Hospitals*, London.

Mesmin, S. C. (1978) *The Leper Hospital of St. Gilles de Pont-Audemer*, Reading University Ph. D. thesis, unpublished.

FURTHER READING

Mundy, J. H. (1965) 'Hospitals and Leprosaries in 12th and early 13th century Toulouse', in J. H. Mundy, R. W. Emery, and B. N. Nelson (eds) *Essays in Medieval Life and Thought* 18–205, New York.

——(1966) 'Charity and Social Work in Toulouse 1100–1250' in *Traditio* 22: 203–87.

Palmer, Richard (1982) 'The Church, Leprosy and the Plague in Medieval and Early Modern Europe' in *Studies in Church History* 19: 79–99.

Richards, Peter D. (1977) *The Medieval Leper and his Northern Heirs*, Cambridge.

Rubin, Stanley (1974) *Medieval English Medicine*, Newton Abbot.

INDEX

171